P9-CFQ-272

By Ved Mehta

Face to Face
Walking the Indian Streets
Fly and the Fly-Bottle
The New Theologian
Delinquent Chacha
Portrait of India
John Is Easy to Please
Mahatma Gandhi and His Apostles
The New India
The Photographs of Chachaji
A Family Affair
Three Stories of the Raj
Rajiv Gandhi and Rama's Kingdom
A Ved Mehta Reader

CONTINENTS OF EXILE

Daddyji
Mamaji
Vedi
The Ledge Between the Streams
Sound-Shadows of the New World
The Stolen Light
Up at Oxford
Remembering Mr. Shawn's New Yorker
All for Love

CONTINENTS OF EXILE

DARK HARBOR

Beach, 1987

VED MEHTA

CONTINENTS OF EXILE

DARK HARBOR

BUILDING HOUSE AND HOME
ON AN ENCHANTED ISLAND

Thunder's Mouth Press / Nation Books
New York

DARK HARBOR: *Building House and Home on an Enchanted Island*

Copyright © Ved Mehta 2003

Published by

Thunder's Mouth Press/Nation Books
161 William St., 16th Floor
New York, NY 10038

Nation Books is a co-publishing venture of the Nation Institute and Avalon Publishing Group Incorporated.

Library of Congress Cataloging-in-Publication Data

Mehta, Ved, 1934–
   Dark harbor : building house and home on an enchanted island / by Ved Mehta.
   p.cm.
   ISBN 1-56025-528-5
   1. Mehta, Ved, 1934–Homes and haunts—Maine—Islesboro Island. 2. Islesboro Island (Me.)—Social life and customs. 3. Dwellings--Maine—Design and construction. 4. Authors, Indic—20th century—Biography. 5.Authors, American—20th century—Biography. 6. Blind authors—United States—Biography. 7. East Indian Americans—Biography. I. Title.

PR9499.3.M425Z466 2003
362.4'1'092--dc21
[B]   2003042624

9 8 7 6 5 4 3 2

Printed in the United States of America
Distributed by Publishers Group West

To Ed and Mary Barnes

ACKNOWLEDGEMENTS

After John Milton went blind, he was fortunate in having
Andrew Marvell and his own daughters read to him and take
dictation from him for hours. As I wrote this book, I was
similarly served by a succession of amanuenses—Valerie
Jaffee, Julia Lee, and Sasha Haines-Stiles—although I can
do no more here than acknowledge their forbearance and
invaluable contributions to the book. My warm, lively, and
grateful thanks goes to them, and also to William Whitworth
and Elizabeth Macklin for their meticulous editorial readings
of the manuscript; it goes without saying that responsibility
for any error of fact or judgment is wholly mine. Last but not
least, I owe a great debt of gratitude to Ed and Mary Barnes,
not only for their indomitable spirit during the vicissitudes of
construction but also for reading the manuscript and gener-
ously giving their blessing to this account of what I often
think of as their house. I salute them one and all, with a
private gesture of love to Linn, Sage, and Natasha.

V.M.
New York
April 2003

CONTENTS

PHOTOGRAPHS

CONTINENTS OF EXILE

DARK HARBOR

I

ENCHANTRESS

T O THIS DAY, I WONDER IF I SHOULD HAVE STAYED away from the eightieth birthday party of the Very Reverend Father Martin D'Arcy, S.J. It was to have far-reaching consequences, and I still cannot work out if they were to my benefit or to my detriment. The party was given in June, 1968. I remember it clearly.

It was orchestrated by Jane Brian Engelhard, the wife of Charles William Engelhard, one of the world's richest men, and was held at a private room at the "21" club, in New York. From the very start, I felt out of place. Not only did I scarcely know Mrs. Engelhard but the dominant timbre of the party was one of moneyed voices. Still, I reminded myself that we were all there to honor Father D'Arcy. I had met him some ten years earlier, when I was an undergraduate at Oxford. He was a revered figure at the university, indeed in England at large, having served as the Master of Campion Hall, Oxford, and later as Provincial of the English Jesuits. It was common knowledge that he liked befriending the rich—staying in their houses, being wined and dined by them, and getting money from them for the Church. Apparently he was one of those worldly priests who saw the wisdom in Jesus' injunction "Make to yourselves friends of the mammon of unrighteousness; that, when ye fail, they may receive you into everlasting habitations."

I negotiated my way to the head table, where I wished Father D'Arcy Happy Birthday and greeted Mrs. Engelhard, an expansive, coquettish woman; she presented me to the Duke and Duchess of Windsor. To my great relief, the grand gathering included a few fellow-writers and friends—Edmund Wilson, Anne Fremantle, Phyllis McGinley.

The party has everything, I thought—fallen royalty and cultural Pooh-Bahs mixed in with literati and professional Catholics. It's the usual Father D'Arcy crowd, all right. I should be happy to be here and so, I suppose, I am.

I was shown to my table and introduced to Annette, Mrs. Engelhard's daughter. I was seated to her left. The chair on my left was empty, and beyond that, to my delight, were Edmund Wilson and Anne Fremantle. I no longer remember who else was at the table, perhaps because my attention was completely engaged by Annette. Just like an enchantress I had read about as a child when I was learning English (my mother tongue is Punjabi), she was ravishing, flirtatious, but completely unassuming. She had a girlish voice and laugh and sounded younger than she probably was.

I wonder if she's married, I mused. I wish I could take her hand and touch her ring finger. Ah, we sly foxes. Or, should I say, sly bats. We have to be ever alert to pick up small signals that people with eyes take in at a glance. The world isn't arranged with people like us in mind.

"I'm sitting down on your left," a woman said. Her voice was mannish, peremptory, and patronizing, as if she imagined that, lacking in one faculty, I was deficient in another too. But I was at a party, and I had been brought up to think courtesy was second to godliness. I excused myself to Annette and turned to my new neighbor, the editor of *Vogue*. "Hello, Mrs. Vreeland," I said.

"How did you know? Annette, you must have whispered in his ear that I'm Diana Vreeland," she said.

"I certainly did not," Annette said.

Why does she have to call attention to something that I would rather forget? I thought. Keep cool. "I think we met once, with some of my *New Yorker* friends," I said aloud to Mrs. Vreeland.

"I know—you are Mr. *New Yorker*," she said.

"No, I just try to write for it," I said.

Apparently finished with me, she turned to Edmund Wilson, and I turned back to Annette.

"What are you doing next weekend?" Annette asked.

I had a flicker of excitement, thinking that perhaps she was hinting that we could do something together, like have a meal or go to a play; but it was inconceivable that she would be asking an odd duck like me to squire her anywhere. A rich woman like her could have no shortage of friends and admirers—anyway, she was probably married.

"Same as I do on weekdays—try to write," I said offhandedly, trying to cover my confusion and, at the same time, to give a truthful answer.

"What do you do for fun?" she asked.

"I go out a certain amount in the evening," I said. "I'm here at '21,' aren't I?"

"You must go away for the summer," she pressed.

"Not really—I can't travel anywhere unless I pay my way by coming up with a piece to write," I said.

"You sound like a workaholic." She paused. "But that's probably not a word that your beloved editor of *The New Yorker* would allow you to use in the magazine."

"How right you are," I said. "You must be a *New Yorker* reader."

"I'm sure you go out every evening," she said.

"Before I started writing for *The New Yorker,* I imagined that writers and artists had glamorous lives—that they spent all their time consorting with society people." As soon as the phrase "society people" was out of my mouth, I realized that she might think that I was being an intellectual snob and putting her down.

But she only laughed, a kind of suppressed harmonic giggle that soared like a fast arpeggio.

"I'm sorry that you don't find me glamorous enough," she said.

"*Au contraire,*" I replied.

She fired back a whole stream of French, which I did not catch.

"You were brought up in France?" I asked stupidly.

"No, we had a mademoiselle," she said.

For some time, I had been listening with half an ear to Diana Vreeland goading Edmund Wilson on her other side. "You don't want to talk to me, I know it!" she had said to him several times. "You don't give a damn! You think I'm beneath your notice!" She had a strident, imperious voice—clearly she was a woman who was used to being listened to and having her way. At first, Wilson tried to excuse himself politely by explaining that he was getting a little deaf, but she would not believe him and would not leave him alone. In the end he was provoked to say, "I really am getting deaf, but you're right that I don't give a damn."

She now pointedly turned her back on him and asked me in a loud voice, as if to be sure that he heard her, "Is your friend Mr. Wilson always rude?"

I wanted to tell her that she was the one being rude to him, but I bit my tongue.

"What are you and I doing here in this aging café society?" Wilson called across her to me.

I did not want to offend Edmund Wilson, the critic I admire most, nor did I want to insult Mrs. Vreeland at such a gathering. I could sense that Annette was waiting to see what diplomatic ploy I would use. I could think of none, so I changed the subject.

"Father D'Arcy says he has set his heart on converting me," I said. "You know he converted Evelyn Waugh."

Everyone became silent, making me wonder if I had committed a faux pas. Edmund must think my remark absurd, Mrs. Vreeland must think I'm dropping names, and Annette must be disappointed that I couldn't think of anything better to say. Wilson abruptly turned to his left and began talking to Anne Fremantle.

"There is as much chance of your becoming Catholic as of my becoming your friend Wilson's lapdog," Mrs. Vreeland said to me. She seemed still to be fishing for Wilson's attention, but he ignored her.

No doubt she's right, I thought, but she scarcely knows me.

"Father D'Arcy is a wonderful priest," Annette said, obviously trying to relieve the tension in the air. "Mummy has him celebrate Mass for us in our chapel, and I love his sermons."

"With your sensitivity, you must have picked up that Annette is a closet intellectual," Mrs. Vreeland said ingratiatingly.

"Maybe that's why I am drawn to her," I said to Mrs. Vreeland. "It's her closeted side that I am trying to explore."

Annette laughed and covered her face with her napkin. If I were in her place I wouldn't try to hide my intelligence, I thought. But, then again, maybe I would in the society in which she must move—a society no doubt dominated by people like Mrs. Vreeland.

"You would like me more if I were shy like Annette," Mrs. Vreeland said provocatively.

I was spared from answering her because, just then, a waiter materialized on my left and thrust a huge platter between Mrs. Vreeland and me, expecting me to serve myself. Annette immediately grasped that I needed help and motioned the waiter to bring the platter around to my other side, and she served me herself. I thanked her.

"You have charmed Annette—how did you do it?" Mrs. Vreeland asked.

"Actually, it is I who am under Annette's spell," I said.

❧

AT THE END of the party, Annette offered to give Father D'Arcy and me a lift home in her limousine. I almost declined, thinking that they must have known each other longer and better than I knew either of them and that I would simply be in the way. But clearly her offer was genuine, and I accepted.

In the car, Father D'Arcy, charming as ever, was courtly and chivalrous toward Annette. If he had been at our table, he would not have worried about himself, as I did, but would have been attentive to Annette and her interests—indeed, would have been equally courtly and chivalrous to everyone, even Diana Vreeland. Charm knows no distinctions; it spreads as evenly as butter on bread. I wished I had his winning ways.

Even as I thought this, I felt I had to guard against thinking that I was always at fault. From my earliest years, it had seemed to me that every mistake I made, big or small, was as irremediable as any damage sustained by my body. Moreover, no matter how much I tried not to want what I couldn't have, I was always reaching for things that were beyond my grasp, even though I knew that all around me people voluntarily renounced things that they *could* have had. Take Father D'Arcy: early in life he must have made a choice to be a Jesuit and to renounce wife and family for the Church. In contrast, I had trouble renouncing anything. Believing in nothing, I never stopped fretting about being unmarried or longing for a wife and a family.

Father D'Arcy was dropped off at the St. Ignatius Residence, a Jesuit lodging house on East Eighty-third Street. Annette made the driver wait until Father D'Arcy was inside.

"It always makes me sad to leave Father D'Arcy here," Annette said distractedly. "I don't know anyone who enjoys the good life as much as he does. After dining with the Duke and Duchess, he comes home to this plain white brick building. He probably has a small, hard bed in some room and has to use a common bathroom."

I was touched by her concern for Father D'Arcy's lack of comfort.

As we pulled up in front of my apartment house on Eighty-second Street, she said abruptly, "You have to come and see me on my island."

"Where is your island?" I asked, trying to sound nonchalant when, actually, I was thrilled at the idea.

"It's in Maine."

There was something exciting about Maine. I had wanted to go there ever since I had come to America at the age of fifteen and had stayed briefly with John and Muriel di Francesco, some family friends, in New York. The di Francescos had barely known me, but they invited me to join them on their summer holiday in Maine and dwelled on the joys of sailing, fishing, and swimming there. I had to pass up their invitation, because I had to proceed to my school, in Little Rock, Arkansas. Now, some nineteen years later, here was Annette, who knew me even less than the di Francescos had, enticing me, with unbelievable generosity, to go to Maine. I accepted Annette's invitation as impulsively as she had given it and agreed to leave in two weeks for a three-day visit.

As I was getting out of the car, she said that she would send a private plane for me. I protested, but she retorted by saying there was no other way for me to get to the island and that it was something she wouldn't think twice about doing for any of her guests.

"ARE THERE NO other passengers?" I asked the air hostess as I stepped into the private jet that was to take me to Maine. It had a pilot and a copilot, an air hostess, and me.

"No, Mrs. Reed sent the plane especially for you," the air hostess said.

"Who's Mrs. Reed? I thought it was Annette Engelhard who was sending the plane for me."

"Engelhard is her maiden name. She's married to Samuel Reed."

Gosh. Am I condemned to commit blindisms? I should have kept my mouth shut and not revealed the fact that I scarcely knew Annette. However much I trained myself to hold my tongue and appear normal, a word here and there always slipped out and betrayed my limitations. How could I have dared to think, just because I couldn't tell whether she was wearing a wedding ring, that an unmarried woman would invite me to her island after just one meeting and then bring me across in a plane as if I were a film star?

Her sheen as a romantic object dulled, but she was left with another kind of lustre, that of an extremely wealthy woman. I had the fascination with money and moneyed people of someone who had been brought up in a poor country and who had to struggle constantly to make ends meet. Like Father D'Arcy, I certainly enjoyed hobnobbing with the rich, as if association with them in itself could be nourishing and there were no price to pay for it, as if I could be wined and dined by them and still keep sacrosanct the plain-fare values of my vocation.

Try as I might, I was unable to rein in my curiosity about Annette. "I didn't know she was married," I found myself saying to the air hostess. "What does her husband do?"

"I'm afraid I don't know. This is her father's plane. It's available to anyone in the family, but we work for Mr. Engelhard."

"From what I hear, he seems like quite a character. He's the fellow who had a birthday party at which a naked girl popped out of his cake."

The air hostess seemed embarrassed. To gloss over my inappropriate remark, I asked if the Engelhards would be staying on the island with Mrs. Reed, as I now tried to think of Annette.

"No, Mr. Engelhard is in Europe, and Mrs. Engelhard is travelling."

"Are the Engelhards a big family?"

"There are five Engelhard sisters, but I don't think that any of the girls are staying with Mrs. Reed just now."

"Then Mrs. Reed is the eldest?"

"Yes."

"Where are the rest of them?"

"I'm afraid I don't know—at school, I think."

Since I had been working as a journalist now for many years, asking questions was second nature to me, but I noticed that the air hostess had suddenly become edgy, as if, having realized that I was not a close friend of the family, she felt she had to shield them from my nosy inquiries. To smooth things over, I turned the conversation in a general direction. "I've never been to Maine. I'm afraid I don't even know where exactly Mrs. Reed's island is."

"It's in Penobscot Bay, near Camden. The island is called Islesboro."

The engines revved up, and the plane started taxiing. It felt grand to be able to hear the squawk coming over the radio from the control tower.

The air hostess buckled me in as if I were too helpless to put on my own seat belt. In other circumstances, I would have insisted on fastening my belt myself, but I let her do it, thinking that such ministrations were standard in a private jet. She sat down in the seat beside me and buckled herself in.

We quickly reached our flying altitude. We were merrily coasting along when, without any warning, the airplane started shaking and weaving, shooting up and dipping. My reason told me that we were merely encountering some turbulence, that in a small plane such unpleasant sensations were magnified. Still, I clutched the armrest.

"We'll soon be out of this bad patch," the air hostess said, taking my hand.

"You don't have to baby me," I said.

"But Mrs. Reed told me that I was to take care of you."

I had never gone anywhere before with so little information, and I asked myself how it was that, on the strength of a single meeting, I had decided to go and stay with Annette. It was uncharacteristic of me. "Think of it as an adventure," I told myself. "How many people in this world can fly in a private jet with two pilots and an air hostess attending them?"

I asked the air hostess how long the flight was.

"We should be on the ground in Portland in less than an hour," she said.

"Portland?"

"The runway on Islesboro is too short for a jet to land so we are only taking you as far as Portland. Mrs. Reed has arranged for a small propeller plane to take you on to Islesboro."

I am being carried off to the sticks, I thought.

"How far is Islesboro from Portland?"

"Not too far. The propeller plane will take you to Islesboro in less than an hour, unless the fog sets in."

"And if it does?"

"The people in Portland will arrange a taxi. I believe it's two hours by road to the ferry slip in Lincolnville."

"Ferry?"

"Yes. It's only a twenty-minute ferry ride."

I wish Annette had warned me about all these complications, I thought. For all I know, I could be trapped in Maine for days by the fog. Time probably means little to her, so she doesn't know its value. That's why she can hole up in some godforsaken island. Why did I ever agree to go there? What will I do there all day long? I don't sail—I don't do any country things.

An Urdu couplet of my father's came to me—he always had an appropriate one for any situation:

It's best to keep away from the rich.
Neither their friendship nor their enmity is good.

But then I remembered Annette's bright voice and her suppressed laugh, her warmth and spontaneity, and felt a bit ashamed of my churlishness.

As we were getting ready to land in Portland, the air hostess took my hand again. I felt that I had given her a bad impression. She seemed like a fresh-faced, small-town young woman. I realized that I did not even know her name.

"It's rather late in the day, but I wonder what your name is?" I asked.

She became all bashful. "I can't say it—I'm sorry."

I could not believe that she fancied I had designs on her and was therefore being coy.

"I only want to know your name. My name's Ved."

"Please don't press. You'll embarrass me."

"Now you've really piqued my curiosity—I really have to know."

"You don't want to know—it's obscene."

"How can a name be obscene?"

"Since we've gone this far I have to tell you that it's part of my service agreement with Mr. Engelhard that, in his plane, I can only answer to one name."

"So?"

"Have you ever read any James Bond books?"

"I have. I can't say that Ian Fleming's my kind of writer. Why do you ask?"

"Goldfinger was modelled on Mr. Engelhard. You know what he called his girlfriend."

"Oh God, no!" I said. I dropped the subject.

II

ISLAND

I N Portland, I was hustled into the waiting one-engine chartered plane. It had no air hostess, and only one pilot, who was seated so close in front of me that I could have reached out and tapped him on the shoulder.

"Are you comfortable?" the pilot asked in a clipped accent as soon as we were airborne. "Do you like flying in a small plane?"

"It's O.K. But I'd feel better if you had a copilot," I said.

"What do I need a copilot for?" he retorted.

"What if something happens to you?"

"We'll go down and be dead on arrival."

I laughed a little uncertainly at his macabre humor but persisted. "I really would feel safer if the plane had two engines, you know."

"Why do you worry about having only one engine? You only have one heart."

His humor got the better of my fears, and I relaxed.

"We're flying low," he said. "The coast around here is jagged and wild. Many of my passengers don't like looking down at it."

"Maine must have more unoccupied land than most places in the world," I said, recalling that the state occupied half the land area of New England but had a population of no more than a million.

"I don't know about the rest of the world, but we've got thousands of islands with no one on them."

"Why don't people live there?"

"They're wild and hard to get to."

"What kind of islands are they?"

"They're just your regular islands, in all sizes and shapes, with rocks and brush and seagulls and pines."

"A person must really love the water to live around here."

"Yup. Fishing, lobstering, sailing—that's what people like to do hereabouts. True Mainers are really water rats. Have you ever been on a sailboat?"

"I can't say that I have."

"What are you going to do here, then?"

"Just visit."

The conversation with the pilot was making me anxious. I suddenly felt frightened of the coastline, islands, and water.

As soon as the plane touched down and the pilot opened the door, I grabbed my suitcase and bravely scampered down the stepladder, hoping to impress upon Annette that I was as independent as any seeing person—that I would be no more a burden to her than any normal guest. I had no doubt that she would be waiting and watching for me from her car.

The pilot shouted out of the open door, "You all right?"

"Yes, of course!" I shouted back.

He rattled the door shut and revved up the engine. I instinctively dashed in the opposite direction as the plane taxied and took off.

I stood listening to the plane gain height until it became a distant rumble and then faded completely. I looked at my watch. It was just eleven, exactly when I was due in. I turned this way and that way, trying to keep my eyes open and to look alert, any moment expecting to be greeted by Annette, or, at the least, by a member of her staff.

Some minutes went by, and there was no sign of anyone. In fact, the silence was so enveloping and absolute that I was unnerved; I could hear my own heart beating.

People had always called me reckless—I could never resist a physical challenge, even if I were totally unequipped to meet it. Perhaps because I was generally a deliberate person and spent most of my time engaged in the sedentary activity of writing, I felt I had to seize every social opportunity that came my way if I were not to be left sitting on a rocker on some porch, like many people in my condition. That was one of the reasons I had accepted Annette's invitation, even though I knew little about her, less about Maine, and nothing about her island. But now I could not remember an occasion when I had decided to do something on the basis of so little information. I had agreed to come to her island without knowing if she was a dependable person or a fickle society woman. I had simply succumbed to my imaginings of her as a sexy, unattached woman—to her palpable aura of fashion, money, and charm.

"You're a lunatic," I told myself. "You left the city that you know like the palm of your hand, where you could go anywhere alone, do anything by yourself, to chase a will-o'-the-wisp. For all you know she's forgotten that she invited you.

"Calm down. Annette is just late.

"Maybe she has forgotten.

"That's unthinkable—after all, the plane arrangements were in place.

"But rich people are notoriously unreliable. She must meet hundreds of people. Everyone must want something from her. She is liberal with her promises but has trouble following through.

"Still, she did not have to invite you.

"Maybe she felt sorry for me.

"But she gave the impression that she liked you.

"People who move in high social circles are adept at giving any impression they want to.

"But didn't Mrs. Vreeland say she's a closet intellectual? She must have read one of your books.

"Someone like her must meet hundreds of writers.

"But how many writers have five books to their name at the age of thirty-four, as you do?

"A legion."

First shyly, and then with rising fear, I called out, "Hello? . . . Is anyone here? . . . Is anyone out there?"

The air was so still, the surroundings so stark, that I did not get so much as an echo. There did not seem to be even a building, a tree, or a rock around—something I could use to orient myself. I walked this way and that but could sense no object of any kind, no sign of another human being.

I stopped and cocked my ear for the sound of water, a cricket, anything at all, but there was nothing but unearthly silence.

Oh God, the wretched pilot has dropped me on the wrong island, I thought. He did say that there were heaps of islands. I shouldn't have let him fly away just for the sake of giving Annette the impression that I was every bit the equal of a seeing person. Now I have no way of getting out of here.

I had no picture of the terrain—whether it was a big or small island, whether it was forest or desert, whether it was mountainous or flat. For all I knew, if I strayed too far I would fall off a cliff. Certainly, the Maine coast was notorious for having steep bluffs. I was not even sure if the island had any amenities like a telephone or if anyone besides Annette's family lived on it.

I was stricken with terror and besieged by all kinds of mad thoughts. Annette's husband was trying to do away with me because he thought I had fallen in love with her. Ian Fleming had dreamed up my plight as a plot for his new book, and he was somewhere watching and taking notes. Annette was a decoy for a vigilante group who were out to get me because I had written a bad review of Rabindranath Tagore, the standard-bearer of their Bengali culture. There was no Annette or house or anything else on the island. I was going to die—a slow, agonizing death. I should not have thought of taking any plane anywhere at all when I was still in the middle of a big book, as I was.

I felt dizzy. My knees began to buckle.

"Get a hold of yourself or you're going to faint. Take sober stock of your situation."

But what situation? I prided myself on being capable, imagining that I could do anything that a seeing person could do. But now I felt as helpless as Helen Keller without Anne Sullivan. My usual way of telling the compass directions, from the sun on my face, was unavailing, for even as I stood there, fog was coming in.

"Stop shaking," I told myself. "Just concentrate on what a seeing person would do under the circumstances." I tried to recollect what Robinson Crusoe had done when he was marooned on his island. Somewhere there must be a tree; maybe I could climb up on it. Sooner or later, an airplane was bound to come, and I could signal my plight by waving my handkerchief.

I put down my suitcase and started walking, taking one step at a time and gingerly feeling the ground underfoot with the toe of my shoe. My hands suddenly shot up, as if I thought I was going to bump into the air. I firmly thrust them in my pockets and started walking normally, as if I didn't care if I went over a cliff. With my facial vision, that ability some of us have to sense objects through sound-shadows, echoes and changes in air pressure around the ear, I discerned a small structure. It loomed ahead like a welcoming oasis in a desert, and I came upon it so quickly that I almost crashed into it.

I touched it up and down, not believing what my hands were telling me. It was a wooden structure—indeed, a shed, with an actual telephone in it. I picked up the receiver and heard the dial tone. At that moment it sounded sweeter than any piece of music I had ever heard.

I got Annette's number from the operator and dialled it.

"Is that really you?" she said cheerily, her voice caressing my ear, with the reassuring sound of dogs barking in the background. "Are you on the island?"

"I am on an island, but I don't know if it is the right island."

"Of course you are on the right island. Didn't Mr. Lloyd bring you in his little plane?"

"Yes, I have been here for at least twenty minutes."

"Can it really be eleven-twenty already? I'm really embarrassed. I'm sorry—you'll never talk to me again. Stay where you are. Marco Polo, Mikey, and I will be right there—you can probably hear them barking in the background."

As soon as I stepped out of the shed, the sun appeared, weak, but sun nonetheless, also strong enough for me to surmise that I was facing west.

Fog seems to lift here as rapidly as it closes in, I thought. My depression lifted like the fog.

All my senses suddenly came alive. For the first time, I noticed a wafting scent of spruce, pine, and birch. The air felt fresh as sweet water; it was so rich with oxygen that I felt intoxicated. It seemed to have blown in from the timeless world of the sea. I did a little jig and jogged around the place.

I heard in the distance the screech and bump of tires and what sounded like a duet of shrill barks.

IN THE CAR, I said, "Tell me a little bit about your island. You own it?"

"Oh no," she said, laughing. "You've never heard of Dark Harbor?"

"No. What is it?"

"It's where people come for summers."

"You mean like Martha's Vineyard or Nantucket?"

"Yes. Our island, though, is called Islesboro."

"What is Dark Harbor, then?"

"It's the village on the island."

"What's on Islesboro?"

"Woods, docks, and cottages."

"Is there a hotel? A shop? A movie theatre?"

"No. There is one grocery shop, one general store with a soda fountain, and one restaurant that is only open in the summer—that's it."

"Oh my God, it sounds as if you've brought me into a wilderness."

"I have."

"I wonder what brings people here."

"The fact that it's so wild and beautiful."

I peppered her with more questions—how big was the island, how many people lived on it, what kind of people summered there, and so on. She was not forthcoming, perhaps because she did not know the facts or because she was not interested in them. But I did slowly gather that it was a long, thin pencil of an island, about thirteen miles long and one or two miles wide, and that it had a summer population of about fifteen hundred.

"The rest of the year—do people live on the island?"

"You mean the natives?"

The word took me aback. "I mean, the local people."

"I think there are a few hundred natives."

I had a sense of déjà vu, as if I had arrived in a forgotten outpost of the British Empire, with British sahibs and mem-sahibs on one side and natives on the other.

ANNETTE'S HOUSE WAS huge and beautifully situated. It faced the harbor to the west, and I could hear the slapping of a sail and the rippling of the water. Although it was summer, a fire crackled at one end of a grand living room.

As I entered, I was greeted by her husband, Samuel, who was tall and had a smooth manner, and was introduced to their two children—Beatrice, about seven, and Charlie Reed, a baby, whom Samuel always addressed by his full name, as if to emphasize his status as son and heir.

Samuel hovered over me, worrying that I was going to trip over a doorsill or a rug, or bang into a table, or confuse my right with my left and set off in the wrong direction. I wanted to tell him to leave me alone and let me fend for myself. Every day I went into strange apartments and houses, travelled on unfamiliar streets and blocks, and managed everything myself. But he was my host, and I felt that I should be tolerant of his ministrations, which were, after all, well-meaning. Still, it took all my self-control to keep from losing my temper.

Annette showed me to a guest room on the ground floor and, as she was about to leave me to my unpacking, said, "We've arranged a little picnic on an uninhabited island."

I've just come to one island and now I have to go to another island, I thought. The rich are wonderfully restless.

"Who's going on the picnic?" I asked with feigned casualness.

"Just the family."

"How will we get there?"

"Captain Quinn will take us."

I wondered if the captain, like the air hostess, had been renamed by the family—in his case, to fit their quaint perception of nautical life. But I said nothing.

Once the door was closed, I took stock of my room. The bed was so large that I could lie in it crossways. The bathtub was large enough for me to drown in.

So much for rustic living, I thought.

I had always imagined that only a life of plain living and high thinking was appropriate to the vocation of a writer. And here I was in a house whose expenses could probably swallow my whole month's earnings in one day—and it was only a summer house. I recalled Father D'Arcy at St. Ignatius Residence. He had taken a vow of poverty for the sake of his religion, and, in a sense, I had taken a similar vow for the sake of keeping my writing "pure," fearing that if I, like the rich, were cut off from the rest of the world, my writing would become detached from my values and concerns.

I washed up and changed from city to casual clothes and stepped out of my room. All over the house, there seemed to be a bustle. Annette had brought along her own staff from New York and supplemented it with local help. The island apparently had none of the usual amenities to maintain the social life she was accustomed to. It seemed that every last servant was now scurrying around, preparing picnic food and muttering about picnic blankets and picnic hampers, coolers and wine.

Soon the staff, the family, and I set out for the boat, everyone carrying something. I walked alongside Annette, who had a dog under each arm—Marco Polo, a Lhasa terrier, and Mikey, a Cairn terrier, from whom she seemed inseparable. I found myself explaining her attachment to dogs in the words of W. H. Auden's poem "Talking to Dogs," in which he apostrophized a pet (perhaps his own) named Rolfi Strobl:

> Being quicker to sense unhappiness
> without having to be told the dreary
>   details or who is to blame, in dark hours
> your silence may be of more help than many
>   two-legged comforters.

From the Reeds' private dock, we all boarded a forty-two-foot-long boat with a high-powered motor and with Captain Quinn at the helm. The water was calm, and there was just enough breeze to make sitting out on the deck under the sun enjoyable. The Reeds had decided upon an island far out into the sea, and we were on the water for about an hour. We could not get close to it, because the water there was too shallow for the draught of the boat. We anchored some distance away, and there was much ado about getting us all, with the dogs and the picnic paraphernalia, into dinghies and onto the shore.

Once on terra firma, the staff began spreading blankets, laying out paper plates in individual wicker holders, and unpacking silver emblazoned with the family crest. Samuel and the other men immediately set off to gather firewood and sticks to roast hotdogs and marshmallows. I felt perfectly capable of joining them, but they seemed to think I was not fit for such tasks, so I didn't make a fuss but obediently perched on a half-rotted fallen tree and listened to the woodsy sounds of masculine activity—the hacking and whacking of brush, the cracking and snapping of twigs underfoot. The happy noise of their camaraderie stabbed me much like the sharp knots of the log I was sitting on.

If I had had any inkling that at Annette's I would not be allowed to hold my own with other men, I would not have come, I thought. But then again, the outdoor life may be too chaotic and dangerous for someone in my situation. The truth was that I wanted to appear at all times self-sufficient and competent, to such an extent that I avoided situations where I might seem helpless and so, perhaps, invite pity.

"Would you like to come exploring with me?" Beatrice asked, as if sensing my discomfort.

"Exploring the island?" I asked.

"Yes," she said.

I was touched by the little girl's concern. Like mother, like daughter, I thought.

She took my hand, and we started toward the woods. We had taken only a few steps when, suddenly, my leg caught fire. The flame leapt up my trouser leg to my thigh as if I were about to be immolated. Oh my God, I thought, I've walked straight into the campfire. I am going to die at a picnic.

Beatrice screamed, dropped my hand, and ran back to her mother as if she, too, were being consumed by fire.

The sea was somewhere behind me, crashing and churning.

Water, I thought, and made a dash for it, almost somersaulting into the sea. Even though I was practically up to my neck in icy Maine water, the burning on my leg did not seem to abate.

Oh my God, it's too late, I thought. I'm never going to be whole again.

I stumbled out of the sea. My leg felt swollen and enflamed.

Samuel was at the water's edge. He was solicitous, but was also laughing, though not in an unkind way.

"I am going mad," I cried.

"You just stepped on a ground nest of yellow jackets," he said.

"What in the hell *are* they?"

"They're these horrible wasps," Annette said, rushing up to me.

"Oh," I said, trying to control my tears. I felt that everyone would think me a sissy for making such a fuss over a few stings. But I could scarcely stand up. I leaned on Annette and walked back to the log.

"Beatrice got three stings on her face," Annette said, as I tried to ignore the mounting pain in my leg.

"Look, her cheek is swelling up," Samuel said.

"Let me see your leg," Annette said.

"It's nothing," I said.

"But you've been stung badly," she said, pulling my trouser leg halfway up my calf. "Let me put some Xylocaine on it."

"It's O.K.," I said.

"No, it's not O.K.," she said, and I felt her cool hand all around my ankle and lower calf like a healing unguent.

"You're flinching," she said. "Xylocaine will help."

"Mummy put some Xylocaine on me and it feels cool and nice," Beatrice said.

She's such a brave little girl, I thought. I can't spoil Annette's picnic on an uninhabited island. I must let mind prevail over matter.

I pretended that the Xylocaine was giving me some relief, but the fact was that my leg was swelling even as I struggled to pull down my waterlogged trouser leg.

The firewood had been gathered and laid out. Paul

Pendleton, Annette's weatherbeaten gardener, put a match to it, and the flames came up so quickly and fiercely that we all had to sit back. Pâté and prosciutto, potato salad and watermelon were brought out, hotdogs and hamburgers were grilled, buns toasted, and white wine opened. Everyone ate heartily, except Annette, who just sipped a Coke.

There was a lot of talking and laughing, and I was able to participate in it fully, perhaps because my leg had now become numb with pain.

As SOON AS we were back in the house and I was safely in my room, I gingerly peeled off my trousers and examined my leg with my fingers. I counted no fewer than eighteen stings—my manhood was spared by just an inch. The stingers were embedded in my flesh, and the welts merged into one another, forming one continuous inflammation.

I should see a doctor immediately, I thought. But there is certainly no doctor on the island, and there is probably no way of getting off the island without making a lot of fuss. Anyway, I mustn't let Annette think that I am not enjoying myself.

I wondered what my father, who was a doctor, would do in such a predicament. No doubt he would apply heat to reduce the swelling, I thought.

I went into the bathroom and turned on boiling-hot water, filled the tub, and tested the water, nearly scalding my hand. I closed my eyes, said a prayer to my childhood god Rama, and stepped in. I had trouble staying in the water, but I valiantly pressed on with my cure. When I got out, the welts were twice as swollen.

I got into the bed, between soft, silky sheets, but they rasped against my skin like sandpaper. I wanted to lie there and just groan and fall asleep, but Annette had arranged a big dinner party for me that night. Even as I was writhing in my bed, Paul Pendleton was out on the mud flats digging up soft-shelled clams, or steamers, for the dinner.

I decided to keep my infirmity to myself and to go through with the dinner as if a few stings were just part of country living. At the appointed hour, I got dressed in my casual flannels and tweeds and appeared at the dinner party.

There were about a dozen guests, seemingly all prominent figures from New York. All of them were affluent and wellborn and seemed to relax around Annette's table, as if they had never heard of the cares of the world—as if they'd spent their whole lives in the wilds of Maine. Ordinarily, I would have been cowed by their company, but Annette's treating me like an honored guest—she put me on her right—gave me self-confidence.

Each guest was served a whole lobster in its shell, and the table practically shook as the guests attacked their meals. I had never eaten one and didn't even know how to hold the special implements for cracking the shell and scooping out the meat. I thought of pretending to Annette that I was allergic to shellfish but recalled that she had seen me eat shrimp at the party for Father D'Arcy. I therefore confessed to her my ignorance.

"Annette, I grew up on the plains of the Punjab," I said, trying to take the edge off my embarrassing admission. "I don't know the first thing about lobsters."

Without a hint of discomfort, she prepared and all but fed the lobster to me.

I was not sure that I liked the taste or texture of the lobster; it was too rich and somewhat slimy. But everyone else seemed to be enjoying it, so I acted as if I did too, washing it down with gulps of exquisite wine. Despite my wretched leg and the humiliation of being fed like an invalid, I enjoyed the dinner. I thought I could get used to the life of the rich easily; I already had a taste for good wine, which had a way of making any food palatable and at the same time freeing me from my overdeveloped self-consciousness. The next evening, Annette invited seemingly all the children on the island for a party. They were served grilled hotdogs, hamburgers, and Cokes outdoors and then shown a film in the boathouse, which had been transformed into a little cinema, with projector, screen, and folding chairs. We grown-ups took chairs at the back and watched the film with the children.

I don't remember what the film was, but I remember feeling grateful to Annette for sitting next to me and, between sips of Coke, whispering to me the bits of the story that were not readily graspable from the dialogue. She had an uncanny feel for what I could and could not follow. I practically saw the film through her eyes.

As the children were leaving, they each came up to Annette and said, "Thank you, Mrs. Reed." "Thank you, Mrs. Reed." "Thank you, Mrs. Reed." I could only add my silent thank-you to theirs. Their polite voices echoed in my head long after I left Maine.

SAMUEL AND I took a charter plane from Islesboro to Boston, and then took a shuttle to New York. The moment I got to my office, I called my doctor.

"Is your leg still swollen?" he asked. I had spoken to him a couple of times from Maine.

"The swelling does not seem to have gone down," I said.

"Then you had better come right over."

At his office, he took one look at my leg and said, "You're lucky to be alive. I once had a patient who had an allergic reaction to a single sting, and he died. Some of your stings are infected. What did you do after you got stung?"

"Nothing much. I took a hot bath to bring down the swelling."

"That was probably the worst thing you could have done. You burnt your leg and aggravated the swelling."

He tried to extract the stingers with tweezers but could not get hold of a single one of them. I asked him what I should do now, and he said there was nothing to be done but to apply some salve and to wait until the stingers worked their way out by themselves.

It was several weeks before my leg was normal again. Nature is all fine and good for people who can see, I thought, but people like me are best off in the city.

Soon after returning from Maine, I went to a cocktail party given by Anne Fremantle. There, I encountered a bouncy, self-satisfied man from Brazil, whom Anne introduced to one and all as the only genuine cannibal she had ever met.

Not knowing what to say to a cannibal, if that was what he really was, I asked him the first question that popped into my head.

"What does human meat taste like?"

"You mean baby meat or adult?"

"Whichever," I said, turning away and hoping to escape him.

"Well, the nearest thing to it is lobster."

For some time afterward, I could never think of Maine without recalling my exchange with the cocktail-party cannibal.

IN TIME, I got to know Annette's mother and sisters and became a good friend of Samuel's. I now had not only Annette as a friend but her whole family. Every so often, the Reeds and I would meet for dinner in restaurants in the city, or sometimes Annette would sweep into my office bringing with her a picnic lunch of several kinds of thinly sliced bread, already buttered, delicious wedges of cheese, smoked salmon, pâté de foie gras, and devilled eggs heaped with caviar. We would sit and have lunch in my office—or, I should say, I would, since she hardly ate anything, just sipped a Coke. Then we would slip off to a movie. I decided she was about the best person to go to a film with; she had a way of explaining just enough, and not too much.

I noticed that when we were together without a planned activity, she would find a pretext—real or feigned, I never knew which—to get away. Indeed, I found her alternately flirtatious and elusive. At one point, in the early days of our friendship, I hugged her and sensed that she was pregnant—she was just beginning to show. I refrained from saying anything about it; she was quite vain about her figure, and, in any case, I thought she would announce it when she was ready to. But then her sister Susan told me the news, and when Annette found out she was furious with her.

"I don't understand," I said to Annette. "Why would you want to keep your pregnancy a secret from me?"

"I just thought that you wouldn't like me as much now," she said. But of course her pregnancy—and, later, the birth of the child, another daughter—made no difference to my feelings about her. If anything, her openness deepened our friendship.

Indeed, I came to see in her apparent flirtatiousness an expression of shyness. It seemed she liked to keep people off-balance, as if afraid that they would get too close to her. Years later, I had an inkling of what the reason for such a fear might be. Her father was Jane Engelhard's first husband, an extremely wealthy Dutch banker and financier named Fritz Mannheimer, whom Jane had married as a girl (she had Annette before she was eighteen, around 1936), and who had died in 1939, at the age of forty-nine. Although Charles Engelhard, whom she had married in 1947, when she was about twenty-nine years old (he died at the young age of fifty-four, in 1971), had adopted Annette and brought her up as one of their five girls, the fact remained that she was not an Engelhard by blood. That might have made her feel a little bit of an outsider; if so, that might explain why she was drawn to me.

In any event, for many years after, I kept returning to the island and the Reeds' for a few days every summer. One of the first times that I was there, I discovered that the Reeds had a fleet of bicycles. I had not been on one since my college days, but the island—flat, with only one main, or town, road—seemed like a perfect place for biking.

I grabbed a bike. Just as I was about to mount, I wondered fleetingly if I would be able to stay on it. But, of course, as soon as I was astride it I realized that one could no more forget how to bicycle than how to swim or how to walk. I set off, and Samuel ran after me, as if he thought I was going to kill myself. Sometime later, he relaxed and we went bicycling together, he riding two or three lengths in front and I following. He kept looking back at me so often to see that I had not ridden off the road that I found the ride as nerve-racking as he did. After that, I left the bicycles alone.

Still, at the Reeds I relished having my every need— spoken or unspoken—taken care of, as if I too were a rich person. At first, I rather presumptuously imagined that the guests, food, wine, and picnics were all laid on for my visit. But I soon learned that that was the way of life in the Reed household. Annette's mission in Dark Harbor seemed to be to entertain, and, having natural elegance and taste, she did that with great aplomb. Indeed, her house was more populated by visitors flown from New York, Washington, or Montana, than by her neighbors from the island. Many of the imported guests were wished on her by her mother, who would lodge wives of her influential business and political friends at Annette's. I recall that Maureen Mansfield, a schoolteacher and the wife of Mike Mansfield, the Democratic majority leader from 1961 to 1977, would stay there for weeks at a time while the Senator was tied up in Washington or was travelling. Yet underneath Annette's immense charm and goodwill I sensed a restless tension, as if she couldn't wait to break out of the responsibility of the Dark Harbor house. For comfort, she always seemed to turn to her little dogs, Marco Polo and Mikey. (Later, they were succeeded by Fairfax, Steppenwolf, and Brünnhilde.)

I SOON DISCOVERED that a stay at the Reed house was different from life in many other American country houses, where people were occupied with athletic activities like tennis, golf, swimming, fishing, and sailing. Although Samuel did play some tennis, Annette played no sports; she did not even swim. Also, life at the Reeds' was different from that at a grand English country house. There, people would go on long walks and hikes, explore historical sites, drop in on local pubs, a nearby cricket pitch, or the village church, and perhaps tour the gardens of old estates; in the evening, there would be games of wit like charades, board games like Monopoly, discussions about politics, and perhaps music and dancing. Even in hill stations in India, where my childhood summers were spent, there was more interaction with the world outside, in that we went for daily strolls along the mall, where we met up with our neighbors and friends and dropped by local restaurants. In contrast, Annette, like a storybook queen, seemed to be happiest seeing people on her own turf, on her own terms, with her own staff. Sometimes, she seemed like a precious child who required a lot of nannying. Other times, she seemed like an exotic flower that needed just the right amount of light and water.

We guests all had the feeling that we were marooned in a little kingdom in the middle of nowhere, the long boat rides, the picnics on uninhabited islands, and the dinner parties notwithstanding. Most of the time at the house was spent sitting in front of the fire; or lounging in the sunporch, watching boats go by; or just staring out to the water, waiting for the fog to lift. It was interesting that for reading most people retreated to their separate rooms, as if public rooms were reserved mainly for social conversation. Yet the idleness had its own magic, and I think it all had to do with a certain ineffable quality Annette had, which was as hard to pin down as the flight of a butterfly.

For short stays, I enjoyed being at Dark Harbor. I slept well. The pure, oxygen-rich air, I imagined, was made for deep slumber and long dreams.

SAMUEL HATED FLYING in small planes, and, after a while, Annette did not want to be running a sort of elegant boardinghouse. They sold their house and bought property closer to the city, in Bedford, New York.

Once she was gone, there was nothing to take me back to Dark Harbor. Perhaps the rich needed their own playground, but by physical limitation, temperament, vocation, and bank account I was not suited to island life.

III

LAND

O NE HOT SUMMER DAY IN 1981, SOME THIRTEEN years after my introduction to Dark Harbor and a few years after Annette sold her house, I was sitting in my office in New York when the telephone rang.

"Honey, how are you?"

There is no word that sets my teeth on edge like the endearment "honey." It sounds saccharine, and, besides, after my stings it conjured up for me a hiveful of mad bees, the cousins of the yellow jackets.

"Is that Mary?" I asked.

"It sure is. I see you haven't forgotten your down-home girl."

Mary was an old college flame. (Her identity, like that of some other characters not central to the narrative, has been disguised.) The daughter of a florist, she was from Nashville, Tennessee. Her speech had deliciously languid cadences, and she came across as a proverbial Southern belle. She had jilted me and eventually married a hometown banker whom I remember making fun of because his formal name was printed on the wedding card as "Earl Foot VII." Mary and I had not been in touch for over twenty years, and her now casually telephoning me gave me a turn.

"Long time, no see," I said lightly, trying to hide my confusion.

"I feel real bad about calling out of the blue like this," she said.

"Really bad," please, Mary, I thought. Her grammar had always left something to be desired.

"How are the children doing?" I said. I had heard she had a boy and a girl, who would both be teenaged now.

"They're doing fine. Morty is growing up to be a true gentleman, but April, I fear, will never be a lady. I'd go stark crazy if I couldn't get away from them and Earl every summer and go solitary in Maine. This year I'm paying my way by taking care of a group of cabins near Camden."

"A chatelaine in Maine!"

"What did you say?"

"Never mind."

"But I'm awful lonesome for company. There is only so much time a woman can spend answering telephones, taking reservations, and making beds."

"Don't you get to know the people staying in the cabins?"

"Couples come here only for weekends, and they're gone before you know it."

"It doesn't sound like a very good job."

"It's fine," she said. "You know I like to be by myself, but I don't like sitting around a group of empty roadside cabins. Would you come up for a weekend and entertain me?"

So that's the reason for her call, I thought. I asked myself if I still had a flicker of interest in her and, in all honesty, I had to admit that I did. Not the kind that would make me want to get back together with her but a sort of residual interest— memories of how she had lighted up my lonely life at college in Southern California. There, the prevailing ethos of conventional good looks and conventional attitudes had made me more or less an outcast from the day I arrived. In my senior year, Mary had turned up, not as a student but as an assistant in the Religion Department, and had surprised me by taking a liking to me. It had all ended in nothing because we were simply too different to get on with each other. I was put off by her parochialism, by her religion—I was an agnostic and she was a fundamentalist Christian—and even by her Southern accent. All that was, of course, history, and was of consequence only because, unlike her life, mine was still unsettled. Despite my long-standing preoccupation with getting married and having children, I was now forty-seven, and an aging bachelor. Something seemed to be stopping me from moving forward in that area of life and creating my own home and hearth.

I was about to beg off when she asked, "Do you know Islesboro?"

"I know a little corner of it. Why do you ask?"

"I camped out there for six weeks last summer. I think it's the most beautiful place on the face of the earth. This summer I'm planning to look for a little land there. My idea is to build a little cottage there one day."

"If I were you, I wouldn't buy anything on Islesboro," I said. "It's very ritzy and old money. I think you would be happier on the mainland."

"But, honey, I like the wild. To me, that's Maine—and there's no place I know that's more wild, more beautiful than Islesboro. I simply love the pine trees there."

"Have you looked at any property there yet?"

"No. I got the idea just recently, and Earl is of course against it. If I did find something, I'd have to raise the money for it myself."

For years afterward, I could not work out why her project interested me. Did I, without knowing it, want a house, and since Islesboro was about the only summer place I knew, was I, too, tempted by the idea of having a piece of ground there to call my own? Such an idea was preposterous. Aside from my not being able to afford the land, the ferry slip to Islesboro was at least a steady eight-hour drive from New York City—and, of course, I wasn't capable of driving. After that, there was the problem of getting on and off the ferry and of getting around the island by myself. I could follow the town road on foot or on a bicycle alone, but, beyond the confines of the road, I could not take a step without fear of tripping, falling, or encountering natural hazards. Did I fancy that I could exorcise my own absurd wish by helping Mary look for a piece of land? I always lived vicariously. Whatever the reasons, there was no denying that it would be pleasant to go back to Islesboro and see it from a perspective other than that of Annette's house.

"So you will come up to Maine for old time's sake?" Mary asked.

"Down to Maine, you mean." I was about to explain that Maine was always Down East because it was downwind—she always brought out my pedantic side—but stopped short.

"Yes, I'll come," I said.

I HAD NEVER been to Maine under my own steam and was staggered to discover how difficult the trip was. The train and boat services there had long since been discontinued. A bus required a change in Boston and all together took nine hours to a point near the ferry slip, and anyway buses made me sick to my stomach. I had no choice but to fly. That required a taxi ride to the airport, the flight to Portland, and a limousine ride to Camden, where Mary picked me up in a rented car. Just getting there took a big bite out of my monthly budget and a day out of my writing. Then, the cabin at Mary's disposal as chatelaine turned out to be only one bare room with an outhouse for a lavatory. Worst of all, being with Mary was awkward. Because we had been close friends, I had trouble being natural with her, although she, being a wife and a mother, managed that better than I did.

In the morning, we drove to the ferry slip, just in time to

be the last of thirty cars to be loaded onto the nine-o'clock ferry. Twenty minutes later, we were deposited on the island, and we drove due south on the town road to the village, where we stopped at the Dark Harbor Shop, the island's general store. We scooted onto a couple of stools at the soda fountain and ordered ice-cream cones.

"I'm sure houses and land in Islesboro are all closely held and are passed on within families," I said to Mary. "I doubt if there is even a real-estate agent here."

"Don't you say that," said the man who was scooping ice cream into our cones. "I might work here as a soda jerk, but I have many house lots and houses for sale."

For a moment, I thought the fellow was having us on. But it turned out that he moonlighted as a Realtor. We had hardly taken our first lick of ice cream when he called to the owner in the back to take over for a while, herded us into his car, and started out on a scouting mission.

"An unusual feature of this island is that you are close to the water everywhere—you can see it through the trees from almost any point," the Realtor told us.

"What kind of trees are they?" I asked.

"The ones lining the town road?" he said. "Pines and spruces and birches. You'll notice that this island has wonderful smells everywhere."

"Do you get a lot of people looking for property here?" Mary asked.

"All the time," he said, as we coasted along the town road toward the southern tip of the island. "But there are two kinds of clients who come to me looking for an island home. There are those who get me to take them to every house and every piece of land and never buy anything. I call them 'kick the tire' folk. And then, there is the other kind. I show them just one thing and they fall in love with it and want to go to contract. I call them 'give me the keys' folk. You look to me like real buyers."

I laughed uncertainly. This fellow is as wily as he is smooth,

I thought. I had never met a Realtor before and I did not want to be carted around by him on false pretenses, so I said, "I've just come along for the ride—it's Mary who is looking for something."

"I sure didn't come here all the way from Nashville just to kick tires," Mary said. "But my husband, Earl, will need a lot of persuading."

"Say no more," the Realtor said. "I understand completely. You've heard of Crane toilets? Well, Mr. Crane, the genius behind the business, was a longtime summer resident of Dark Harbor. His second wife was a Japanese woman named Mine"—pronounced Mina. "She's a widow and owns the Crane cottage. It has a swimming pool and is beautifully furnished with antique pieces. Mrs. Crane loves the cottage, she loves everything about it, but she's an artist and spends a lot of time in Japan, so she's put it on the market. Anyone who buys it will get the priceless antique pieces, because she wants it maintained just the way it was when Mr. Crane was alive. She said to me, 'Bud'—that's what everybody calls me—'find someone who will feel about the cottage the way Mr. Crane did. That's what he would want.' You see, I don't think she just wants money, she'd like someone who will give the cottage tender loving care. Now, Mary, anyone looking at you would know that you are the T.L.C. kind."

A cottage—perhaps because of my English associations—made me think of a little peasant dwelling, which did not square with a house with a swimming pool and antique pieces, so I asked, "How big is the cottage?"

"Not so big. Summer cottages here have eight or ten bedrooms."

"They call that a cottage?" I exclaimed.

"That's what the big old summer houses on this island are called," he explained.

"That's far too big for little old me, Bud," Mary said, flustered. "I don't need one of your 'cottages.' I'm just looking for a small house, or maybe even a campsite."

"But, Mary, you won't find a better deal. Mrs. Crane has put it on the market for just three and a quarter."

"You don't mean three thousand two hundred and fifty dollars!" I exclaimed. I was staggered at the low figure, but then I had no idea about the price of real estate on a remote island.

"No, three hundred and twenty-five thousand," Bud said, without a hint of condescension. "Now, I'm saying that from memory. It could be a little more or a little less; I'd have to check my records, so don't hold me to it."

Mary flinched.

"That's not too much," Bud said, unfazed. "That's what you would pay for a small apartment in a big city without land, without a swimming pool, and without its own private dock. It's nice to bring in your boat to your own dock after a hard day's sailing."

"I don't sail. I just want a place I can sleep in," Mary said, trying to impress upon him that she was interested in buying something really modest.

"Say no more," he said. "I understand completely. You want a hideaway on an island where you can meditate and walk, breathe wonderful island air, and gaze at the moon."

"How did you know that, Bud?" Mary asked.

"I know just the right spot for you," he said. I thought for a moment that he was coming down to earth, but, immediately, he was up in the clouds again. "As it happens, Mrs. Crane is also selling seventy-five acres on the other side of the town road from her cottage, with three or four thousand feet of prime shorefront."

"But I only want a small piece of land," Mary said, aghast.

"I always say to my clients, there is no harm in thinking big," he said. "In order to get an idea of the market, you have to start with the prime properties."

He turned east, onto a dirt road next to dense woods, and we followed him out of the car.

"You've brought us to the Black Forest," Mary said.

"This is the Crane land," he said.

"But where is the water?" she asked.

"Down a piece," Bud said. "We can walk down to it."

"But you can't see the land for the trees," Mary said. "It's so dark and ugly."

"The land is thick with trees, alders, and brush because no one has walked on it since the first planting was done sometime in the thirties," he said.

"I can't imagine anyone wanting to live here," Mary said. "It's so doggone dark."

"But people here like the seclusion that woods offer, Mary," Bud said. "You could build yourself a wonderful little house and look out onto the water through the trees."

"I really want to find a small piece of land already prepared for a house," Mary said.

Bud turned, switching his interest from Mary to me so fast that I was caught off guard. "Have you thought of buying some island property for yourself? Shore property in Maine is as scarce as hens' teeth, and it is a safer and better investment than stocks. You could double your money in a year."

I was taken by surprise by his interest in me as a prospective client. I had never owned land or a house—I lived in a rented apartment. Whenever I had a little money left over from my writing, I invested it in stocks, but perhaps because I was averse to risk—in my experience, people who earn money the hard way tend not to be gamblers—I had not done well in the market. I now found myself stepping, however gingerly, into Bud's net by innocently observing, "It's true. Maybe land is a better investment than stocks, but I know the kind of people who live on this island. Mrs. Crane probably wants to sell the seventy-five acres as a unit. I couldn't begin to afford that."

"No, sir," Bud said. "We're in the process of surveying and subdividing the seventy-five acres into eight or nine house lots, but the best piece of land is this fifteen-acre parcel along this dirt road. It's like a wedge of pie—broad along the town road and narrow along the shore. Its beach is very desirable. Mr.

Crane and his family used to use it for their picnics. In fact, he put this dirt road in here so that they could drive their picnic supplies right down to the beach. I wager it's the only sandy beach at this end of the island."

I scarcely knew how big an acre was, but fifteen acres sounded like a lot. If shore property is as scarce as Bud says, maybe it would make sense to buy it and hold it as an investment, I thought. I could not resist asking how much the parcel was.

"This particular parcel is listed for seventy-five thousand dollars. The other Crane lots are less expensive. Would you be interested in seeing them?"

"I was hoping to get half an acre for two or three thousand dollars," Mary said anxiously.

I thought Bud would be insulted by Mary's pitiful figure, but I had misjudged him. He soothingly said, "You leave it to me. I'll find you something. It will probably be a little piece up-island. Maybe not on the water, but with a view of the water. But you'll be able to enjoy everything that the island has to offer."

"Is seventy-five thousand dollars for this land negotiable?" I asked.

"I'm glad you asked," Bud said. "You hear the airplane up there? That's Mr. Morris looking over the land for his grandchildren. He's probably going to make an offer for this parcel this evening, but if you make an offer to me now, you'll have the first call."

"When you say 'an offer,' does that mean Mrs. Crane would entertain an offer under seventy-five thousand dollars?" I asked.

"I can't speak for her, but I reckon there might be a little give, seeing that Mr. Crane left her plenty. I'll be talking to her lawyer this evening. Would you like to make a verbal offer? I won't hold you to it. It'll just be between us as an indication of your interest."

One of the things I missed about India was the cut and thrust of bargaining. Hardly anything had a fixed price, and one proved one's mettle by haggling. I recalled that when my parents haggled for a special acquisition like a carpet, they would ask questions like how many knots it had per square inch, whether the dye was vegetable or chemical, whether its fringe was original. They thought that by sounding knowledgeable they would win the respect of the rug merchant, avoid being cheated, and, perhaps, eventually talk down the price. As if I were merely haggling over a carpet, I bombarded Bud with what I thought were the kinds of question my parents would have asked.

"Wouldn't it be expensive to clear a couple of acres as a house site?" I asked at one point.

"You could make a heap of money by selling the trees you would take down. The pulp and firewood alone would justify the cost of clearing the house site. None of the trees have been figured into the price."

"But you wouldn't want to send a bulldozer in here—wouldn't it ruin the land?" I asked.

"That's exactly what I was going to say," Bud said. "You would have to do selective cutting—clear a space for a house, then take down some other trees so that you could have a romantic view of the water through the woods."

"I've never known anybody to buy land without walking it," I said.

"Affirmative," he said.

"But how can that be done when the land is impenetrable, what with the trees, alders, and brush?" I asked.

He seemed, for the first time, to be ruffled, but rallied quickly. "I myself would never buy land until I had walked every inch of it," he said. "However, there's only one problem. I don't carry liability insurance, and, as you can see, Mary, there are a lot of roots, stumps, and suchlike sticking up. If someone fell and hurt himself—or, I should say, herself—I'd be in mighty big trouble. So, as I always say, we can't be too careful when we walk in the woods."

I immediately lost interest in walking the land. It was as

if, by a conjurer's trick, he had produced a swarm of yellow jackets to keep me away from the land.

It was later, much later, that I realized that if I had been able to walk the land—or, indeed, to see it for myself—I might have resisted his blandishments. While beautifully situated and perhaps an excellent investment, this parcel of land, no matter how it might be improved, would remain rough and hazardous.

Bud, as if sensing my disengagement, changed his tack. "You would love the island life. People come to summer here from Colorado, California, Hawaii, even France and Belgium. The island's natural beauty tugs at people everywhere."

The plane overhead swooped down low, circled, gained height, and streaked away.

"That was Mr. Morris taking a closer look," Bud said. "He's now probably rushing back to the mainland to have a conference with his grandchildren."

As a rule, the thought of competition galvanized me, but the idea of competing with a Mr. Morris for this land left me cold. I was ready to get into the car and go back to the mainland, and so, I imagined, was Mary, since it was quite clear that Bud had nothing in his inventory that was within her price range. But Bud was not so easily shaken off.

"I think you should at least walk down with me and see the beach and the ocean view," he said. "After all, the value of the land is calculated on the shore footage."

"What do you mean?" I asked. I hated to expose my ignorance, or indeed my interest, but I had never heard of land being measured in feet.

"Shorefront here sells for about a hundred dollars a foot, give or take a few dollars," he said. "This parcel of land has, if I remember correctly, nine-hundred-plus feet of shore footage."

Soon Mary and I were following Bud away from the town road, along the gradually sloping dirt road that cut through the north end of the property.

"Just eyeballing this road, I would wager it was eight

hundred feet long," he said, pushing back or breaking the shoots and branches that were hanging over the road. "If you had to put this road in yourself, it would cost you at least ten dollars a foot. I reckon you would be out of pocket a total of eight thousand dollars. And this road is just being thrown in, like the trees. I am not even sure that Mrs. Crane is aware of its value."

"How close can you build to the shore?" Mary asked.

"Pretty close to the beach," he said.

"Wouldn't it be washed away in the winter?" I asked.

"It could, if you didn't sink the foundation too deep," he said, equably. "But, as we say on the island, we come here because we like the life by the water."

"I seem to have read that there are federal regulations about setbacks," I said. "Don't houses have to be built back from the shore?"

"Affirmative," Bud said. "But only seventy-five feet from the high-water mark."

At the bottom of the dirt road, there was a little turnaround for a car, and at a right angle to the road was the beach, which was, indeed, sandy, though the sand was interspersed with rocks. There was a cove, which formed a natural tide pool. Beyond the cove, to the south, the beach turned wild and rocky.

"Those rocks mark where your shore land ends," Bud said.

"Oh, the beach is beautiful!" Mary exclaimed. "The islands out in the sea look stunning."

I stood on the beach with Mary, trying to see what she was seeing.

"It's unspoiled, it's virginal, it's so pure," Mary said rhapsodically.

At that moment, the water was still, the beach free of even a single seagull or sign of any life, making me feel that I was having a primordial experience.

"This is what I imagine the world must have been like when He created Adam and Eve," Mary said.

Land, 1981

Adam and Eve certainly would not have been in Maine, I thought. Yet, for a moment, I had an illusion of our being in the Garden of Eden, surrounded by an all-enveloping silence.

"Don't you think this is worth seventy-five thousand dollars?" Bud asked. His voice broke the trancelike atmosphere like a pistol shot, reminding us that we were taking up a lot of his time and, perhaps, wasting it.

We immediately walked up the dirt road, and Bud drove us back to Dark Harbor Shop and to Mary's car. As we were leaving, I said to him, "I'm sorry we ended up being kick-the-tire kind of folk."

"Don't you say that," Bud said. "I have a feeling that we'll be doing business together one of these days."

I HAD SCARCELY returned to the city when Bud started sending me listings of all the properties for sale in Dark Harbor, along with notes about the island, its tides, its lighthouse, and its lobster boats. He also called me and asked if I had reached a decision about the Crane land.

"Even if you buy it, you won't be committed to the sale."

That sounded like doublespeak, and I asked him to explain.

"A sale doesn't go through if the perc test is negative."

"What's that?"

"The perc test tells you how quickly the water percolates through the soil, and that tells you whether you can have a septic tank or not. Without a septic tank, you can't build."

"How is the test done?"

"You get hold of Dennis Small, the soil scientist. For eighty-five dollars he'll do the test and write up a report."

When he said "you," I flinched. He seemed to take it for granted that I was going to buy and build on the Crane land, while I was hoping only for a tip that would enable me to buy some land somewhere and quickly sell it and pocket the profit.

I now realize that that was naïve of me. Land cannot be bought and sold in a minute like a stock on a stock market. But it was a tribute to Bud's talent that he had made me entertain the fantasy that land was as liquid as stock—indeed, required as little attention.

At one point, I told Bud that my total savings were about equal to the price of the Crane land and that they were invested in common stock—all long-term holdings. I could not bear to liquidate them. In fact, I daily checked in newspapers the changes in the prices of the companies in my portfolio, as if Texaco, U.S. Steel, and I.B.M. were Stella Dallas, Ma Perkins, and Lorenzo Jones—characters in the radio soap operas I used to listen to as a schoolboy in Arkansas.

"Who's ever heard of spending one's real money to buy property?" Bud said. "Everyone takes out a mortgage and deducts the interest from their income tax. It's one of the great benefits the government offers to home buyers and property owners."

Bud's solution did not appeal to me. Aside from the fact that I had grown up hearing my father say, "Neither a borrower nor a lender be," my income was so unpredictable that I was terrified about taking on a debt that I might have trouble paying off; I was not confident that I could even meet regular interest payments. As a writer, I lived at the pleasure of my editor, who lived at the pleasure, ultimately, of the publisher. Indeed, I felt that my income was no more stable than that of the hawker who used to go up and down our gulli in Lahore, crying, "Special powder will cure headaches, backaches, stomachaches, and foot aches!" Some people who bought the powder swore by it; others swore at it. Anyway, like my writing, it was not a necessity. No doubt my writing nourished some souls, but there were many more souls who got along perfectly well without it. Most important of all, there was no way that I could get to the Crane land by myself, let alone survive there. Consequently, it was much easier to sit in my armchair in New York and dream of having a summer house on the island. Still,

I hoped and prayed all the time that Mr. Morris or someone else would buy the wretched parcel and relieve me of ever having to think about the subject. But the winter had set in, and, as Bud pointed out, that was a dead season for real-estate sales on the island, and also Mr. Morris—if he had ever been interested—was out of the picture. That left me the sole prospective buyer.

I do not have a good explanation for why I led Bud on or, rather, allowed myself to be led on by him. Did the fact that the island was favored by the rich stoke the same competitive spirit that had made me strive to surpass in education my sighted siblings? But then, owning a baby Black Forest could not compare with achieving academic success and so proving to them—and, by extension, perhaps, to the larger world—that I was to be respected rather than pitied. Was I lured by my sense of how beautiful the island was, much as I sought out women who I sensed were extremely beautiful? But I felt that owning property in the middle of nowhere could not compensate for feeling like a piece of damaged goods in the way that being seen around town with beautiful women did. Was I tempted by the thought of having a holiday place like everyone else I knew? But I could not play tennis or golf, did not sail, or even swim very well, had never taken a vacation, and had scarcely done anything physical in my adult life—indeed, was afraid of vacations and worried that if my mind were ever not engaged in work I would sink into a trough of depression. Was it the fact that, even after reading and writing for twelve or fifteen hours a day, I still had energy left over that needed an outlet? But then, thinking about buying the Crane land and what I might do with it was hardly mentally taxing.

None of the explanations, in and of itself, was persuasive. If I were in the market for a summer place, East Hampton, Nantucket, Martha's Vineyard, Provincetown—or any number of places—would have suited me better than Islesboro. They were refuges for writers, artists, journalists, actors, and intellectuals—the kind of people I generally met and associated with in New York. But then, I scarcely knew any of those resorts firsthand. My friends who summered there rarely asked me to their houses, leaving me to speculate about the reasons. Did they think that I was a city person who could not be pried away from his work, or did they think that, because I was handicapped, I would not enjoy the outdoor life? For whatever reasons, my friends did not invite me. Anyway, it had taken a private plane and Annette's imagination to get me to Islesboro. Now it was Bud who, like Annette, was extending himself to me, but who, unlike Annette, had an ulterior motive for offering me, as it were, a bite out of the apple.

Eventually, I mastered my temptation and informed Bud that I had decided, once and for all, against buying the Crane, or any other, land on the island.

"Affirmative," he said. "I assume you don't want me to call you or send you any material on the island."

"That's right."

"Affirmative. It's been nice doing business with you." He was affable as always.

I felt relieved to have put the whole business of the island out of my mind.

ONE EVENING EARLY in 1982, some seven months after I had visited the island with Mary, I was having dinner with Annette at an elegant French restaurant in New York and mentioned that I had heard that her mother had been upset at Samuel and Annette's selling the Dark Harbor property.

"That's not true," she said. "Mummy only visited Dark Harbor four or five times. She had no interest in keeping the property."

Suddenly, there was a certain awkwardness in the air, making me feel that I might have overstepped the boundary of good manners by referring to something that was a private family matter. Things were made worse by the absence of

Samuel, who at the last minute had begged off, pleading an overlooked prior engagement. In order to cover up my faux pas, I launched into a sentence without knowing what I was going to say.

"You know, I have always meant to ask you . . ." I did not know how to go on. There was awkward silence—generally, when I was with Annette, there was a lot of talk and laughter. I pressed ahead and found myself saying, "Do you know the Crane land?"

"In Dark Harbor? I think I know the land. But I don't remember it clearly. Why do you ask? Are you going to buy it?" Her tone was teasing.

"I'm thinking about it," I said, surprised by my own answer. I thought I had long since dismissed the subject from my mind. But the truth was that the prospect of owning a piece of ground of my own had even more resonances than I had initially acknowledged. I was gradually becoming aware of them through deep and continual introspection. In India I had grown up hearing that a poor man who owned even a postage stamp of land could never starve and that there was no curse greater than being landless. On top of that, there was the personal trauma of the Partition, in 1947, when every last member of my extended family who lived in what became Pakistan fled the Muslim country with only the clothes on their backs. Practically the first thing all my relatives did was to try to acquire a small piece of land, where they could build a little replica of the house they had lost in Lahore. Later, at Oxford, I had spent considerable time trying to puzzle out how the English landed gentry in the sixteenth and seventeenth centuries had got hobbled by debt, become impoverished, and lost their land and position to a new merchant class. The idea that I could own land of my own, and thereby even become part of a landed gentry, kept haunting me.

As I write this, I realize how ludicrous that idea was. I was living in rich America, not poor India; and the landed gentry was associated with old families, county seats, and inheritances, whereas all I was aspiring to was a forest on a island in some remote corner of Maine. But the state of my mind was determinedly self-deceptive when it came to the question of owning land.

"Wait till I tell Samuel that you're buying the Crane land. He'll fret about your bicycling all around the place."

I found myself backtracking. "Actually, it's not at all certain that I'll ever buy it. I don't have the money, or, rather, I have the money but I don't want to blow it on just one thing."

I looked away. Money was one subject I always avoided with rich friends. I felt that, in order to be friends, we had to maintain the illusion of being on equal footing. In the early days of my friendship with Annette, I had once made an issue of paying for dinner, fully aware that what was a substantial layout for me was loose change for her. That gesture had merely drawn attention to our basic inequality. After that, I resigned myself to accepting her hospitality without protest—flowers for her and occasional presents for her children being about all I let myself offer in return.

"I think I can swing the Crane land, though," I said. Saying this was nothing more than a ploy to divert her attention from the subject of money. "I hope you will come and stay with me there sometime—I mean, once I build a house."

"What are you saying?" I asked myself. "Are you mad? She'll take you at your word. Now you might have to buy the land and build a house just to prove to her that you can." It occurs to me now that I was indeed trying to become more a part of Annette's world, as if I fancied that, by buying the Crane land, I was putting up an ante to join her and her friends at a poker table, conveniently forgetting that the ante was all I had while they had unlimited resources.

My father, although he was a mere government servant with a commensurately low salary, had always played high-stakes poker with some of the richest men in India. He claimed that he had, on balance, won and had used his winnings to educate us children well. Perhaps I had absorbed his gambling spirit. Indeed, I thought that it was because of that spirit that I had been able to get out of India, where the blind were condemned to beg or be family charity cases, able to get myself to the West and to Oxford and Harvard, and able to embark on the exciting, if dangerous, profession of writing. There was, however, no correlation between that gambling spirit and the cautious way I had always managed my money. But now, under the influence of Annette's company, I was about to bet everything on one throw of the dice, when there was nothing to win and everything to lose.

"Those were wonderful times we had in Dark Harbor, weren't they?" she said.

I expected her to go on and ask me what I would do with the land, how I would get to it, a hundred other practical questions, but I forgot that such mundane problems exist only for those of us who do not have money to spare—that people in her world are shielded from such practical concerns, are in fact barely aware that they even exist for ordinary people. Of course, many artists I have known are also impractical, but for them there is always a day of reckoning. In any case, I imagined that I was not like them, that because of my blindness I had had my nose rubbed in reality early on. I sometimes thought that as a result I lacked the capacity for lighthearted enjoyment, something that everyone around me, whether of modest means or lavish resources, took for granted.

"I can't wait to see what Samuel will say."

She doesn't seem to realize what a serious step I am contemplating, I thought.

"What do you think Samuel will say?"

"He'll say, 'Oh my God, those horrible little planes. I'm glad it's Ved who'll be taking them and not me.' " She laughed her harmonic laugh.

It is the way of the rich to talk down their privileges, I thought.

Soon we were talking about how any land in Dark Harbor was a good investment, about how Beatrice missed the island, about how nice it would be if Annette had a foothold there for the children. At some point, the idea emerged of our going halves on the Crane parcel, which was big enough for two houses with plenty of acreage around them. I would like to think that I was not the first to raise the idea, but, truthfully, I cannot be sure now. All I remember clearly is that she seized the idea eagerly. Buying the Crane land suddenly seemed manageable. I would now have to come up with only half the purchase price—thirty-five thousand dollars (Mrs. Crane had dropped her price to seventy thousand dollars)—and I would not have to wean myself off all my stocks. I could sell half my shares and still keep all the names I was attached to in my portfolio. I was determined to avoid getting into debt—to avoid taking out a mortgage.

The next day, I called Bud and told him that I was buying the Crane parcel with Annette. The moment the words were out of my mouth, I forfeited the chance for second thoughts. The train pulled out of the station so abruptly that all my normal hesitations and deliberations fell by the wayside. The day after my forty-eighth birthday, I made the down payment for my share of the Crane land.

Annette was impatient with the technicalities of the division. She barely listened when I told her that there was no way to divide the land horizontally since that would mean that all the valuable shore land would be in one half, and the much less valuable land along the town road in the other. Consequently, the only option was to divide the land vertically, but, in that case, the more desirable half was clearly the one with the dirt road and the cove. I pressed her to take that half, but she wouldn't hear of it. Then she turned the matter over to her lawyer, who simply followed her wishes, and so I ended up with the more desirable half. It was then that it struck me that she had bought the land only to help me out. Indeed, in due course, she deeded her half over to me as a gift, ignoring my offer to buy it from her.

Her generous action revived my complicated feelings

about being an object of charity. Since there was no way I could pay her back, she had unwittingly reminded me that we were not—and never could be—equals. Her hospitality, whether at her house or in a restaurant, was something I could gloss over, but a gift of land was an act of another magnitude. No matter how I rationalized her gift, I felt that my pride had been injured. Although she never acted any differently toward me— by word or gesture—and although I struggled against my feelings of being indebted to her, still our friendship cooled off. Perhaps, I reasoned, it would have changed anyway. In 1983, I got married, and in 1989, she divorced Samuel and married the internationally acclaimed fashion designer Oscar de la Renta. Whatever the reason, after the land business, I saw much less of her than I had before.

IV

ENGAGEMENT

I SLESBORO WAS FIRST SETTLED IN THE SEVENTEENTH century by a small tribe of Indians who belonged to the Abenaki Confederacy and who were called the Taratines, or Tarratines, possibly meaning "traders." At the time, the island was thick with woods, teeming with ducks, foxes, and minks. In the mid-eighteenth century, it was settled by some enterprising Americans, who cleared land, built simple houses, and sired large families. About these settlers, John Pendleton Farrow writes, in his "History of Islesboro, Maine" (1893), "They had one chimney in the center of the house, which would take ten thousand bricks to build. The fire-place in the kitchen would burn cord wood six feet long. The kitchen was ornamented with a pole hung from the ceiling used for drying pumpkins, herbs, clothes, etc., with a gun hung up on the partition. They used sand on the floors and cedar boughs for a broom. . . ." Because of the prevalence of sedimentary-rock shelf and marshland, only one-third of the island was deemed cultivable. Potatoes were one of the main crops, and they were shipped to and sold in markets in Boston. In the early years of settlement, who owned what in Islesboro—or indeed, who owned Islesboro itself—was tied up in litigation. Then, in 1789, the residents preempted the court case and incorporated their settlement as a township, appointing, among others, two constables, three selectmen, a surveyor of wood and lumber and a surveyor of highways, a registrar of deeds, two tythingmen, two hog-reeves and two fence-viewers. In the first year, the town levied taxes, elected two island residents to begin laying out town roads, and chose a representative to send to Congress. In the following years, it established school districts, built a meetinghouse, and dealt with such arcane problems as whether hogs should be allowed to run at large and how to combat the nuisance of the crows. In the War of 1812, it kept the British ships anchored near Castine supplied with provisions, although the settlers on the island were neutral. As Farrow writes, "their action on this occasion was not patriotic, but considering the hard times they had to get along, they were excusable in a manner; and in those days, as well as the present, they sacrificed principle for money."

In 1820, Maine was admitted to the Union, and Islesboro became part of Waldo County. After the American Civil War—because of improvements in transportation, both by train and by steamship; an increase in leisure time for the nation's middle and upper classes; and a desire to escape the oppressive summer heat and rampant disease of East Coast cities—seaside resorts in Maine became popular places to go. Initially, the most popular resort was Bar Harbor, but gradually Islesboro acquired a following. Eighteen-sixty-eight saw the building of the island's first summer hotel—a simple, two-and-a-half-story structure catering to visitors from the mainland—at Ryder's Cove, on the eastern shore. Then steamboat service to Islesboro from the nearby town of Bangor improved, and several Bangor residents erected modest cottages on the island. Around the same time, a second settlement of summer cottages clustered around another little cove, Hewes Point, to the south. Hewes Point, like Ryder's Cove, was on the eastern shore, and both had deep, protected ports, where steamboats could safely dock. In 1882, Jeffrey Brackett, a junior at Harvard College, started a third settlement, when he bought two hundred acres at Pendleton's Point, on the southern tip of the island, and moved a one-and-a-half-story house onto it, in time adding onto the house and enlarging it. Subsequently, Brackett's property was divided and subdivided and sold off—our land was part of that subdivision—making way for more houses, this time mostly on the west shore.

In 1885, the Boston real-estate developer James Murray Howe visited the southern end of the island with the wealthy Philadelphia steamship owner James Winsor. Struck by the area's development possibilities, Winsor had Howe purchase property for him in the area and, in 1888, founded the Islesboro Land & Improvement Company. Winsor sold shares in it to approximately twenty-five Philadelphia businessmen, including Anthony J. Drexel, of Drexel & Co. (a family bank); Alexander Biddle, of the Pennsylvania Railroad; Clement A. Griscom, of the American, Inman, and Rio Star Steamship Lines; George Philler, of the First National Bank of Philadelphia; and Charles Platt, Sr., of the North American Insurance Company. Once the money had been raised, Winsor had Howe accumulate hundreds of acres of shorefront property. They lured similarly influential families from Philadelphia, Boston, New York, and St. Louis to summer there. Consequently, the whole southern quarter of the island got developed on a much grander scale than Ryder's Cove or Hewes Point. Along the way, the area came to be known as Dark Harbor, so called after a harbor of the same name on the eastern shore, considerably south of Hewes Point. It was more or less concealed between two tall bluffs and ringed by tall spruces. Taking advantage of the cover, American boats had been able to slip in and out of the harbor unobserved, their masts hidden from pirates and from rival European powers that, at one time or another, had laid claim to Castine, a few miles north and one of the first trading posts on the coast of Maine. Late in the nineteenth century, a building boom on the western shore of Dark Harbor was set off because, among other things, the newcomers realized that the sheltered sea-lane between the island and the mainland was ideal for boating. The Belfast, Maine, *Republican Journal* for August 15, 1901, exclaimed, "Imagine an island, barren save for a few scattered houses and settlements three or four years ago, to have grown to be a beautiful villa-dotted paradise where $500,000 has been expended for summer cottages alone." And Thomas J. Lyons, Maine's Commissioner of Industrial and Labor Statistics, wrote in 1908, "Islesboro is now the wealthiest town in Waldo County and all through the coming of the summer visitor. The improvements brought about by the increase in the town's resources are plainly visible. . . . In addition to all this, land values have increased so that there is no farm in town valued at less than $5,000." Charles Dana Gibson, who had first come in 1903, remarked to the press, "One summer in Dark Harbor is worth a dozen summers abroad."

As FAR AS I could imagine, there was no chance of my ever spending any summer in Dark Harbor, but as soon as I acquired the land, I started thinking about what I should do with it. Holding it just as an investment seemed sterile. I thought I should make use of it and enjoy it—perhaps put a platform tent on it and cajole a friend into coming up for a weekend or two during the summer to picnic on the beach, as the Cranes had done. But then, I did not have many friends who could fork out five or six hundred dollars for travel to and from the island. Even if I somehow could get a friend to bear the expense, I had no resources to call on for hospitality. Annette had had a big staff at her command and had been in a position to lay out a dazzling array of activities. What did I have to offer: licks of ice cream from the Dark Harbor Shop and a sleepover in a tent—that is, if somehow I was able to get a patch of the land cleared and a platform put up? Anyway, camping was not my style, and I was not sure that it was the style of any of my friends. Perhaps if I had been married with small children, I might have felt differently, but I was not.

I now started dreaming about putting up a simple seaside cottage, as I thought of it. I could not actually hope for a house with a fireplace in the master bathroom—a feature much commented upon in Annette's erstwhile house—but I could hope for something modest and romantic. The idea of laying down roots in the New World, in my adopted country—and in Dark Harbor, where the likes of Annette migrated and congregated—was exciting. I conveniently ignored the facts that it was a resort, that the summer people went there for only a couple of months, and that their real roots were in the places where they lived year-round.

I called up Bud and asked, "How much would it cost to put up a simple, cheap seaside cottage on my land?"

"Some people do it for as little as twenty thousand dollars."

What he did not say was that he was talking about something like a fisherman's hut, without plumbing or other modern conveniences, and I did not have the wit to ask him what kind of house he meant. I only fastened on the idea that, having saved thirty-five thousand dollars on the land, I could perhaps afford to splurge some of that found money on a house.

I started asking friends about architects who might be interested in building me a house on a remote island. All the architects I consulted—like my acquaintance Harry Cobb, a professor of architecture at Harvard—turned out to live in old houses. They all advised me against a new house, saying that, knowing my sensitivity to sound, they doubted if I would ever be happy in one. In order to educate myself in the differences between new and old houses and other matters architectural, I went to see a close friend who had a successful architectural practice in New York.

"Your advisers are right—a new house would be torture for you," my friend told me. "New American construction uses

Sheetrock for internal walls. It's such a thin, flimsy plaster-board that it scarcely serves as a barrier against sound. Knowing you as I do, I think there are other things you wouldn't like about Sheetrock. If you banged a chair hard against the wall, you would be likely to punch a hole in it."

"Then why do people use Sheetrock?"

"It's cheap, it's easy to install—you just stick it on the studs and tape over the joints of the boards and paint it. And it gives the house a nice, clean, uncluttered look. And contemporary architecture is mostly about appearance. I just built a palace for a lady in the Hamptons. She's tickled pink. The poor dear doesn't realize that she's living in a cardboard palace whereas someone of her ilk a hundred years ago would have lived in a stone or marble palace."

In New York, I had once lived in a new apartment building, and I had hated it; I never understood why it was so noisy. The voices of my neighbors travelled as if there were no wall between our apartments, and when my neighbor who lived two floors above me, a saxophonist, practiced his instrument, it sounded almost as if he were playing in my living room. Clearly the apartment house had had Sheetrock walls.

"Could you build me a new house with plaster walls?" I asked my friend.

"I could, but it would cost you the earth to have a New York architectural firm build you a house on an island. I suggest you get a local Maine architect. Besides, plaster walls are hellishly expensive and, in this day and age, something of an anachronism. In this country, the craft of plastering has gone the way of the stonemasons. I doubt if you could find a plasterer in New York, though Maine is one place where you might still be able to find one. I think you'll have to lower your sights for the kind of house you want to build."

"Are you suggesting that I build myself a cheap Sheetrock house?"

"What do you mean by 'cheap'?"

"I was told that you could slap up a house for as little as twenty thousand dollars."

"Someone must be pulling your leg. I doubt if you could build any kind of house for less than a hundred thousand dollars. And you would probably have to add a premium of another twenty or thirty per cent, because all the materials would have to be transported from the mainland in boats. And if your island didn't have a local electrician or a local plumber you would have to hire them from the mainland too."

What my friend was telling me was so staggering, so contrary to what I had imagined, that it took me some time to absorb. Finally, I said, weakly, "Is there anything I could do for twenty or thirty thousand dollars?"

"Nothing. Even a mobile home probably would set you back twice that, and you would be run off the island if you rolled up there with a trailer."

"What have I got myself in for!" I cried. "I had no idea just building a little seaside cottage would be so expensive. Why is it all so complicated?"

"You see, when you write a book, if you don't like parts of it, you can just rewrite them. But when you finish a house, even a simple one, and you find a mistake, it's expensive to correct it. And I don't know a single architect who doesn't make mistakes. Say you put a window too high. Every time you look at that window, it will irritate you, but if you decided to change it you'd not only have to fix the inner wall but also have to do something to the outer skin and perhaps the trim." He must have noticed the dejected look on my face, because he immediately said, "I have an idea. West Virginia, I read recently, is going through some pretty bad times. The coal miners are out of jobs and are hard-pressed. You could buy one of their log cabins and move it up to Maine."

"Be serious."

"I am. I've heard that the coal miners' cabins are exquisite nineteenth-century items."

"Yeah, yeah," I said. "First, how would you find one, and then how would you move it?"

"You would get hold of a local newspaper and look for advertisements for cabins for sale. Go down there, select one, buy it. You probably could pick one up for twenty or thirty thousand dollars. Then you get a builder to dismantle it, log by log, and number the logs. Then you get a trucker to bring up the logs to your island, and then another builder could assemble it like an Erector set."

"But I don't think that anybody on that island lives in a log cabin—any more than they live in a mobile home."

"You could be the first. A nineteenth-century cabin would have much more character than a mobile home. And you could pretend that you are a little Lincoln."

"For God's sake, be serious. Anyway, even if I got a cabin, it would be totally impractical in Maine, with its fog and its cold air."

"The kind of cabin I have in mind is made of seasoned wood. When they were built, the logs were seasoned outdoors. They were probably left out for a few years."

"And nowadays?"

"I don't know. Some mechanical way with compressed air or something."

"So? How does that help with insulation?"

"The logs don't warp and they fit tight as a drum."

I was getting interested in spite of myself. "What about a bathroom?"

"An outhouse, my friend."

"Don't think that would suit me."

"But didn't you tell me that you'll be living in the woods? You could think of yourself as a latter-day Thoreau."

"For God's sake, I don't want to be Lincoln, Thoreau, or a coal miner. I just want a simple seaside cottage."

"Ved, you know as well as I that simple things are hard to achieve and often come at a price."

My FATHER USED to say one must cut one's coat according

to one's cloth, so I set about investigating the option of a coal miner's log cabin. I called up the West Virginia Chamber of Commerce and got hold of a local paper. That's as far as I went, because, when it came down to it, the idea of travelling to West Virginia, locating the right cabin, negotiating the price, hiring someone to dismantle it, someone else to truck it, and still another someone to clear the site on my land and put it up— without knowing what would be the best site for it, how it would fit into the landscape, and whether, in the end, I would really like it—was extremely daunting and seemed, in its own way, expensive. In any event, the unhappy memory of staying in one of the cabins in Mary's care made me decide that I was simply too soft for living in a cabin, however well-seasoned its logs were.

In total frustration, I called Bud and told him to sell the land. In everything to do with the island, I seemed constantly to be doing things that were uncharacteristic of me.

"Affirmative," he said. "But you will have to absorb a little loss because of your quick turnaround."

"How much?"

"That's hard to say. The market has softened since you acquired your property. Anyway, selling will take some time."

"I don't know what else to do but to sell it, because I now realize that I'd hate living in a new house, even if I had the money to build it. I need plaster walls and such."

"Affirmative. That's no problem. You buy the Crane cottage I told you about, and, like the Cranes, you use the beach with your land for picnics."

As if Bud were not satisfied with having sold me my land, he was now trying to sell me a house suitable for a family of ten. Next, he will be trying to sell me furniture and drapes, a car and a boat, I thought. He must think I'm rich, like Annette.

"Come off it! I had trouble raising money to buy the Crane land. Where am I going to get the money to buy a cottage?"

"I could put you in touch with a fellow at Camden

National Bank whom I know. He's giving thirty-year mortgages to my good customers at a reasonable rate."

"Now, look here. I'm a mere writer. I have no steady stream of income. I could never afford to take out a mortgage."

"That's no problem. I have five inexpensive houses for sale on the island. You can buy one of them and move it onto your property. They have lovely plaster walls and moldings—just what you and I like."

It is one thing to move a cabin log by log, quite another to move a whole house from one site to another. The idea was startling, arresting—even riveting.

"You can't just pick up a house and move it as if it were a piece of furniture," I said. "A house must weigh tons."

"Houses are moved here in Maine all the time. We're lucky on this island because we have a good blacktopped town road. You could wheel a twenty-ton truck on it, and it wouldn't crack."

"Still, how do you move a whole house?"

"Like everything else, there is an art to it. You jack up the old building, put it on wheels and roll it onto the new site, which, of course, has to be made ready to receive it."

"What do you mean?"

"You have to clear a site, break ground, and pour a foundation."

"Where in the world would I find someone to undertake such a risky venture as moving a house?"

"We have a famous house mover in Maine. His name is Jim Merry. He's moved a whole village down a mountain."

"He can move a house without damaging it? That's hard to believe."

"Now, I'm not saying that the plaster walls won't settle down or develop a crack or two, but there is nothing that a painter can't fix by applying a coat or two of paint."

"But isn't the landscaping part of the house? Wouldn't a house wrenched from its site and moved somewhere else look out of place?"

"Affirmative. But you can duplicate landscaping. It's not so different from making a Xerox copy of your manuscript."

It was vintage Realtor-speak. He made everything sound easy and simple.

"Has anyone ever moved a house on this island?"

"Affirmative. Liberty Redmond, who lives near your land, and who belongs to one of the great families on the island, sawed her house in two, picked half of the house up, and moved it down to her shore."

"How can you saw a house?"

"With a big electric saw."

"Why would she do that, anyway?"

"She liked one part of the house and not the other, so she took the part she liked and left behind the part she didn't like and then sold it. And the people who bought that half of the house didn't like their view, and they upped the house and moved it and cleared the trees to get a better view. Liberty hadn't reckoned on that, and was she upset."

Bud made the island sound like some kind of a game in which people moved houses around like pieces on a board.

"The houses you say you have for moving—how much are they?"

"They're all under thirty-five thousand dollars—one-tenth the price of the Crane cottage. But, as I said, the market has softened now. I would be honor bound to convey to the seller any good-faith offer you made, however low."

"What do you mean?"

"I mean, you might get a house for much less than it's listed for. There is always give-and-take in price in any transaction."

"Why are those five houses so inexpensive? There must be something wrong with them."

"They have no land to speak of with them, and they were built for islanders to live in, so they are on a much smaller scale than the summer cottages."

"What condition are they in?" I was getting drawn in in spite of myself.

"I would say they're in excellent condition. They're solid as a rock. But that's something you'd have to judge for yourself."

All my conversations with Bud were conducted on the telephone. Indeed, I had bought the land over the telephone. That had not been a great disadvantage since, even if I could have visited it a second time, I could not have learned much beyond what I already knew from my first visit, even if the thick forest had not obscured the features of the land, much as a cataract obscures eyesight. But buying a house was different. I felt I was equipped to judge its character if I could spend some time walking through it. But that would mean more gruelling travel and more expense.

Not for the first time, I excoriated myself for getting involved in a project that was so far away, and so fraught with difficulties for someone who was blind that it might as well have been on the moon. The reality was that, almost for the first time, I was coming up against my limitations, which, by and large, I had generally ignored and, in many ways, had overcome. Indeed, without the convenience of Annette's planes or Mary's car, I did not know how I could get to the island. Even if somehow I got there, where would I stay? There was now an inn on the island, but that only raised the problem of how I would get from it to my land. On top of it, I had no time that I was prepared to take off from my writing, no real interest in ever living in any summer house anywhere. It was dawning on me, as if I were waking from a long sleep, that whether I was keeping or selling the land, moving or building a house, everything would have to be done from an armchair in New York or otherwise involve more expense than I could afford. But I was still not awake enough to tell myself to cut my losses and run.

"But there is no way I can get down to the island," I said to the Realtor now.

"Affirmative. I would be happy to supply you with all the information about the houses, along with some pictures, but I think you also will need your own architect in Maine who can look over the houses for you and give you his professional opinion."

"Are there any architects on the island?"

"No, sir. But we have some of the finest architects in the country on the mainland. I believe Camden is now considered one of the ten best cities for retirement, and people are moving there from all over the country and building."

I was leery of having the Realtor recommend an architect, who would then evaluate the houses that he, the Realtor, was trying to sell me. When I was casting about for a lawyer to act for me in purchasing the Crane land, I had ended up using the lawyer whom Bud had recommended and who was representing Mine Crane, the seller. When I asked the lawyer, Stanley Brown, Jr., of Brown & Crowe, if there was not a conflict of interest in his representing both the seller and the buyer, he had said, "No. This is a sparsely populated state, and, as your Realtor will tell you, all of us here are called to do just about everything."

Aside from the Realtor and the lawyer, I knew scarcely anyone else in the state, so I now found myself asking, "Do you know any architects in Camden?"

"Yes, sir." He rattled off several names but specifically recommended Dick Zimmerman, an architect who he said had designed a much-admired house in Blue Hill, a couple of hours' drive from Camden.

When I got off the phone, I passingly wondered if the Realtor and the architect might not recommend clients to each other as a professional courtesy and if this architect was really as good as the Realtor claimed. Maybe it would have been better for me to ask around for a good architect. But then, I was in no position even to judge how well an architect drew. And, moreover, I was not hiring an architect to design a house for me but merely to look at houses that I might never buy. Even if I did end up buying one, I would eventually have to go and evaluate it for myself.

ON THE TELEPHONE, Zimmerman sounded young, friendly, and well-spoken. He said that he had been trained at an Ivy

League university and had settled in Rockport, Maine, because there he could work independently and design houses, whereas in Boston or New York he could expect to be only either a draftsman in the basement of a large architectural firm or, at most, a junior architect in charge of window-treatment details of some building.

"You sure you want an old house?" he said. "I could design you a great island house that would suggest a boat with portholes for windows."

I could not imagine myself living in a house in the shape of a boat. Anyway, wouldn't that kind of design wear thin quickly? I thought. But then, I suppose, he's young and eager to be experimental.

"Your ideas sound interesting," I said. "But it is only fair that you know my taste. I am an old curmudgeon and I grew up with heavy, sombre architecture."

"But you're going to be by the sea."

"Bay, I think." (In due course, I was to learn that although, technically, the island was in Penobscot Bay, people tended to speak of the narrow, sheltered sea-lane on the western side as the bay and the body of water on the eastern side as the sea or ocean, perhaps because beyond the islands was the open sea extending all the way to Europe.)

"On water, anyway. You want something light and airy with a lot of glass and something that would stand out—would be admired by people sailing past your neck of the woods."

Glass was, acoustically, about the worst material I could think of. I came right out and told him that I could not imagine living in the kind of house he had in mind. "I have decided never to build a house," I said. "I only want your help in looking over some old houses, as I am thinking of buying one of them and moving it to my land. There are five possible houses that I could apparently buy and move. If I can't do that, I'll probably sell the land."

"Don't do that," he said. "Coastal land here is such a good investment—"

"I know—it's rare as hens' teeth," I said, falling into Realtor-speak.

"My wife and I enjoy going out to the island. It's so beautiful there. The first good day we get we'll take our car out there and look over the houses for you."

I thanked him and asked him to get in touch with Bud.

❧

WITHIN A WEEK, Zimmerman called me.

"I don't think that I've seen a more beautiful piece of land than yours," he said.

"That's music to my ears. But did you see the five houses? What did you think of them?"

"They're all well-constructed nineteenth-century buildings. Two of them are classic New England Capes—one and a half stories tall with bedrooms in what amounts to an attic. One of them is too expensive for what it is. I think I would scratch it out on that account. The other one I have no problem with, but it would be lost on the land. You really need something more generous, with more mass, than a Cape."

"Do you think any of the three other houses will do?"

"They're all two stories tall, and it wouldn't be easy to pop them off their foundations and wheel them to your land."

"Bud says that he knows someone who can move mountains." That was how I had begun to think of Jim Merry, the village mover.

Among the three two-story houses, Zimmerman felt that the most desirable was the so-called Reidy house, which had spacious public rooms downstairs and five small bedrooms upstairs. Its only blemish was an L-shaped wing, which had been added later and was poorly constructed, but which he thought could be lopped off without damaging the original structure.

"It is interesting that it's the new construction that's not as well-built as the old," I said.

He was silent, as if put out by my observation, but then retorted, "Old houses have their drawbacks too—the Reidy house has only one bathroom, and that's upstairs. A modern architect would put at least one bathroom on the main floor so that guests and old people wouldn't be inconvenienced. He would also probably have a bathroom adjoining every bedroom."

"If we lopped off, as you say, the new construction of the Reidy house, could we build a new wing with a second bathroom?"

"That would be no problem. I think that I could come up with a good design. But what I really recommend is a whole new house."

"The more I learn about the Reidy house, the more I like it. What I also like is that I would not have to make any major architectural decisions. The whole house would come all built and ready for use."

"But people like making architectural decisions. People love building customized houses. Once we started working together, you'd enjoy the process and you could end up with something really special, beautiful, and distinctively yours."

Gosh, these people who live in Maine are all salesmen, I thought. I had imagined that the Realtor was sui generis. But here I am slowly being reeled in by Zimmerman, as if I were a fish on a fishing line.

"I am from the Old World, where people just adapt themselves to whatever house they are born into or find themselves in. I thought it was only Californians who like to build their dream houses."

"Not at all. I would wager there are dream houses on every inhabited island in Penobscot Bay, and people love living in them."

"Did Bud say how much the Reidy house would cost?"

"Bud asked me to tell you that the asking price was a mere thirty thousand dollars. What's more, he thought that the owner would accept a lower price."

"Why is that? Is there something structurally wrong with the house?"

"No. Although most everybody on the island has their own individual septic system, there is a municipal sewer system—it's in the backyard of the Reidy house. Its filtration system is aboveground and is a real eyesore. And yet the house has a wonderful view of the water to the west. In the summer, you could see all the boats sailing past."

I was excited at the prospect of getting a ready-made old house—and on the cheap.

I DECIDED THAT before I could make up my mind what to do about the Reidy house, I had to see it for myself. So, that October, about six months after I had bought the land, I called up Jim Merry and arranged to meet him, together with Zimmerman and Bud, at the house, to see if and how it could be pried loose from its foundation and if and how it could be moved to the Crane land. I got to Camden after a horrendous effort, all the time worrying about what I was spending on the visit. The expense was all the greater because, given the vagaries of the airplane and ferry schedules, I had to stay a night in a motel on the mainland on the way out and back.

From Camden, I rode with Zimmerman and took the early-morning ferry. When we pulled up at the Reidy house, Merry and Bud were already there.

Mr. Merry, a charming man with a strong Maine accent, hardly greeted me before disappearing with his tools to examine the foundation, while Zimmerman walked around with me pointing out details, taking notes, and making sketches for a new wing—Bud staying discreetly in the background.

The house was complete with a porch on two sides, a music room, a living room, and a dining room—even a little sunroom. Each bedroom upstairs had its own dormer window. As I went around, I listened to the echoes, which indicated that the rooms had high ceilings. I touched and tapped the walls, doors, and windows and was cheered to discover that the walls were made of thick plaster, that the interior doors slid easily into pockets in the walls, that all the doors were heavy and of solid core, that the mullions dividing the lights of the windows and the French doors that opened onto the front porch were handmade—indeed, all the moldings and fittings were graceful and well-turned. I climbed onto the roof, which was shingled in asphalt, and which I would probably have to have redone in time.

In contrast to my tiny apartment in New York, the house seemed like a palace. The music room alone was so large that it could easily have accommodated all my furniture along with a grand piano. If one closed all the doors in any room, there was a silence the like of which I had never experienced in New York City. Indeed, I had visions of writing in the sunroom and preparing meals and eating in the large kitchen, overlooking the fact that I could never write without an amanuensis, that I could scarcely boil an egg, and that, on my own on the island, I would indeed be like a fish—beached, writhing, and dying.

"I'm going to make an offer for this house," I said to Zimmerman.

Immediately, Bud stepped forward and said, "I knew you'd say that."

"I think you'll find that any two-story house will be too tall to move down the town road," Zimmerman said. "It's about two miles from here to your land, and you would have to take down the power lines, cut down many of the old trees, and severely cut back the branches that hang over the road."

"Goodness, I hope you're wrong," I said. "If I did anything like that, the neighbors would run me off the island."

"You're both being unnecessarily alarmist," Bud said smoothly. "This is the off-season here, and the trees could be cut back and the Reidy house rolled along the road to the Crane land without the neighbors being any the wiser. When they returned in the summer, a certain amount of foliage would have come up on the trees. Anyway, it would be long after the fact. And who's to say that the overhang of the trees on the road doesn't constitute a public hazard? You could certainly make that argument if you had to in a court of law."

"For God's sake, I don't want to get involved with courts and arguments," I said. "What I like about your island is its serenity."

"Affirmative," Bud said. "Even if you decided not to move the Reidy house onto your land because of the disturbance to the trees," he resumed, "you could still buy it and hold onto it as an investment and move it when you found a suitable piece of land closer to the house. Mr. Reidy, who used to be the superintendent of the school here, has already moved off the island and, boy, he's anxious to sell. You just have to name your price. Like in love, timing is everything in real estate."

"Listen," I said. "I never wanted to buy the Crane land in the first place, and now you are trying to sell me a house that it seems I can't move and is on top of a sewer system."

"But you love this house, and if you move it I could help you to sell the land under it and get some quick cash," Bud said. "Boy, it must be a good half acre, and it's quite desirable—it's in the middle of the village. Or you could temporarily keep the Reidy house where it is and, while you were waiting for a good little piece of land close by to come on the market to put it on, I could help you rent the house. That would provide you with monthly income and a tax break to boot."

"Wait a minute," I said. "Do I understand you correctly? You are trying to sell me the Reidy house and also trying to find me another piece of land somewhere else?"

"It was just an idea for you to consider," Bud said.

"But who would want to rent a house on top of a sewer system?" I asked.

"Plenty of islanders," he replied. "Not all people can afford to care about what's in their backyard, and I have to tell you that this sewer system is a sand filter, so, as you notice, there is no smell of any kind."

"But, while waiting, what in the hell do I do about the Crane land?" I asked him.

"You hold onto it as an investment. Before long, it will start appreciating a few dollars every day," he answered.

How I wished at that moment that I had never bought the Crane land! Yet my experience with investments was that, at the time of investing in anything substantial, one was always unhappy. It was only in retrospect, when the investment realized its potential and appreciated, that one felt happy. Even so, the tendency was not to credit the adviser who had initially put one onto the investment. I did not want to be one of those ingrates, especially toward Bud, who for months now had been available on the telephone anytime I wanted to talk to him, had been free with his advice and opinions, and had always been friendly and in good humor. No doubt he was governed by self-interest, but I calculated that the broker's commission he would make from, for instance, selling the Reidy house, and perhaps also another piece of land to put it on, was not all that much. I had just received a big bill from Zimmerman and discovered that his meter had been running at the same rate whether he was talking to me on the telephone, travelling to the island, or looking over the houses, and that rate was the same as if he were doing creative work, like drawing up a new house. I was learning, to my cost, that that was the custom in his profession and that I was wrong to take umbrage. Still, it was hard not to compare him unfavorably with Bud.

"If moving an old house to the Crane land is not possible, why did I buy the land in the first place?"

"But at the time, we didn't know your feelings about Sheetrock and the trees. We didn't even discuss the question of an old or a new house for you."

Zimmerman, who had stood patiently doodling on his notepad, now spoke up. "I think you're going to end up asking me to build you a new house."

"That's what any good architect would want to do, Dick, but that's not an option for Ved since he hates Sheetrock," Bud said. He turned back to me. "I don't think you should do anything you don't want to do. That's a principle I've always lived by, and it has made for a happy life."

I was never unmindful of the fact that I was a freelance writer who could dry up or lose his *New Yorker* association without any warning. Yet, throughout my discussions with Bud—indeed, with my New York architect friend and Zimmerman, too—I acted as if I were a man of substantial means. Perhaps I was driven by an impulse to lay claim to the things that my friends had—many people besides Annette had summer houses—not so much because I thought I would enjoy them but because I didn't want those friends ever to think that I was lacking in anything. This feeling might have had its origin in my lack of sight. In any event, it is my experience that when people like me, who have spent their whole adult lives working in a salt mine, as it were, come up for air, they cannot get their bearings and are apt to do something rash and foolish, and on a big scale. That is what I did. Although I told myself that my involvement with the island was total insanity, still I could not leave it alone. There was something thrilling about having one's own Realtor and architect. (The telephone messages they left always said, "This is your Realtor calling," or "This is your architect calling.") They fostered the illusion that I was Emperor Shah Jahan planning the Taj Mahal, even if, in my case, it felt like my own tomb. Intellectually, I despised rentiers—I thought people should live off their own earnings, not off someone else's rent. Yet there was also something exciting about the thought that I might be able to pick up the Reidy house for little money, rent it, and have a monthly income coming in without doing any work for it. Imperceptibly, I was being drawn like a fly into Bud's web. The more I thrashed about, the more tightly I was caught.

I was so preoccupied with the minutiae of the Reidy house and the question of trees and neighbors that I had almost forgotten that Jim Merry was under the house until he emerged and announced, "This house is going nowhere."

I was stunned at the finality of his statement.

"I've never known you to admit defeat, Jim," Bud said.

"Nothing anyone can do," Merry said. "She's simply too broad in the beam—I reckon half as much again as the width of the road."

"Can't we tip it and ease it along the road?" Bud asked.

"For two miles to the Mehta land? No way," Merry said.

"I wonder if you have taken into account, Mr. Merry, that we plan to lop off the L before we move it," I said, now thinking a little like the Realtor in my turn.

"That ain't going to make any difference," Merry said. "She's just too broad in the beam."

I wish I had never seen the house, I thought. Now I will never be able to get it out of my head.

"Jim, what would you think of sawing the house in two and moving it in two bites?" Bud asked.

"Then you'd be moving not a house but a wreck," Merry said.

"I'm relieved," I said. "I didn't want to nick even a single tree." What I said was at variance with what I was feeling—it was if a manuscript of a book I had worked on for many months had been irretrievably lost.

"I think you're looking unnecessarily downhearted, Ved," Zimmerman said. "I can build you a custom house with pocket doors, double doors, and nice moldings—with many of the features you like about this house."

"But your new house will have Sheetrock walls," I said.

"There's bound to be a plasterer in Maine," Zimmerman said. "In fact, if you don't want fancy plasterwork, anybody can build plaster walls. It's just a matter of labor and how much money you're prepared to spend."

"How much would a new house on the island cost?" I asked Zimmerman.

"Say you wanted a basic house," he said. "If you didn't go in for a lot of fussy details, the construction costs would run you about eighty dollars a square foot. If you wanted a regular house—say, with a covered area of thirteen hundred square feet—that would come to a little over one hundred thousand dollars."

"But that would not include the plaster walls," Bud said.

"That's true," Zimmerman said.

"And that won't include your fees," Bud said.

"But my fees would be only the standard fifteen per cent of the construction cost," Zimmerman said.

Merry started to leave, saying, "I guess I'm no longer needed."

"Can I pay you something for your trouble?" I asked.

"I wasn't able to do anything for you. Why should you pay me anything?"

He's a true Mainer, the kind one reads about, I thought.

"I've never known you to give up, Jim," Bud said.

"Yes, I hear you can move mountains," I said.

"There's always a way," Merry said, scratching his head. "If we take off the new wing, we could stud and cover the exposed area with plywood to keep the weather out, then slide the building onto steel stringers and push it along down to the western shore. The slope of the land is just right."

"Oh my God—you can't be thinking of floating the house?" I cried.

"That's an option," Merry said tersely.

"That way, you wouldn't have to disturb the trees, which you don't want to do," Bud said.

"But wait a minute—how can you float a house?" I asked.

"At the waterside, we load the building onto a barge," Merry said.

"Are there barge people around who could take on such a job?" I asked.

"I reckon Prock Marine, in Rockland, could do it," Merry said.

"How would the cost of a new house compare with the cost of buying and floating the Reidy house?" I asked Bud.

"I think you could get yourself the Reidy house for twenty or twenty-five thousand dollars," he said. "Prock Marine will probably do the job for a few thousand dollars, don't you think, Merry?"

"I reckon ten thousand dollars is closer to the price," Merry said.

"Then you have the cost of preparing the new site, pouring the foundation, and putting in a septic tank," Bud said. "But you'd have those costs with a new house anyway."

"You're overlooking Merry's costs for jacking up the house and setting it up in the new site and the cost of taking off the old wing, adding on the new wing, and putting in an additional bathroom," Zimmerman said.

"With the Reidy house, you would have a really beautiful old house on a beautiful piece of land," Bud said. "And, with a new house, you would have a beautiful new house on a beautiful piece of land. In either case, you will have an excellent investment."

BACK IN NEW YORK, I got in touch with Prock Marine, or, rather, with its president, Wallace Prock, and a couple of weeks later I was again on the island, this time to get his assessment of both the cost and the feasibility of moving the house by water. Prock, Bud, and I took a shortcut from the Reidy house to the western shore, about a thousand feet away, and Prock looked over possible spots where he could anchor a barge.

"It's doable," he said. "But it'll be expensive."

"Why is that?" I asked.

"Since this building is sitting on the west side and you told me that your land is on the east side, we would have to float her down to the southern tip of the island and go around it," Prock said.

"Ved's property is only two miles south from here," said Bud.

"But that's by land," Prock said. "From the map, it appears that, by water, it'll be twice that, since you would first have to drift along the west side of the island those two miles, plus an additional mile down to circumvent the southern tip, and then an additional mile up to reach your land on the east side.

Then there's the problem of catching the tide, which would have to be high enough for the barge to float with such a heavy load. If it took a much longer time to load the house on the barge than we calculated and the tide were to go out, the barge could be grounded, and we would have a real job floating it again. Then we have to take into account the variation between the sheltered waters on this side of the island and the open waters on the other side, where your land is. If my bargemen didn't catch the tides just right, they might have to spend a night or two on the water with the house."

"Are there any risks in moving the house on a barge?" I asked.

"As long as the house is properly balanced and lashed on the barge, there should be no danger to it on the water," Prock said. "But there's always a danger of the house catching fire on the land when it's being jacked up and moved."

"Why is that?" I asked.

"A worker can be careless with a cigarette, a match, electrical tools, or something, but an even greater danger than fire is that the house will slip into the sea when you're loading it onto the barge or unloading it at the other end."

"But you can insure the house against such accidents," Bud said.

"The insurance companies will write you a policy on land and on water but, as far as I know, not between land and water, and that's the point where you can really lose the house," Prock said. "I don't think that category even exists in their vocabulary."

"I need to get some idea of the cost of your share of the work," I said. All the talk about the barge getting grounded and bargemen having to spend nights on water was making me nervous.

Prock said he could not give me any estimate of the cost until he had seen the unloading site.

Mindful that Zimmerman's architect meter was still ticking, I said goodbye to him, and Prock, Bud, and I drove down to the Crane land.

As soon as we arrived at the beach and Prock surveyed the conditions of the shore, his enthusiasm noticeably cooled.

"I had imagined that your coast was like a bluff, so that I could bring my barge right alongside it," he said, "but I see now that your bank gently slopes into the water and the water stays pretty shallow for a piece. No barge with a heavy load could get closer than a hundred feet to your shore without being grounded. Even if we were to catch the high tide, we still couldn't get much closer."

"Are you then saying that we can't get the house from the barge to my land?" I asked.

"No," Prock said. "If you want to go through with the project, you'll have to get someone to fabricate a steel ramp for you."

"A ramp extending out a hundred feet into the open sea?" I said. "How would you support such a monstrosity?"

"The fabricator of the ramp would have to come up with ideas about pilings and such," Prock said.

"I think I could come up with the names of a couple of good fabricators," Bud said.

The whole project of floating the house was beginning to sound increasingly hopeless. Yet, oddly, the more it seemed so, the harder it was for me to let go of it. Most of the time that trait served me well, but occasionally it also tripped me up and landed me flat on my face.

"The ramp will only get the house to the shore of your land," Prock said. "But, as you know, the law requires that you have the house set back at least seventy-five feet from the high-water mark. That's going to create a problem for you since your land is sort of a hill and the house would have to be moved up it."

"How would you do that?" I asked.

"You'll need something like a flatbed truck to roll it off the ramp and up to your chosen site," Prock said.

To assess the condition of the land, Prock and I made a foray up the hill, Bud following behind good-naturedly. The brush was so thick that even though we valiantly fought through it, we couldn't get far. Moreover, at every point, we seemed to sink, as if we were stepping on marshland.

"The whole wretched place is a bog!" I cried.

"You have to remember that you're on a narrow island," Prock said, "and there probably is a lot of groundwater underneath. There could be springs down there, artesian wells, you can never tell."

"Affirmative," Bud said. "But that's not just true here but in many parts of the shore land."

"Frankly, the land is too wet and too rough for me to tell how the house could ever make it up to the setback required by the law," Prock said.

"Would the land be drier and better up near the town road?" I asked.

"Very likely," Prock said. "But you could never get an old house anywhere near it from the shore. It would sink or break up long before you got it there. Even to get the house to somewhere near here, you would first have to get someone to clear the land and let in some sun and air to dry it out. If I were you, I would seriously consider building a new house and putting it near the town road. Then you'd have a good prospect of your acreage and shore. Besides, in the winter, a snowplow could get to it, but no plow could ever get down here."

My heart began to race. I had gone out and bought a bog on nothing better than an impulse. In New York, I used to make fun of people who bought expensive co-op or condominium apartments and imagined that they had bought "property," when in fact all they had bought was a hole in the air, as if they were midair gentry, as opposed to the landed gentry of old. But here what kind of status was I laying claim to with my marshy land?

We more or less slid down the hill in a heap and returned to the beach, all muddied, wet, and scratched up.

"Since you're trying to sell Ved the Reidy house, you must have some idea of how to get it up the hill," Prock said to Bud pointedly.

Bud was thrown for a moment, but he rallied quickly. "I always thought you would have to put in a road to take up the house."

The idea of the road would have been the proverbial last straw if I hadn't all but taken leave of my senses. But I asked, "Who could build such a road on such land?"

"Rodney Leach," Bud came back, without a moment's hesitation. "He's your man, and he's right here on the island. I guess he's about the best road builder in Maine. Sooner or later, you'll have to meet him, because he's about the only one on the island who can install a septic tank. If you like, I'll go and find him for you. I'm sure to spot Rodney's truck parked somewhere along the town road."

I asked Prock if he thought it was worthwhile getting the opinion of a road builder.

"You've come this far," Prock said. "You might as well go the last mile."

Bud drove off. I was feeling guilty for having dragged Prock all the way from Rockland to the island on what was increasingly appearing to be a fool's mission.

"I'm sorry to keep you here," I said.

"I have time," Prock said patiently. "It's just two, and the last ferry's not until five o'clock. Besides, I'm enjoying being on the island."

"It's probably now academic, but can you give me some idea about how much it would cost to bring the house over by water?"

"Now, I can only give you a price for the barge part of the job. The insurance, the steel ramp, the possible road, and whatnot—you'll have to negotiate those costs separately with other contractors."

"I understand."

"I've had a lot of experience estimating such jobs and I can give you a flat contract price of eleven thousand five hundred dollars. Whether my barge is used for one day or three days, you won't have to pay anything extra."

If Prock's estimate were added to, say, twenty-five thousand dollars for the purchase price of the Reidy house, I thought, I would still come in under a third of the price of the new house Zimmerman wants to build me. Still, I felt that there was no way I could make an informed decision until I got a firm price for the ramp and the road, not to mention for the foundation to receive the house.

Bud returned with Rodney Leach, a blustery, rugged man, who took one look at the job and said, "I know the Reidy house. She's got a big gauge and it's going to require a wide road to get her up from the shore, and the area around here is all wetland. The truck hauling her will get stuck and, boy, you'll need a crane to get the truck out, and I don't know how you'll ever get a crane down here."

"Where there's a will, there's always a way," Bud said.

"Before you even think of putting in the road, I reckon you've got to cut down all these trees."

"Disposing of them won't be a problem," Bud said. "Somebody would haul them away for Ved and sell them for pulp. That would cover the hauler's cost."

"But after you hauled away all that wood, you'd have to do one heck of a stumping," Rodney Leach said. "Whenever you pull out stumps, you tear up the earth like nothing you've ever seen. And then you still got the problem of getting rid of the stumps. It can take a season or two before you can dry them out and burn them."

"But you could haul the stumps to a stump dump," Bud said.

"Yeah," Rodney said. "But then Ved will have to pay first for hauling them away, and then for disposing them in the stump dump."

"Moving the Reidy house would certainly be an adventure, as Rodney points out," Bud said, fastening on me, "but you give me the impression, Ved, that you like adventure."

This is no adventure, I thought. It's a nightmare. Then, why am I clinging to the whole idea of buying, building, or moving a house? Is there something exciting about having all these knowledgeable experts leading me, as it were, blind-folded through the forest?

I turned to Rodney Leach and asked, as a final gambit, "What about that road?"

"I was coming to that. If you want to roll up that house of yours, I basically have to build you an I-95 all the way from the high-water mark to wherever you want to set down your house. That would mean digging out all the topsoil until I get to some hard surface and levelling it, probably, with a bulldozer. After that, I'd have to truck in shale and stones and pack them all down in order for you to have your road. Now, once the house is up you won't want to look out onto an I-95, so I'll have to dig up the shale and everything and find somewhere to put it all. Once I've done that, your front yard will be an eyesore and you'd have to do some kind of planting to hide the fact there ever had been a road here! So you see, by that time you could easily be out of pocket twenty or thirty thousand dollars. Now, I don't want you to misunderstand. I'd like to build you a road. It's good for me, it's good for my wallet, it's good for the economy of the island—people here need work in the winter. But I don't feel good about sticking it to you, seeing as how you're just getting to know the island."

He didn't so much speak as shout, as if he were lecturing to some greenhorn who didn't know the first thing about what building a road entailed. I did not know what conclusion Prock and Bud had reached, but I thought the road builder had made a good case for not building a road.

"I guess Rodney has hit the nail on the head," Prock said.

"Well, I think I'll be going along now," Rodney said. "I'll leave it to Bud to show you how to put your money into the ground. I reckon there's no one better on this island to help you do that."

WHAT TO DO about the land? I considered several options. I could leave it alone for a few years and let it gain (or lose) in value. I could put it on the market immediately and absorb the loss, in which case I would be honor-bound to give to Annette half the proceeds (in the event she refused to accept her share, I decided, I would donate the money to her favorite charity). Or I could postpone the whole decision until I had a clear picture of how I would fit into the Islesboro community. As an Indian who had grown up during the Raj, I felt that politically my lot was with the natives—the likes of Bud, Rodney Leach, and Paul Pendleton—but I'd already sensed that they would no more regard me as one of them than the Indians in my childhood would have regarded the British colonizers as one of them. And yet, with my small bank account, my disability, and my lack of interest in any island sports, I couldn't aspire to be one of the summer colonizers, either. I had no doubt that I had survived on the island thus far because of Annette's sheltering riches and kindness. But, even in her house, after a few days I would get bored and yearn to get back to the city and my work. I hated the whole idea of resorts, with their artificial, unreal, privileged life cut off from the way most people lived in the rest of the world. I always knew that my lot as an Indian, a blind person, and even a writer, would have been with the have-nots of this world if I had not managed to escape that lot. Whenever I met a poor person, I would think, "There but for the grace of God go I." Father D'Arcy at least had a Biblical justification for hobnobbing with the rich—for making to himself "friends of the mammon of unrighteousness." He was trying to collect donations for the Church. But what could be my justification?

But the project of a house on the Crane land, without my actually willing it, had got so far along, and had got so many people involved, that I felt I couldn't draw back—couldn't just forget about it, as if it had been a passing whim. The irony was I still couldn't think of the land as my land. Despite all my qualms about the island society and my own predilections, I decided to let things ride, wondering where they would take me.

I recalled, almost as an afterthought, that I would be able

to live in any house on the island only if I were married, even though with the passing of each year—I was now past my forty-eighth birthday—I had to reconcile myself to the idea that I might end up single and alone. Still, I never stopped nursing the hope that I would make a permanent connection with a woman. I even rationalized that maybe I would be more likely to find her if I were able to offer her this refuge—a private piece of ground in the woods, a private beach. But then I castigated myself for my low sense of self-worth. Did I really believe I needed worldly inducements to entice a woman?

I had barely put that ghost to rest when I began fretting that the woman of my dreams might not like the house I might have an architect design for me—that she would have her own taste and preferences. But how could I plan a house according to the taste and preferences of someone who was only a figment of my imagination? Immediately I was struck by a whole other thought. What if she detested resorts, detested islands, wanted nothing to do with the kind of people who decamped for summers there? For all I knew, the kind of woman who would be attracted to me might be happier in a cold-water flat than in a flashy place in Islesboro or, for that matter, Manhattan. I was rattled until I remembered Annette's harmonic laughter, the exquisite wines at her table, and the lively conversation at her house. I recalled how she would appear in my drab office with her ambrosial picnics and then whisk me away to a movie as if all work and no play would have indeed made this Jack a dull boy. After all, if I were wedded to my writing and hated to look away from it—and that was in fact the way my life was before my vacations in Dark Harbor—there could be no room for "another woman." Consciously, of course, I always yearned for a wife, but unconsciously, if I were that inflexible, perhaps I would be incapable of adapting to the demands of another person—or, rather, many persons, since I wanted children, too.

At the time, I was seeing a psychoanalyst. I put before him all my conflicting feelings about Dark Harbor and told him I felt I was on a rack, being pulled this way and that way. The tension was insupportable.

He was reflective and then said, "As I hear you talk about getting yourself a house, you sound like the proverbial wanderer who reaches a stage in life when he is ready to settle down anywhere, anyhow, anyway, irrespective of what would be right for him. I can imagine that, in your loneliness, you have got yourself engaged to your land in Dark Harbor, with the wedding bells ringing loudly in your ears and suffusing you with pleasant feelings. There are no doubt some unpleasant feelings, too, but that's to be expected in any new relationship. Most people get a house after they get married, but you want to get a house ready before you have found a woman who will have you. In your unconscious, the house is the surrogate for the wife you may never find. It provides you a refuge in case you end up alone. At the same time, it is also the ring all wrapped and ready in your pocket in the event you do find her."

"Are you telling me, then, that I should hang on to the land?"

"I'm not your lawyer or your financial adviser. I'm only your analyst, who tries to offer you an interpretation based on the material you bring here to me."

WE ONCE HAD a family house in Lahore—my father had built it. My older siblings had been born there, but since my father's government job as a public-health official had involved frequent transfers, most of the time I was growing up we made do with rented houses wherever he was posted. Indeed, as often as not, all my six brothers and sisters and I slept together in one room. For a brief spell, my father was posted in Lahore and we did live in our own house, where we each had a room of our own, but within two years we lost our house in the Partition and became refugees. Two years after that, I came to America and entered the Arkansas School for the Blind, where I slept in a dormitory with thirty other boys. Although later, at college and university, I had individual rooms or suites, I had always lived simply, as behooved the student that I was. Still later, as a writer mostly living hand-to-mouth, I had made my home in small apartments, which I had furnished with care, myself, but where I did little more than sleep. So the idea of designing a whole house of my own was exciting. But had a blind person ever built a house on his own? I'd heard of only one—the businessman Gordon Gund of Princeton, New Jersey—but he was married, rich, and had lost his sight when he was thirty-one years old. People who go blind later in life are much less mobile and require many more aids to get around, even within their own house. Indeed, Gund's architect had installed sculptural railings along the walls to guide him from room to room.

I thought if I were setting out all over again looking for property in Dark Harbor, I would have bought an already-built, old house, where all the architectural and design decisions had long since been made—where the house was well-established in its landscape and terrain. I certainly found the ambience of an old house comforting. Not only did I like the acoustics but an old house reflected what I imagined was my architectural taste. In a sense, my taste could be a reflection only of other people's taste, but then, everybody's taste was influenced by someone or another. And taste mirrored one's general level of sophistication (for instance, even a blind person of some sophistication wouldn't put gargoyles in his bedroom). Still, there was no denying that eyesight was indispensable when it came to important architectural issues, like the play between light and space. My imagination could compensate for that lack—and I had plenty of imagination—but it could take me only so far. At that point, I would hit a wall and would have to fall in with the architect's taste and present it as my own.

To use an inexact analogy between houses and clothes, I dressed with other people in mind. I made sure that my clothes were tasteful according to accepted norms. Almost like a spy, I could quickly and discreetly find out what kind of clothing was considered appropriate in the various places I had lived—

Claremont or Berkeley, Oxford or London, Boston or New York. I was not born mimetic, but I had trained myself to be mimetic, thinking that civility required looking to the comfort of others. Intellectually, I was a nonconformist, but I felt that I had to conform to the standards of others so as to be accepted despite my blindness. Other people's special concessions to my condition were even more hateful than conformity. It was simply easier to merge, at least where outward appearances were concerned, as long as I could keep my inner identity sacrosanct and inviolate.

Of course, building a house was many times more complicated than, say, choosing a suit of clothes, with more chances to make glaring mistakes. Naturally, there would be an architect to guide me, but he would be a little like the tailor who cut and sewed a suit, while it was I who would have to wear it. If it looked good on me, someone might ask, "Who is your tailor?" If not, people might say nothing but secretly think that I understandably lacked taste. Similarly, if the architect built an elegant house, it would reflect well on both of us. But if he built an inelegant house it would reflect badly only on me. "Poor fellow—he couldn't know better," people might say. No wonder I had been so hung up about the Reidy house, had made expensive trips on account of it, involved so many different people, and wasted a lot of money and energy. Maybe it hadn't been so much a matter of falling in love with the Reidy house as of not wanting to take the plunge into building a new house. It was as if I had walked to the edge of a high diving board and were paralyzed there.

In any case, the nagging question remained—could I ever tolerate living in a new house, even if it were only for summers? Not only would it be built of new, flimsy materials but it would also probably have low ceilings and small rooms, since I couldn't afford to build anything more ample. There was no telling if it would suit my taste, or what personal touches or eccentricities the architect might be tempted to introduce. I felt that I would have to be involved in every architectural decision and to have everything I couldn't see for myself explained to me so I could grasp it conceptually and prevent horrible mistakes.

I was bedevilled by many other questions: How would I set about making design decisions? How good was my visual imagination? How well could I see in the abstract what would look right—for instance, how the exterior and the interior could be coördinated? How would I go about siting the house? There was a great deal of difference between a city house and a summer house—between building a house in which one lived all year round and building a house in which one lived for one short season. I fretted that the kind of house that would suit me in the city—something that was enclosed like a cocoon, padded with carpets and curtains, and so was soft, quiet, and snug—would be out of place in a resort, where I imagined bare wood, glass, and light were prized. But, then again, I scarcely knew what a resort was, or how the Dark Harbor resort differed from other resorts, or what my needs in Dark Harbor would be. Would my friends and family enjoy visiting it? In a new house, whether I liked it or not, I would, I concluded, have to surround myself with wooden, uncarpeted floors and the hard, dry sound of glass. The difference between a traditional and a contemporary house would be a little like that between the rich tones of a wooden violin and the screech of a violin made of glass.

There was no way a contemporary architect could produce a replica of an old house, even if somehow he could get hold of all the old materials and even if cost was not an object, any more than a contemporary poet could compose in Miltonic verse. Even if he somehow met the challenge, the effect would be one of pastiche and parody. Architects, like poets, had to reflect the spirit of their age, and the better they were, the more accurate that reflection would be.

Then there was the question of what kind of house I would tell the architect to design for me. Could I point to a new house I liked? I couldn't think of one. I recalled visiting acquaintances who lived in what they called their dream houses in Los Angeles. Their houses were as discordant as the individuals who had dreamed them up. These dreamers seemed to lack any sense of community or landscape, civics or town planning; each was concerned only with doing his or her own thing. I felt that it was just a matter of time before the next lot of dreamers would come along, sweep away the airy castles of their predecessors like so many cobwebs, and start all over again. It was a blueprint for a perpetual architectural wasteland. In contrast, I wanted my house to fit into the Dark Harbor community and landscape and also to have the classical values of truth, clarity, harmony, and courtesy—the values to which I aspired in writing. There I was again, dreaming of tradition, longing for an old house.

If there was any solution at all, it was in finding an imaginative architect who would approach my personal needs with as much sympathetic understanding as I would have in approaching his professional needs. Of course, in a sense, architects and clients are always in a tug-of-war, but in my case the stakes would be much higher.

I COMMISSIONED ZIMMERMAN to make some preliminary sketches, and on one sunny May day in 1982 I met him in Camden and drove out with him to the land in order to look over a possible site for the house. We walked together down the dirt road and, about two-thirds of the way down, he noticed that the road levelled off a bit. He pointed to the forest and said, "This is the site for the house."

"Where?" I asked.

"I would say about fifty yards from this point into your land. This seems to be the only level bit. If you put your house anywhere else, you would either have to have the footings on many different levels or build a house on many levels. In either case, construction will be complicated and you'll add to the cost of your house."

"Wouldn't the house be more accessible during the winter snows if it were higher up?"

"It would, but you wouldn't be able to see the water, because you'd be closed in by trees, unless you did some major cutting."

I wanted to do a minimal amount of cutting, not because I had any principles about preserving the forest as such but because I had a naïve and sentimental attitude that something growing, like a tree, should not be sawed down to make room for a house, especially a summer house that I might nearly never occupy. Lately, I had come to think of the house as a painting or a sculpture, which would exist to be admired and written about in architectural magazines but would serve no useful purpose.

I expected Zimmerman to venture into the land and walk through the proposed site, but he didn't make a move. He was not robust physically and today he had a cold. In fact, it was easier to imagine him sitting behind a desk than stomping through the bush. Later, I reflected that if he had taken just a few steps into the land, I would have followed him and realized that, although the dirt road was level there, the land itself sloped down precipitously and, therefore, couldn't be a good site for a house. Instead, on his say-so, I got hold of Rodney Leach, whom I had typed in my head as the I-95 man, and asked him to put in a driveway to the house site that would also serve as a construction road for supplies and for the builder.

Later that day, as we watched, Rodney whacked his way through the land, checked the slope with a level, measured the stretch for the driveway with a tape, and boldly announced, "I would just as soon pass up this job as build an unusable driveway." Generally, contractors were respectful toward architects, deferring to their higher education and professional qualifications. But Rodney, as a road builder and, therefore, a practical man, seemed to think he had the prerogative to challenge Zimmerman's judgment.

"What did you say?" Zimmerman asked, as if his hearing had been affected by his cold.

Rodney backed off a bit. "I was saying I wouldn't recommend putting a driveway here. It would be so steep that you wouldn't be able to get even a four-wheel-drive out."

Zimmerman told him firmly that he thought that was the best site for the house.

"You're the architect," Rodney said with mock deference. "I'll do what you tell me."

A few weeks later, Rodney called me in New York and told me that the driveway was in and he was sending me a bill for twenty-two hundred and thirty-one dollars.

"I can't get up there for a while," I said. "What's your opinion of it?"

"My opinion? You might as well have thrown your money down a rat hole."

My heart sank. I asked myself if I had ever had a choice between following the advice of my architect or heeding the warnings of a road builder.

I directed Zimmerman to go back to the site to look at the driveway and tell me what he thought of it and also whether he still felt that that location was the best site. When he called back, he told me that he was sorry, because he had now decided that the driveway was a mistake—just as Rodney had said, it was simply too steep, and now that Rodney had cleared the land, he, Zimmerman, could see that the land beyond it was a continuation of the slope.

"I should have listened to the road builder," Zimmerman said sheepishly. "One should have respect for men who do hands-on work."

"What do we do now?" I asked.

"I think the driveway should be taken away."

"That will involve more expense."

"That's true: If you left it there, it would look like the abandoned house site that it is and be an eyesore."

I was furious—I had just sent Rodney the check for putting in the driveway. Still, I couldn't help but grudgingly admire Zimmerman for admitting his mistake before we had gone further with the house. In the meantime, he continued to work on sketches. One house looked like a tall ship, another like a series of connected lighthouses. I had difficulty evaluating them as works of architecture, but I had no doubt they were as unsuited to me as a frock coat and top hat for going to the office. He had such a pleasant, personable manner on the telephone that I was lulled into believing that he was sketching as a pastime, much as a person might do watercolors. But then I received his bill for his professional services—for his sketching hours, for his travel time to the island when he had scouted for new sites, and for incidentals like phone calls, Xerox copies, and postage. I had once had the fantasy that I would buy the land for a set price and build the house for another set price, and that that would be the extent of my total financial commitment. But I was discovering that every time I turned around there were new bills coming in and eating up my resources faster than a termite went through a piece of untreated wood. Then and there, I wanted to disengage myself from Zimmerman and from his billing machinery, but I couldn't bring myself to dismiss him, perhaps because I had become a prisoner of the island, Odysseus on Aeaea—though, in my case, Circe existed only in my imagination.

I SHOWED ZIMMERMAN'S sketches to Patrick, yet another architect friend, who had won a couple of architectural prizes and was climbing rapidly up the professional ladder in New York.

"You can't judge an architect by his sketches," he said. "Anyway, the mettle of an architect is not only in what he dreams up and sketches but also in the precision and elegance of his working drawings. It is from those drawings that the actual house gets built."

"So what do you think I should do?" I asked. "His houses don't reflect me, but for all I know they are right for the island."

"But it's you, not the islanders, who's going to live in the house. You say Zimmerman has built a house in Blue Hill, Down East. I'll check into it and tell you what I find out."

He later told me that his findings about Zimmerman were not reassuring. Zimmerman had no real office and functioned as a one-man band. He did not have the staff or the time to make proper working drawings. As a result, the contractor for the Blue Hill house had ended up building just from Zimmerman's sketches. Patrick felt that such a method was fraught with dangers for both the architect and the owner, since, as likely as not, the contractor would improvise on the spot and cut corners. Alternatively, if a contractor were conscientious he was apt to be on the telephone constantly with the architect and depend on his ad-hoc oral instructions. If the owner was backed up by drawings, the contractor would have to correct his mistakes, but with improvisations and verbal dealings, anything was possible. In any case, the owner was put at risk.

"If you want a carefully designed house, you need a good New York architect whose drawings will control where the contractor puts each nail," Patrick concluded.

"Oh God, Patrick, no!" I said. "I can't take on the bills of yet another architect. Can you imagine what the travelling bills to Maine of a New York architect would be?"

"Maybe I could do the drawings for you and we could get a local architect to supervise the construction. I'll tell you what—I'll come up with you and look at the land, as a friend, and advise you. Your only initial expense would be my fare."

It seemed that whenever I mentioned my land on an island in Maine to an architect I got an immediate expression of interest, as if the idea of building a house there was irresistible. At the time, I would have denied that the interest might have had to do with the challenge of building a house for a blind person. Instead, I assumed that an architect's interest in the land was aroused because the project was on a remote island. Certainly in myth and literature islands had a romance about them.

Almost impetuously, I decided to replace Zimmerman with Patrick, reasoning that, just as an architect would have more control over a contractor if he had made good drawings, so I would have more control over an architect if he and I lived in the same city.

In July, 1982, Patrick and I flew to Maine, hired a car, and went across to the island. The trip, along with a night or two in a hotel on the mainland, was by now a routine.

As soon as we pulled up on the dirt road, Patrick jumped out of the car and rushed onto the land. The usual sounds, like twigs and leaves snapping and rustling underfoot, seemed to disappear in the blanket of forest, like Patrick himself. He was gone for nearly half an hour, all the time making me feel that I had even less control over the project than I had had when I was dealing with it, long-distance, on the telephone.

"My God, I had no idea you had bought such a rough, intractable piece of land," Patrick said, emerging from the forest, breathless. "If it were anywhere else, I would just send a bulldozer in and level all the trees and the land, and turn it into a meadow or a farmland. But on this island people are probably as attached to their trees as New Yorkers are to their pets."

"So what would you do here?"

"I would clear madly, put the house on the top of the hill near the town road, and then maybe build you a boardwalk to get you down to the shore."

"Boardwalk!" The word conjured up Coney Island or Atlantic City—overrun beaches with hotdog stands, cotton-candy machines, and amusement-park rides. For better or worse, I thought of myself as a formal person who wanted a formal house, even if it were in a jungle. It was maybe the old tradition of my father, no doubt inherited from our British masters in the preindependence days, that, even if one was living in the bush, one maintained certain forms and standards.

"I don't think a house with a boardwalk is my style," I finally said.

"But then maybe this land isn't your style, either," Patrick said.

Patrick may be a rising star in his profession, but maybe he's not right for me, I thought.

It had been a ravishingly sunny July day, but, as is the way in Maine, the wind changed, the fog came in, and it started raining, and raining heavily. We sat in the car hoping that the rain would let up and he and I could spend some more time on the land, reconnoitering and discussing the kind of house, but the rain kept coming down steadily.

Day trips to the island were always governed by the ferry schedule, and, before we knew it, we had just enough time to drive through the rain to make the last ferry. Since our flight had been booked in advance, we had no flexibility to return to the island the next day.

When I got back to New York, all I could recall from this architectural visit was the idea of the boardwalk and the uneasy feeling I had got from Patrick that building a house for me on the Crane land was a little like trying to fit a square peg into a round hole. Soon after, I told Patrick that I was abandoning the project of a house and that I would not need his services, but my relief at his departure was temporary. Temperamentally, I was not one ever to give up on anything—in fact, the more impossible something seemed the more doggedly I pursued it. Still, for two or three months I could think of no way to revive the project. Then, just about the time I had made up my mind yet again to sell the land and be done with Islesboro, I happened to hear that the architect Edward Larrabee Barnes had designed a house on an island in Maine for the journalist and public servant August Heckscher; that one of Barnes's most respected works was Haystack Mountain School of Crafts, on Deer Isle in Maine; that Barnes himself had a summer house in the state; that he was a disciple of Walter Gropius and Marcel Breuer, with whom he had studied at Harvard; that his name would appear in any list of a dozen distinguished American architects; and that although most New York architects who were burdened with the heavy expenses of running an office in the city would not consider taking on a small project like a house, Barnes might and occasionally did, if he saw it as a challenge.

I asked around about him, and everyone I spoke to said that he was the last of the gentleman architects, with a great generosity of spirit. They said he was very much his own man and gave as an example the I.B.M. Building he had designed on East Fifty-seventh Street in New York. "When the brass of I.B.M. were choosing an architect for the building, Barnes went to see them," one friend said. "Any other New York architect would have come with an impressive group of people, but Barnes arrived alone, much as an artist would. That's the kind of person he is. In fact, he generally eschews commercial projects in favor of commissions from colleges, museums, and art galleries."

I rang Barnes up and immediately got through to him, without having to explain the reason for my call to any inter-mediaries. We had lunch, and by the end of it he had agreed to be my architect on the house. Before we parted, we made plans for him, his wife, Mary—also an architect and his colleague—and me to go to Maine to look at the site. In due course, in order to formalize our relationship, he sent me the Abbreviated Form of Agreement Between Owner and Architect for Construction Projects of Limited Scope. It was technically a legal document, but I regarded it more as a token of my emotional commitment to Ed Barnes. The truth was that I had fallen under Ed's influence, rather like a dutiful son, and I felt I could no more abandon him than I could disown my father.

Although I signed the contract, which bound me to pay him fifteen per cent of the total cost of construction, which was, of course, as yet unknown, I scarcely had the money to build any house. Taking out a construction loan or a mortgage, together with selling my securities, was the only route open to me. But even that seemed academic, since I probably would not be able to generate the income to meet monthly interest payments. I therefore tried not to think about construction itself. The only thing I cared about was not disappointing Ed, as he had insisted I call him. In fact, I had a hard time thinking of myself as a property owner retaining any architect, let alone one of Edward Larrabee Barnes's distinction and reputation.

Ed could not get away from the office on weekdays, so we had made plans to catch the last plane to Portland on Friday, December 10th, at eight o'clock, spend the night in Camden, catch the first ferry out the next morning, the last ferry in that night, and fly back on Sunday.

V

ARCHITECT

I THOUGHT IT WAS ABOUT TIME THAT I EXTRICATED myself from Bud. The only other native I knew well was Paul Pendleton, who now worked for the new owners of Annette's house as a gardener and extra hand, much as he had done for Annette. I called him up and told him that I would be coming with an architect and asked him if he could meet us at the ferry and lead us in his car to the Crane land. I asked him what his hourly rate would be.

"You don't have to pay me," he said. "I'll do it because you were a friend of Mrs. Reed's." He added, "It's mighty cold here nowadays. You won't want to be on your land more than an hour or two."

"I suppose we could warm up in the car."

"But you're going to need some lunch. People on the island get especially hungry when they've been outside for a while."

"Perhaps we can pick up some sandwiches in Camden."

"I don't know if there'll be anything open there if you're

planning to catch the first ferry. I can get my wife, Marilyn, to prepare a little lunch for us."

I gratefully accepted his invitation.

❦

THE BARNESES AND I had agreed to meet at LaGuardia airport, where I now waited for them. When the flight had been called not once but twice, they still hadn't turned up.

Maybe they're just delayed in traffic, I thought. Or maybe architects are like poets—they can't be depended upon. Whatever the case, I am going to be stuck with the cost of air tickets and of the inn in Camden for nothing.

Just as the gate was about to close, the Barneses showed up. They had no luggage to check, and we went straight to the plane. Mary, an extremely dignified and warm woman, wanted to sit alone and read a magazine, so I sat next to Ed. He had a pad and pencil with him and wanted to get right down to work.

"What kind of house would you like?" he asked.

"I don't have the slightest idea," I said.

"Do you have any particular needs?"

"I don't want you to make any special concessions. I just want a normal house, designed for a normal person."

"There must be something you would want in a custom-designed house."

"I would love the rooms to be totally soundproof. In fact, I like old houses because they have plaster walls." I told him that in New York my office was on busy Forty-third Street. All day long, it seemed, trucks were thundering through, fire engines were blaring out of the fire station below, and sanitation trucks were picking up and pulverizing the day's accumulation of office garbage with hellish crashing and grinding. On weekends, there were parades near my apartment on Fifth Avenue, with piercingly discordant and dissonant sounds. City noises travelled though my dreams as if my bedroom were a subway station.

"But I suppose there is no such thing as a totally sound-proof house built with modern materials," I said.

"We can use five-eighths-inch Sheetrock rather than the regulation half-inch, and since it doesn't come any thicker than that, some places we could double it up."

"But it still will be Sheetrock."

"Plasterers are very hard to find, even in Maine. If you didn't care about the cost, we could use wooden panels, but Sheetrock has a better look to it for modern architecture. Anyway, wouldn't you like to hear the sea? The outside sounds in Maine are lovely."

"I once stayed in East Hampton with a friend who had a house close to the sea. I found the sound of the surf day and night terribly wearing."

"That's interesting. Some people go to the sea just to hear the sound of the waves."

"Since I get around with the help of different sounds, any kind of continuous noise is disorienting. As you can imagine, I have oversensitive hearing."

"I've written down 'SOUNDPROOF' in big letters. What other qualities would you like in your house? Generally, when I ask clients this question they're full of thoughts." That was Ed's delicate way of prodding me.

"I would like you to make the best house you could—I mean, within the limits of my meagre budget."

"Since your house is on the water, it would be nice to have bedrooms with balconies so that you could roll out of bed, step out in your bathrobe onto the balcony and have breakfast in the sun, overlooking the sea."

"That sounds wonderful," I said aloud, but silently wondered how I would get my breakfast, who would drive me to the store, how I would find the items that I wanted there. In New York, I would either pick up breakfast from a coffee shop or telephone a grocery store and ask for things to be delivered.

The air hostess came around with a cart, and the distraction of ordering drinks—we both had juice—allowed me to switch off from the whole problem.

We landed in Portland around nine-thirty in the middle of a heavy snowfall. The airport was deserted, but we were able to rent a car and to set off quickly, with Ed at the wheel.

Although we had good road maps and Mary was an excellent navigator, it was so dark and the snowstorm was so severe that we kept losing our way. Sometimes, we weren't even sure whether we were headed toward Camden or away from it. The gas stations and restaurants along the road all seemed to be closed, and there were no road signs for miles. The few times Ed was able to find someone to ask for directions, that person told us we were on the wrong road.

The distance between Portland and Camden was about a two-hour drive, so we should have reached Camden at the latest by midnight, but at one o'clock in the morning we were still driving. I was famished (in my excitement over working with a distinguished architect, I had not allowed myself time for dinner), anxious, and utterly worn out, but both Ed and Mary, who were nearly twenty years older than I was, remained in good humor throughout, laughing and making jokes about Maine's winter doldrums and its lack of road signs.

Finally, Ed caught sight of a snowplow with "Camden" written on it and, pulling alongside, got the driver's attention and asked him the road to the town.

"You're on it," the driver said. "I'm going to Camden myself. Follow me and you'll get there."

After that, we just followed him to the Camden Harbor Inn, where I had booked two rooms for two nights, and we arrived there at around two in the morning.

The front door of the inn was unlocked, but there was no one at the desk or, apparently, in the whole inn. It had the feel of being closed up for the winter. Ed and I went upstairs and downstairs trying all the doors in the hope of finding some rooms left open for us, but every one of them was locked.

I felt responsible for the well-being of the Barneses. My immediate concern was where to spend the night. For all I knew, the ferry might be cancelled because of the snowstorm, and I wasn't sure when, if ever, Ed would find the time to come back again. I hated the thought of going back to the city the next day, having spent the money but having accomplished nothing.

Ed was unfazed—indeed, he seemed to treat our predicament as an adventure. There was something boyish in his enthusiasm.

"It's terrible—I don't know what we are going to do for beds," I said to Mary, who was sitting in an easy chair in the lounge.

"I'll just sleep sitting right here. This chair is quite comfortable."

"I found some camp beds on the top landing," Ed called from upstairs. "They're very light. We can carry them down and set them up in the lounge."

I ran upstairs. Ed grabbed one bed and I grabbed another. As we were carrying them down, I said, "I am surprised that the owners would leave this inn unattended. What would happen if there were a fire?"

No sooner were the words out of my mouth when there was a clatter. A door swung open, and a man in pyjamas came dashing out.

"Fire! Where's the fire?" he cried.

It transpired that he had been fast asleep but that the mention of fire had roused him. He apparently slept in the inn for just such an emergency and seemed to be, as it were, programmed to wake up at the sound of the word.

He came downstairs with us and got us keys to the rooms reserved for us.

As I was going to bed, I looked at my watch. It was three-fifteen.

I thought I had just dropped off to sleep when there was a knock at my door. It was Ed calling me to say that it was seven-fifteen and we wanted to catch the eight-o'clock ferry.

My head was still full of sleep. I was cold—the heating system in the inn must have been left extremely low. I was also hungry and anxious about getting breakfast, wondering if any place would be open that early on a winter morning. I certainly didn't relish the thought of walking the snow-covered land on an empty stomach.

I jumped out of bed, shaved, dressed, and was in the car in less than twenty minutes.

As we were driving to Lincolnville and the ferry slip, Mary spotted a place called Marriner's Restaurant that was open. Ed pulled over and we ran in and got coffee and a bag of freshly baked blueberry muffins for the road.

We reached the ferry slip just as the last car was being loaded on—it was a small, winter ferry and so had room for only a few vehicles. We abandoned our car and walked on.

"It's so nerve-racking catching planes and ferries," I said.

"That's the charm of living on an island," Ed said.

"We have a house in Somesville up the coast here," Mary said sympathetically. "We can't get away much, but when we do, it's wonderful."

"It would be just my luck to have a white elephant sitting on an island some eight or nine hours away from my apartment in New York," I said.

A huge gust of bitterly cold wind swallowed up my words. When it subsided, Ed asked me what I had said.

"Nothing," I replied, thinking that it was neither diplomatic nor courteous to undermine a project in which I was trying to enlist his help.

We stepped off the ferry into a foot of snow on the ground. The wind was so strong and so piercing that all of us were shivering. The weather in New York had been mild and none of us had thought to bring proper boots, overcoats, or umbrellas. Mary was actually wearing high heels.

"You're all dressed for the tropics, and you couldn't get your car on the ferry, to boot," Paul Pendleton said, coming up to us with a laugh and hurrying us into his warm car. "I suggest that we go to my house and I'll outfit you with snow gear. There's no way you can start off for the land dressed the way you are."

Paul's voice, like his face, was craggy, with lots of rises and falls, and he spoke in a slow, almost languid way, with a strong accent, dropping "r"s and broadening "a"s so that "start" came out sounding like "staaht."

"Are you really able to outfit us all?" Ed asked.

"Think so," Paul said. "When you live on an island you save things thinking that you might need them someday. You might never use them, but they're there."

Paul's house was modest and simple but cozy. There, he introduced us to Marilyn, a shy-seeming woman who was as gentle as Paul. It turned out that she had been the housekeeper for Mine Crane. It was when Marilyn announced to her that she was going to retire that Mrs. Crane had decided to sell her property and leave the island.

"You mean if Marilyn hadn't retired Mrs. Crane would still be here?" I asked.

"Marilyn would prefer not to think about that," Paul said. "But anyone will tell you that it's hard to get good, dependable help here. She did almost everything for Mrs. Crane—sewed her quilts, cleaned her house, and cooked for her."

"Without local help, it must be difficult to survive on the island," Mary said.

I wish Marilyn had hung on for another year or so, I thought. Then I would have been saved from buying the Crane land.

Between Paul and Marilyn, they dug up a lot of old, moldering outer garments—boots, galoshes, and waterproofs—and as we were setting out for the land Marilyn said, "I'll have lunch waiting for you at noon."

Suddenly, the whole experience of coming to a desolate island in the middle of the winter and taking shelter and succor with an elderly housekeeper and gardener—the kind of help who made life on the island possible for summer people—seemed romantic, if unnerving. Once outside, I thought about how fresh the air felt and what a hearty spirit it must require to live on the island year-round.

❦

THE LAND WAS knee-deep in snow. While Mary went off on her own, Ed tromped through the snow, seemingly determined to cover every last inch of the property.

Compared with me, Paul seemed to be as surefooted as a yak, so I attached myself to the back of his belt, and we followed closely behind Ed.

The cold air stung our faces. Everywhere we stepped, there were fallen trees, jutting roots, broken trunks, huge boulders, and deep gullies. One could hardly move without catching one's clothes on brambles, bending aside branches, ducking under limbs, and elbowing through thick brush. Underneath the freshly fallen snow, the terrain rose and fell away suddenly and unpredictably. I was walking for the first time into the interior of this land and was stunned to discover how rugged and hazardous it actually was.

I held fast to Paul, sliding, tripping, and almost falling as he tried to keep within shouting distance of Ed. Even Paul, who could see where he put his foot and was familiar with the island terrain, found walking extremely difficult.

I had always heard that good architects combined the traits of an artist with those of an athlete—a good eye with physical stamina—but I was still astonished by the energetic way that Ed proceeded with his work. He ran rather than walked, jumped over logs and boulders, and, to get a better view of the land, climbed trees, making Paul gasp. Although Ed picked his trees carefully—strong, broad spruces rather than weak, slender birches—Paul claimed that he had never seen anyone, even a local islander, clamber up a tree the way Ed did. Then, oblivious of the snow underfoot, the sting of the wind, and the wetness of the occasional flurries, Ed trudged from the dirt road on the north to the property line on the south, from the beach on the east to the town road on the west; and then traversed the property again. His crisscrossing of the land was not so much systematic as ruminative, as if he were following his nose, taking stock and sizing up the different possible sites for the house.

In the meantime, Mary was doing her own exploring of the land, most of the time going her own way. Now and again, Ed would call out to her and point out a spot where he could imagine siting the house: near the shore, near the town road, somewhere in the middle of the woods. Mary seemed to consider Ed's suggestions attentively and each time would enthusiastically call back her approval, but then add a little reservation. That would make Ed think again, and he would look for another spot. Throughout, Mary served as a kind of a sounding board for Ed's spontaneous ideas. As a person, Mary seemed to be composed and deliberative. She had a touch of the English about her, perhaps because she had once been married to an English barrister. She had now been married to Ed—who was her second husband—for nearly forty years, and one had the sense that they had a close personal and professional relationship. If he had the eagerness of a boy, she had the calm of a mother.

Although the air was still, Ed's and Mary's voices would reach me as if from a great distance, fading in and out as if I were receiving them on a shortwave radio.

I was struck by the thought that I hadn't heard a single bird since we came onto the land, and though I was lurching behind Paul and it was hard for us to talk, I asked him, "Why don't we hear any birds?"

"I suppose they don't like the cold," he said over his shoulder. "Anyway, there's no food for them here in the winter."

"Shouldn't I at least hear a seagull shriek?" I asked.

"The seagulls are probably at some harbor close by, scavenging," he said.

"Will the birds reappear in the spring?" I asked.

"Guess so," he said.

I felt sad at the absence of birds and, for the first time in my life, had an impulse to commune with them—to talk to them about their freedom in the sky and my loss of freedom on the ground, on the island. As a child in India, regardless of the season, I could scarcely take a step without hearing the chatter and song of birds. I sometimes missed those sounds in America, much as I missed the music of the church bells of European towns I had lived in. As I thought about birds and church bells, I wondered whether pleasant sounds shouldn't have been one of my considerations in owning a piece of land.

They say this is the most beautiful island, I thought, and I am sure it is. But shouldn't I have ended up somewhere where my particular set of senses would be excited?

When I was away from my familiar surroundings, as I now was, contemplating designing "a beautiful house," I came up against my limitations in a way that I otherwise hardly ever did. So I resigned myself to the fact that even if I did build a beautiful house, the island would remain for me a literary construct, conjuring up unencumbered free spirits and man's return to nature—something in which I generally could not participate. That made me remember that, in the schools for the blind I had sporadically attended, we had been judged on the basis of how well each of us adapted to and became integrated into sighted society, which there consisted of our dreaded sighted masters. In those schools, we used to dream of a kingdom where everybody was blind. But we were sure that even in that kingdom the person who could function most like one of the sighted masters would be the king. Sooner or later, as we were bound to remember, in such a kingdom there might be a person with some vision, just as there were some children in our school who were partially sighted. If a one-eyed person, indeed, were to appear, he would immediately become the king. In that case, we would be no better off than we were before.

Rather absurdly, I wondered if I were still in the grip of an unconscious fantasy that by living on as wild a piece of land as any sighted person could choose, I would win the right to accede to the throne of that imaginary kingdom. After all, I had a renowned architect in my employ, and buildings were what kings were remembered by. Even as I thought this, I realized how vaporous the fantasy was—all it would take to dethrone me would be the appearance of any sighted person, even a wife. But then it occurred to me that the wish for a wife underlay that fantasy in the first place. The whole idea of getting the land must have been to find her, and once and if she appeared, the question of whether I did or did not have a kingdom would become irrelevant.

Ed was calling us over. He had found an especially large, handsome, almost majestic spruce tree.

"Look at this," he said. "Do you think we could site the house next to this tree?"

"You mean build a sort of a tree house in the shadow of the spruce, Ed?" Mary said. "That'd be nice."

Ed walked to a big, bare, vulnerable birch to the south of the spruce and paced the distance, which came to about forty feet, and then down thirty feet or so to a huge boulder that rose out of the ground as if it had been there in that precise form since the emergence of the island from the sea.

"This would make a wonderful house site," Ed said.

From the car, Ed got hold of a survey of the property and scaled the site. It was seven hundred feet up from the shore, a hundred feet down from the town road, a hundred feet in from the dirt road, and seven hundred feet from the property line to the south.

"But we'd have to do something so that you would be able to see the water from the house," Mary said.

By "you" she means me, I thought. I want to feel that I "see" the water and I want people to feel that I do, in fact, "see" the water. I have never wanted any allowances for my blindness, so she's right on target. She and Ed grasp that instinctively.

"Maybe we could make a sort of allée, a sort of architectural room, from the house to the shore," Ed said.

"What do you mean by 'architectural room'?" I asked, coming closer to him.

"You'd do a selective cutting—a little wider than the footing of the house all the way to the shore. That would give the impression of something designed carefully rather than something wrought haphazardly by nature. In other words, you would carefully cut back or prune all the brush and dead trees and save these lovely white birches. The cutting, if it's done right, would have distinct contours, like a room, and you would see the water through the branches and the standing trees."

"The view through the white birches would look like a Russian seascape," Mary said.

"What do you think of the idea of selective cutting, Paul?" Ed asked.

"I think in time you'll end up cutting much more than you think," Paul said. "In the spring and summer, there's a lot of foliage. Regardless of how much you cut, when that foliage grows in again you won't be able to see anything past it. In the fall and winter, of course, when the leaves have all fallen, then you would get a good vista. But then Ved wouldn't be here to enjoy it. Still, there's no question that a house up here would be much better than down near the shore because you'd have a broader vista of the water."

"I think once we've got your house here and done the initial cutting, Ved, you'd have to live here and experiment to see which trees got in the way of your view, and which trees you fell in love with and wanted to protect and keep," Ed said.

Ed is playing along with my fantasy that I will be living in this house and waking up every morning and looking out the window down to the shore, I thought. He is perhaps also sensing that I am not just in the process of building a house but am looking toward the building of a whole life. He might even understand that people who could see would do things the right way around—build a life and then look for a house— but that I have to move crabwise, surreptitiously, through life.

Ed was backtracking. "It may be, Ved, that you might like to live in a house in the woods, and decide that you didn't need to see the water—just having the feeling that it's out there would be sufficient. Maybe you would enjoy faintly hearing the waves."

Not surprisingly, Ed veers from my eccentric notion that I can appreciate the view like anyone else to the all too common, if reasonable, notion that I should concentrate on enjoying what I can, I thought. Still, if I ever do live in the house I will have guests, all of whom will be sighted. I would want them to enjoy the sea view and, through them, I would certainly enjoy it, too. Much of what I enjoy is, by necessity, vicarious.

"Unless you clear out a lot of these trees, I don't think you would be able to hear waves up here in summer," Paul said. "We don't have crashing surf here like in Long Island. It gets wild in the winter, though. But that's when you wouldn't be here."

"I think the architectural room, if made wide enough, should help to open up the land so that you would be able to both see the ocean and hear it," Mary said.

"It'll also help to dry out the land," Ed said.

"Who could do the cutting for us, Paul?" I asked.

"I reckon Jack Leach. He has the men and the machines," Paul said. Jack Leach turned out to be Rodney's brother. Practically every islander, it seemed, was named either Leach or Pendleton.

"Can we get a competitive bid?" Ed asked.

"I reckon not on the island," Paul said. "And you wouldn't want to get the reputation of going off-island for your work. Then you wouldn't be able to get anyone on the island to work for you."

"Yes, I know," Ed said. "Building something on an island is different from building something on the mainland."

"Yup," Paul said. "I reckon you got to add twenty per cent just to get things across the water."

That was an extra expense I'd forgotten about. I now recalled that on Islesboro summer people were at the mercy of the islanders.

"From your experience, what would it cost, Paul?" I asked.

"Oh, I couldn't possibly say that," Paul said. "Only Jack Leach can put a price on it, but I reckon, for a start, you'll be out of pocket a good bit of money."

"Can you get in touch with Jack Leach for us?" Ed asked.

Paul said he would go and get Jack to look over the job and price it.

"But how will you find him?" I asked.

"I'll just drive along the road. I'm sure to see his truck parked at home or wherever he's working."

While Paul went to get Jack, Ed set about defining the edges and the center line of the architectural room, and tagged the birches and spruces near the shore that were to be saved.

When Paul arrived back at the site with Jack, a short, stocky, and powerfully built man, I asked him what he thought the cutting would cost.

"Oh, I don't have any idea, Mr. Mehta—you know what I mean," he said, cagey as a weasel.

"No, I don't know what you mean," I said.

"Oh, Mr. Mehta, I can't have any idea until I can get my tractor and a man and a chainsaw in here."

"But you must have some idea how long the job would take."

"You got to pay for the tractor by the hour, and you got to pay for the man and chainsaw by the hour. And that's all I can say. I'm sure you know what I mean."

He skillfully ducked practically every question Ed or I asked, but eventually we did pin him down to an estimate of twenty-two hundred dollars. But he kept protesting that it was only an estimate and that he couldn't be held to it.

I later asked Paul why Jack was so evasive.

"Oh, I'm sure I wouldn't know," he said. "He's one of our best businessmen and has his finger in every pie on the island."

"What do you think, Ved, is this a good time to break for lunch?" Ed asked. "I think we've done a good day's work."

"We certainly have," I said. I checked my watch. It was one-thirty. We had been on the land for nearly four hours. My hands, feet, and face were almost numb. In the excitement of scrambling after Ed, I had forgotten about physical discomfort, not only my own but also that of my guests.

I had bought the land like a pig in a poke. But that day,

attached to Paul's belt like a mountain climber, I had walked the land, experienced it underfoot, and grasped some of its features for the first time. Despite the snow on the ground, I now had a clear sense of its dales, hillocks, and gullies. Indeed, I felt that if I thought more about the land than about myself, more about creating something than holding back, and more about taking a risk than protecting my resources—such as they were—I might discover a union between the land and me.

The word "union" came to me just as we were driving away from the land and I felt sad that Ed had stopped work, that we had stopped work, in order to go and eat. That was the first real feeling of commitment I had had toward this property. Until then, in my head and in my discussions I had always referred to it as "the land" or "the Crane land," but, now that I had stood by the spruce tree where there might actually be a house, I could almost begin to think of the land as "my land," as a piece of ground that would carry my footprint, along with the footprint of a house.

The thought alarmed me, as if I were transgressing my karma by trespassing on the preserve of the likes of Annette. Whatever my inner vaulting aspirations, I had always felt that it was better for me to present a meek and humble face to the world, as though if I gave free rein to my true feelings I would be struck down by the wrath of the sighted. After all, they took it for granted that the blind could not compete with them—were no threat to them—but, rather, needed to be helped and taken care of. However much we told ourselves that we were no different from the sighted, the mere fact that the sighted could see made us think that they had an awesome power that we blind people denied only at our peril. I certainly felt that there was something unseemly about a blind person competing head-to-head with the sighted for worldly things. In fact, I was so superstitious about this that I feared that if I openly laid claim to more than the world thought was due to me, I would be guilty of hubris.

As soon as we got to Paul's house, we rubbed our cheeks and ears and hands to get our circulation going and lined up for the single bathroom. Then we all sat down at a table for the lunch that Marilyn had prepared in our absence.

I was so hungry and numb that I scarcely knew what I ate. I just knew that the soup was deliciously hot and the meat filling. All of us took several helpings.

We had coffee sitting at the table, and Paul said that after he had dropped us at the ferry he would go back to my land and spray paint on the spruce tree to mark the house site.

"That'll also provide Jack Leach with a marker for where the cutting should start," Paul said. "That way, he'll be able to send you an informed estimate."

I suddenly felt scared. With the marking of the tree, the house was moving into another stage—a stage beyond my control. It was a little bit like a book. If it were well begun, after a while it had its own momentum, and the author had to run to keep up with it.

There is now a designated site that Ed, Mary, Paul, and I have all walked over, and all approved, I thought. It's so different from the way Zimmerman decided upon the old site with its expensive, ill-fated driveway. And no doubt soon I'll start to receive bills for clearing the land.

I wished I could somehow put brakes on the whole project, even as I realized that once I had signed the Abbreviated Form of Agreement with Ed, there was no turning back.

I asked Ed what kind of house he felt would be appropriate for the land. I felt it would be helpful for Paul and Marilyn to hear Ed's ideas, since, as islanders, they would serve as a good sounding board.

"The house that would fit your land best would be one that would melt into the woods—that would not stick out like a foreign element," he said. "I would like the house to give the impression that it had always been there. I think a ranch-style house, which would be appropriate for perhaps Texas or Arizona, is wrong for your land and wrong for Maine. Anyway, as you noticed, there is certainly no level place by the town road where it makes most sense to put the house, both from the point of view of accessibility and the vista. The land near the road falls away quite precipitously, so we'll have to set part of the house back against the hillside, about a hundred feet from the town road. Since the design would be vertical rather than horizontal, I think the house will have to be two or two and a half stories high. It will have to be simple, and, of course, shingled. That's the traditional Maine material. Shingles age well and they are relatively easy to maintain."

Paul and Marilyn said that they thought his ideas about a tall house with shingles sounded just right. I reflected that there would still be a lot of work left to do before we settled upon the exact shape or site, but that the house was a step closer to becoming a reality. In my excitement, my dread about the house was again somewhat assuaged.

"After our trip here, Mary and I have to fly out west," Ed said. "I'll have more time to think about your house there. I'll do some preliminary sketches on the plane."

We caught the last ferry and returned to Camden Harbor Inn for the second night. The inn, which we had barely noticed the night before, was a handsome nineteenth-century building with views of Camden Harbor, Penobscot Bay, and Mount Baldy. We had a drink in the empty tavern and then a leisurely meal at the empty restaurant, which featured fresh catches from the bay and served a passable table wine. The waiter, perhaps to reassure himself as much as us, kept muttering that the Inn, though dead in winter, was lively in the summer.

Ed and Mary showed no ill effects of the previous night's short sleep or the day's hard work in the field. Throughout the evening, they seemed relaxed and cheerful and warm. I felt that I had found in them wonderful new friends. I judiciously kept off the subject of the house to calm my own nerves.

EARLY IN JANUARY, 1983, a few weeks after the visit to my land, Ed sent me a sketch of the house and then, a little later, the rough plans. From these it appeared that, on the west, the basement would back up against the hillside to the south of the spruce and that the house would rise two and a half stories, becoming narrow at the top level. The first floor would have a kitchen, a dining room, and a living room—all equal in area and arranged in a row. They would open onto a front deck that would run the width of the house from the kitchen on the north to the living room on the south. The rooms and the deck would look out east to the bay. The next floor would have the bedrooms—two of them, with sloping, cathedral ceilings, separated by a hallway—and the attic floor would be half a story high and contain just the study, with a similar kind of ceiling. The front wall of the dining room would be set back about seven feet, to form an inset to the deck, and the back of the house would jut out equally, to form a tower, which would house the stairs. Because the tower would go all the way to the top of the stairs and therefore be bigger in volume than the deck inset—whose ceiling, in combination with the dining room's, would form the underside of the attic-study floor— together they would keep the house from looking monotonous and box-like. The stair tower and three and a half feet of floor space borrowed from the back of the dining room would be an entry hall, with doors into the kitchen and the living room; near the top the tower would have a fixed half-moon window, which would look out west onto the woods and flood the tower with afternoon light. Once the decision had been made to set the house back from the water and to have the trees cleared for the allée down to the sea, it seemed only natural to stack the rooms so that practically every one could have its own, open vista. The land elevation was such that the stair tower helped to anchor the house—"visually tie it to the ground," as Ed put it. At the same time, the vertical element afforded Ed the opportunity to give the roof a nice pitch and to fashion a broad gable to accommodate the attic study.

Initially, Ed had spoken about having stacked, hanging porches above the deck—"sort of balconies" opening out from the bedrooms. But he had abandoned the idea of hanging porches because they would have cast a shadow on the deck. Instead, for less obtrusive shelter, he had indicated a tent-like awning extending over the middle of the deck from the ceiling of the inset.

For economic reasons, the rooms on the main floor were kept small—the living room, the biggest of them all, was twenty-one feet long and thirteen and a half feet wide—and I didn't like the idea of giving up half of the dining room to the deck inset and the entry hall. I called Ed and told him that.

"I know what you mean," Ed said. "There's no way to do without the entry hall. And we need the inset to break the conventional rectangular form of a modern house and at the same time to balance the stair tower. If the inset weren't there, the tower would just stick out at the back like a bump, as if the architect didn't know how to handle its geometry. If you want a bigger dining room, we would have to increase the width of all three rooms on the living level. But that would increase the footprint of the whole house, with a corresponding increase in the cost."

"How much do you think the house will cost?" I asked anxiously.

"From the informal soundings we have taken, we should be able to bring in the house for about a hundred and twenty-five thousand dollars, excluding the architectural fees and expenses. We could save a little money if we didn't finish the attic and the basement, but I know you want a completely finished house so you're not stuck with construction later."

I felt squeezed between the aesthetics of his geometry and my need to keep my costs down. No doubt, he felt squeezed in his turn, having, perhaps for the first time, a poor client. I reluctantly settled for a mingy dining room, about half as deep as the living room, that could comfortably seat only six. Still, it was exciting to hold in my hand, as it were, my house. The thought of the tower and the cathedral ceilings made me feel grand.

I gave my approval to Ed for the rough plans, and subsequently he designated as project architect an up-and-coming twenty-seven-year-old member of his staff named Henry Myerberg. Thereupon, Henry started the long and arduous process of preparing detailed working drawings that the contractor could follow to build an actual house.

I visited the land with Henry in March, so that he could check the elevations and familiarize himself with the site. Unlike Ed, who had seemed relaxed and made the site visit into a sort of holiday outing, Henry was intense and seemed to regard the house as an important step in his career path.

When I got back to New York, I sent my father the working plans and described to him how Ed and Henry were involved with the house. I thought he would be thrilled that his son was planning a home in the New World. As an Indian, he had always wanted me to own property. Also, as a nominal Hindu, he believed that man's life was divided into four twenty-five-year stages—celibacy and learning, marriage and child-rearing, community service, and spiritual contemplation. The second stage of my life—the point at which I should be a householder—was nearly at an end, but there was no sign of either wife or family. That was a source of great sadness to my parents, especially since a man's life could be cut short at any time and the Hindu ideal was to complete all the stages. Anyway, I was so certain that my father would welcome the idea that I might be on my way to becoming a householder—though only in form, since without a wife and family one couldn't be a true householder—that when I received his response, a couple of weeks later, in April, I was stunned. He wrote:

MY DEAREST VED,

I feel that I would not be doing my duty as a father unless I express myself unreservedly. Sixty years ago I learnt that children are their parents' continued growth. I feel myself as if I am you, and questions such as the following keep popping up in my mind:

1. For what purpose am I building a house and investing my money? Is it to go and live there? If so, given my commitments in New York, for how long during the year?

2. Am I building it with the idea of renting it or selling it and, if so, what return am I likely to get?

3. Who is going to look after all the carpets, furniture, books, souvenirs, etc. etc. when I am not there?

4. Considering that value of life and respect for property is decreasing every day, what safety factors can I depend upon in such a secluded place?

I presume that you have gone into the pros and cons of your decisions deeply.

I had often entertained the questions raised in my father's letter but had pushed them aside as I was driven by my own quixotic search. Like Orpheus, I tried not to look back at Eurydice, or Annette, or, if the truth be told, my hoped-for wife, for fear that she would disappear—and my dream with her. From childhood, I had thought of myself, as indeed people around me had, too, as mature beyond my years—as having learned the harsh lessons of life at an early age. Yet the opposite side of that maturity was, as I now realize, a great immaturity, the tendency toward a certain impetuous, bullheaded dash for things that were far beyond my means and abilities—a sort of craziness, which had now manifested itself in my throwing money at building a house, much as my father used to bet the value of his savings and my mother's jewelry at the poker table. When we were growing up, he was often at his club and at the card table from seven or eight in the evening until two or three in the morning, playing for high stakes with a smile and an empty wallet, as if there would be no day of reckoning—and there never was, because whatever he lost one night he won, and more, by luck or by skill, the next night. I had always resisted playing cards, or, rather, playing cards for money, but here I was, doing much as he had done—in a different sphere and under totally different circumstances, to be sure. In later years, how often I would wish that I had not followed his example in this respect, especially since I didn't seem to have his knack or luck in recouping my losses! Whatever my conflicting feelings, I now resolved to get rid of the house project along with the land, but, as so often before, I was uncharacteristically, inexplicably paralyzed by the prospect of conveying my decision.

I called Ed, intending to tell him that I was having second thoughts about going ahead with the house. When it came down to it, however, I couldn't bring myself to say that. He, along with Henry, had put in so much time, thought, and energy on my behalf that I felt I couldn't let him down. The most I could tell him was that I had decided to postpone beginning construction for six to eight months—until the end of the year. That was cowardly of me, but I rationalized that a slow rather than a precipitous disengagement was better under the circumstances. I imagined that Ed would protest and point out that at this late date the house could not be taken off the schedule just like that. Instead, he was accommodating, saying that the delay would give his office more time to revise and improve the working drawings. The effect of his response was to further entangle me with him and with the house and so to prolong the risky game of chance.

In August, Henry completed his working drawings. Ed thought that the only island contractor capable of reading and following them was Yeaton Randlett and had the drawings sent to him. He also wanted to stake the house himself, so Ed, Henry, and I flew to Maine and, as arranged, met with Yeaton, who came to the site equipped with stakes and a hammer.

Ed and Yeaton measured out the area for the foundation and Yeaton hammered in stakes to outline it. Ed and Henry walked uphill from the stakes a stretch and marked out the area to dig for a well. Then they walked many steps downhill from the stakes, and Ed paced an area for the septic tank. The land there rose abruptly before falling away in the direction of the sea, and Ed asked Yeaton if that would present a problem, since the sewage would have to be pumped up the hill to the septic system. Yeaton, however, would not volunteer an opinion.

I later asked Ed why Yeaton was so unforthcoming, and he said that contractors were always fearful of liability problems— they thought of their job as only executing decisions the architect had made.

At the time, Yeaton did not have a project, and he naturally thought that since he had staked out the house, he would get the contract to build it. In fact, he thought I was ready to break ground. I, however, continued to have cold feet. Although I told myself that staking was, in a sense, merely a necessary step in preparing the drawings, I seemed to be on the way to being trapped in construction. I knew if I ever put my name to a contract with a builder there would be no turning back. The mere thought of that was petrifying. I wanted to get away from Yeaton as quickly as possible. How long, I wondered, could I hold off beginning construction? I began hoping something outside me would make the decision and take it out of my hands.

As we were flying back to New York, I told Ed that I might have to postpone the construction yet again, explaining that I was in the middle of a big change in my life and that I might not be able to take on the building of the house. I was afraid he would ask me what change that was—it was something still so fragile I was reluctant to go into it. A gentlemen as always, Ed didn't press me for further explanation, but he suggested we pay Yeaton something for his time. That was clearly the honorable thing to do, but I'd become so anxious about all the money that was flowing out of my bank account on a foolish project that I said without thinking, "He'll make plenty of money off me if I build the house. He should consider the time spent with me as an ante for getting the contract."

I immediately realized my outburst was childish, but I'd been unable to help myself. Some months before, Ed's office had sent me the charges for Mary's air ticket to Maine. Ordinarily, I would have paid them without thinking twice about it. After all, she had contributed a great deal by being at the site. Instead, I queried the charge in a polite letter to Ed, and he immediately apologized and took it off. But later, whenever I saw Mary helping with the project in her own way, I always felt guilty and excoriated myself for having acted meanly. I had a similar feeling about Yeaton now. Rather like a schoolboy, I thought Ed would instruct me about my duty, forgetting, as so often I had, that he was not my headmaster but my architect— that, as his client, I was in the driver's seat. He said nothing more about my compensating Yeaton, but for days afterward I had a lingering feeling that I had done something wrong and yet couldn't bring myself to put it right.

VI

COMMITMENT

I N THE SPRING OF 1983, AROUND THE TIME I
received the cautionary letter from my father, my
friend the writer Ruth Prawer Jhabvala invited me to
a private screening of the film "Heat and Dust,"
which was based on her novel of the same name, and
for which she had written the screenplay. I occasionally went with her to private screenings of films with
which she was involved. But in the case of "Heat and Dust,"
because of a prior engagement, I could not go to the private
screening. Then the late Senator Daniel Patrick Moynihan—
whom I had got to know when he was serving as an ambassador
in India—and his wife, Liz, invited me to a party they were
giving at an Indian restaurant on the occasion of the film's New
York opening. As it happened, Ruth avoided such social
events, and although I had read the novel and so was capable of
following the story, I didn't relish the thought of going to the
première alone. At the time, I was not romantically involved;
indeed, I had almost decided that it was better to renounce

romantic relationships altogether than to risk the excruciating kinds I had barely survived.

I suddenly thought of asking Linn Cary to the film and the party. Linn was the niece of Henry S. F. Cooper, Jr., a *New Yorker* colleague and close friend of mine, and she had been to India a couple of times for the Ford Foundation, for which she worked. Through Henry, many years earlier, I had met Linn's parents, Katherine and William Cary, Henry's sister and brother-in-law, and we had become friends. Now and again, Linn and I would go on a ramble in Central Park. There was hardly anyone I enjoyed talking to more than her. She had a lovely voice and an agreeable, vaguely English accent. I recall once asking her why that was. She told me that she and her younger sister, Katrina, had been brought up in part by Irish nannies and that their mother, who came from an old New York family, had not been a traditional hands-on mother, though she worried about them incessantly. This was so different from my Indian upbringing, where women considered mothering their children in the early years to be the best way of insuring their happiness in later years, that I found myself wondering what our families—and, by extension, she and I—could have in common. I also recall that she was refreshingly forthright and that she laughed a lot, sometimes at things that didn't seem all that funny to me, making me wonder if, like me, she was covering up some sadness—in her case, perhaps the existential loneliness that I had also noticed in many of my English intellectual friends who came from a privileged background. My heart went out to her, though not in any romantic way. She was almost twenty-eight, and I was forty-nine. Besides, she was the daughter of a friend and so, I felt, off-limits to me.

I had never taken her to any public function, so I hesitated to ask her to the opening, but, as the day approached, I dreaded the thought of attending the film alone. I never gave a second thought to going to a party or a dinner alone, but going to a film alone seemed gratuitously provocative. I wondered what people would think if they saw me walking alone into a movie. I shouldn't have cared, as long as I enjoyed the dialogue and could imagine what was happening on the screen. What difference did it make what people thought? But I did care. I generally avoided calling attention to myself. Somehow, having a companion seemed to allay people's discomfort and so mine, too.

In any case, I mastered my nerves and asked her, and she accepted with such grace and simplicity that I felt reassured.

After all, good friends of the opposite sex often go to films and parties together nowadays, I thought.

I remember that her occasional whispered descriptions of what was on the screen were terse and elliptical—but, then, she was new to the role. Still, we both enjoyed the film, and the Moynihans' party turned out to be so full of friends that it had a familial, cozy feel. In addition to Ismail Merchant, the producer of the film, and James Ivory, its director, New York Indophiles, along with well-known Indian expatriates, seemed to be there in force. Although I had a good time introducing Linn to my friends, I found the party hard going. When I was younger, I used to bluff and bluster my way through any social situation, but lately, perhaps because I was doing more introspective writing, I had become shy, self-conscious, and oversensitive about what I said to people and what they said to me. To mask my unease, I ended up drinking too much.

Around midnight, I took Linn home. Although she had her own apartment, in the East Village, she was staying with her mother on the Upper East Side—her father had just died of cancer, at the age of seventy-two.

As I was leaving, I kissed her. She let me, and even responded. The kiss was so passionate that I went home lightheaded and buoyant. But when I stopped to think about it, I couldn't work out what exactly had prompted me. Was it just a goodnight kiss that had gone out of control? Was it due to the wine in my blood? Was it because, having enjoyed my time with her, I had a general sense of well-being? Was it because of some unconscious wish to get closer to the Coopers and their collaterals? (Through Henry, I had met his father, a great-grandson of James Fenimore Cooper, and mother, and his other sister, Susie, his brother, Jimmy, and their spouses and children.) Was it because, all along, I had found Linn attractive and had not acknowledged it? Was it because of my loneliness, something I felt I could no more escape than my nearly lifelong exile?

When I woke up the next morning, there was a poem from Linn under my door, which read:

A DIFFERENT CHILDHOOD

If we had been children together
in London or New York,
our houses eight blocks apart,
both facing the park,
surely we would have played
by the reservoir—or, later,
run in the evenings, as the sun
set—against the well-lit skyline
that rises from the evening like a wall of light:
and cups us, firmly
in its own well-lined palm.
. . . But we weren't.

And those blocks were as distant
as India and New York;
and twenty years, almost.
Perhaps blocks shorten
as our strides grow longer;
the sun strikes the wall
westward as it rises
casting the backs of eastern buildings
in blinding shadow.

The still reservoir catches
our houses' morning reflection
as I run. . . .

for Ved
March 30, 1983

I was stunned. I could only admire the self-confidence and strength of character that had allowed her to open herself affectively in a way that I had never felt able to. Indeed, my overwhelming feelings about the kiss had been guilt and embarrassment, all the more so since she was the kind of woman with whom I would have difficulty in brushing it off as an uncharacteristic lapse.

I thought back over the seventeen years that I had known Linn's family. I feared that by kissing her I had betrayed her family's trust, particularly that of her recently widowed mother. (It had been barely a month since Bill Cary had died.) Katherine would be furious that someone as old as I, and blind, and Indian in origin, had taken liberties with her daughter. I might deny that such factors should be considerations in matters of the heart, but, knowing Katherine, I feared she would take a more conventional view. I feared that because of my transgression I might even lose Henry as a friend—that his affection for me might not be able to withstand his sister's anger. For years I had trained myself to tread carefully and to be circumspect in my conduct and actions—to veil my desires along with my disappointments—so as not to give offense to anybody. Perhaps because I kept such tight control over my actions, on the rare occasions when I strayed I really seemed to risk all. In one rash, inebriated moment, I had forgotten my place, reached above my station, and transgressed what I believed was my karma and dharma.

On the one hand, all this concern over one kiss seemed overwrought; on the other, why would I have such a reservoir of guilt unless I had had more feelings about Linn than I had acknowledged—feelings that Linn, having perhaps sharper instincts than mine, had discerned? I could only be grateful that she had interpreted the kiss in terms of kindness.

I called Linn, thanked her for the poem, and teased her, saying that my apartment did not face Central Park. I stopped myself, for I was doing what came to me so naturally—camouflaging my emotion.

Direct as always, she wanted to know why I had kissed her. "I was just drunk," I said disingenuously. "I am so sorry."

But she didn't drop the subject. She wanted further explanation. But even though we spoke on the telephone several times that day, I was not able to come up with any good reasons. As we talked on, however, that didn't seem to matter. At one point she mentioned my coming to tea at her granddad's and perhaps coming for Easter with her family to Stockbridge, where her father's sister had a house. Then in the evening she sent me this letter:

March 31, 1983

Ved,

I just meant to say
that I got home safely
and thank you,
and good night.

That I tried to reach you,
but others intruded
and your line was busy,
but I wrote you a poem,
instead.

That maybe next Monday
would be a good time to see
Granddad; and maybe

Tanglewood would be better
than Easter in Stockbridge

And there was something else,
somewhere else I might see you;
but I have forgotten again,
—soon.

Linn

I HAD FIRST met Linn at Henry's wedding, in 1966, when she was eleven. I remembered her clearly. She had been a slight girl in a velvet dress, shy but effervescent. She laughed at everything and dashed about engaging people in conversation like a grown-up.

Subsequently, I got to know her father, Henry's brother-in-law Bill. Although our paths didn't regularly cross, we were members of the Century, then a men's club on West Forty-third Street. In fact, we served on its board together for a couple of years. In addition to being a professor at Columbia Law School and counsel to the law firm of Patterson, Belknap, Webb & Tyler, he had served as the chairman of the Securities and Exchange Commission under President Kennedy. Bill had a reputation for being a puritan. He never smoked, scarcely tasted wine, and dressed simply. As a young man, he worked in Washington for a time and shared a house with a group of other young men; he was so abstemious that they ironically nicknamed him Whiskey Luke, the Luke being derived from his middle name, Lucius. Later, he lived in Riverdale, a bucolic neighborhood in the Bronx, and for many years would not move to Manhattan because he thought that life in Riverdale was simpler.

Katherine, having grown up in the city, was always urging the move on him. She was a great-great-granddaughter of James Fenimore Cooper and, as a young woman, was so beautiful, was so sought-after, and had such difficulty deciding among her suitors that Henry quipped that beauty was her profession. Finally, when she was thirty-four years old, Bill, ten years older than she was, successfully wooed her.

The Carys were known for their hospitality and had a wide circle of friends. Once or twice a year, Henry and I and some of our *New Yorker* friends would be invited to dinner at the Carys' and we would drive up to Riverdale. I recall that their parties were always remarkable for the variety of guests, drawn from the academic, political, and social spheres. After dinner, a fresh reinforcement of guests would arrive, and we would all circulate, with Linn and her sister, Katrina, joining the party. When I started going up to Riverdale, Linn was thirteen and Katrina ten. Even as a young girl, Linn tended to speak about ideas and poetry with precocious seriousness. I remember thinking what an unusual child she was.

Later, she went to a boarding school in Massachusetts for a couple of years. From there, she got into every college and university she applied to. Her mother wanted her to go to Harvard, Swarthmore, or another place where women undergraduates had been part of the established scene for a long time, where she could expect to be looked after like a proper young lady, but Linn eventually decided against them, and went to Yale, which had just graduated its first coeducational class. Like so many women attending Yale in the nineteen-seventies, she felt she would be a pioneer and considered herself a feminist—although she did not much like the fact that she would be attending a university that her father, her grandfather, her uncle Henry, and even her great-great-great-grandfather James Fenimore had attended (according to college legend, he had been expelled for putting a donkey in the Dean's chair).

When she was at Yale, she would sometimes come into New York and drop by the office, and Henry and I would take her out to lunch. She would always bring along a girlfriend, as if she were too shy to have lunch with her uncle and another

man alone. There was a kind of virginal, high-minded reti-
cence about her. Indeed, she came across as at once idealistic
and rebellious. She gave the impression that she was single-
mindedly devoted to her intellectual pursuits, much like her
father, though, in her case, they were literary rather than legal.
Although she was intellectually and socially mature beyond
her years, she always seemed physically and emotionally
younger than she was—in fact, she had a waiflike quality that
I found touching. She certainly brought out my protective
side. Since I always saw her with Henry, I behaved with her
much as an uncle would.

I recall that at Yale, along with her studies, she threw herself into extracurricular activities, joining the Yale Glee Club
(she was a high soprano), the diving team (she had grown up
swimming, running, and riding), and a literary group that met
regularly to read Joyce's "Ulysses" aloud. She kept herself so
busy from morning to night that her friends complained that
she never sat down for a minute just to talk. At the end of her
sophomore year, she travelled with the Yale Glee Club to Central America, then went with a childhood girlfriend to Lima,
Peru. There, she tried to meet up with an English nun named
Sister Mary Otteran, who had worked with her maternal
granduncle Linn, after whom she was named. Linn Cooper, a
medical doctor, had had no family. In later life, he wanted to
do charitable work, but, because he was an atheist, no Protes-
tant organization would accept his services, so he went with a
Catholic relief organization first to China, then to the Gold
Coast in Africa, and then, in 1952 or 1953, to the jungles in
Sarawak in the Malay Archipelago. There he worked in a mission that served the Dyak Indians, until his death from
encephalitis, in 1959, at the age of fifty-nine. Throughout his
Sarawak years, Sister Mary had worked alongside him as a
nurse—and later ministered to him at his death. Although
Linn herself was four when he died, she had grown up hearing
stories about his kind nature, his dedication, and his practical
efforts on behalf of the poor. By the time Linn got to Peru,

Sister Mary had gone back to England. Still, as if inspired by her granduncle's selfless work, Linn decided to take some time off from Yale and volunteer with the Franciscans. That fall, she ended up in a high jungle mission, the journey to which had involved a twenty-four-hour bus ride over the Andes and an hour's flight in a one-engine supply plane. She worked at a mission in the village of Cutibireni on the River Ene, and she stayed there until Christmas, helping the nurse with the medical mission and running the store where the local people, Campa Indians, were just being introduced to a cash economy. The work at the mission appealed to her unconventional and adventurous nature. I recall her telling me that for two whole weeks she lived on a diet of papaya. (She liked their taste, and they grew in abundance near the mission.)

Linn's parents had a traditional view of women's place in society. They expected Linn to become a mother and homemaker, but, after graduating from Yale with a degree in English and French literature, in 1977, she did a second undergraduate degree in English at Oxford. I had taken the same route after finishing my American degree twenty-one years earlier, and at dinner with the family I applauded her choice. Like me, she had difficulty adapting to the cold, wet climate of Oxford, where she had ended up at St. Hilda's, an impoverished women's college. Intellectually, the curriculum disappointed her—the university did not welcome her interest in theoretical criticism, which had been her academic forte at Yale. Moreover, she was put in graduate-student lodgings that had no heating to speak of, and most of the time there she was besieged by bronchitis. But she stuck it out, enjoying many aspects of life in Oxford: she was the stroke of a college boat and published some poetry in the Oxford literary magazine; she indulged her passions for books and bicycling by working in a bookshop in Burford, a village in the Cotswolds, bicycling there and back, a distance of some twenty miles each way, on weekends.

After Oxford, she spent a year in Berlin working for

human-rights organizations and consolidating her German. From there, she travelled to Austria, where she hiked and climbed mountains. When she finally returned to the States, she stayed with her parents for six months. In December of 1980, she got her Ford Foundation job and lived on her own with roommates in run-down, bohemian neighborhoods where young people congregated. She eventually enrolled in a Ph.D. program at Columbia.

A year after Linn returned to New York, Hans-Peter, a boyfriend she had met in Germany, came here. He wanted to marry her, but she was still undecided. As soon as I met him at her parents' house, I liked him, but I remember feeling a twinge of something akin to jealousy when he assumed certain family prerogatives, like pouring the wine. That was the first time that I became conscious of Linn as a young, beautiful woman, though my predominant feelings remained those of an avuncular friend.

In the spring of 1980, a year before I met Hans-Peter, Henry's father, also Henry S. F. Cooper, a general surgeon and amateur sculptor who at the time was eighty-five years old, offered to sculpt a bust of my head. Over fifty years, he had done some two hundred heads of his family members, friends, and fellow-doctors. I was overwhelmed; I knew him only as Henry's father or as a much revered figure at the Century, to which he and Henry also belonged. In order to sit for him, I would generally arrive at his duplex apartment on Park Avenue and Seventy-seventh Street and have breakfast with him. Then we would climb the stairs to his studio and he would begin. Having built up a ball of viscous clay about the size of my head on an armature, he would mold and shape the clay, walking around, talking, and telling stories all the time, stopping only to check the measurements of my face and head with a pair of calipers. A charming raconteur, he had an alert mind and laughed easily. Despite the nearly forty-year difference in our ages, he treated me like a contemporary, asking me to call him Fenny, his nickname at Skull and Bones, the secret society he had belonged to at Yale. He made the dozen or so sittings, which would have otherwise been a tedious ordeal, into an entertaining experience. When the head was finished, he had it cast in bronze and presented it to me, saying that his custom was to give the bronzes to his subjects but to keep the plaster models for his "rogues' gallery," in case the police ever needed our likenesses. I didn't know what to do with my head, which, to my fingers, seemed like a strange likeness of me. Anyway, I put it on a shelf in the hall of my apartment, with a hat on it as if it were a hat stand, though I knew scarcely any men who wore hats anymore.

That summer, Fenny invited me to come and stay with him in Cooperstown, New York, which had been founded by his great-great-grandfather, William Cooper, James Fenimore's father, in 1789 and was regarded as the Cooper family seat, so to speak, and where Fenny had a five-hundred-acre farm and Henry, Katherine, and their recently widowed sister, Susie, all had houses. I had never been there, and I accepted enthusiastically.

I went up for a long weekend, and I remember feeling as if I had arrived at a well-staffed English country house. Fenny and his wife, Kitty, had brought their cook, waitress, and chambermaid—all of whom had worked for the family for many years—from New York, and Heathcote, as the house was called, was imposingly big; it even had a servants' staircase and servants' quarters on the third floor. To one side of the house was a big garden with fountains and a great variety of flowers.

Kitty had always been an avid gardener. A highly energetic woman in her younger days, she was now eighty-five and mostly stayed in bed, or sat in front of the fire in the living room, reluctant to make the effort to go even a few steps to the dining room for meals. To go up and downstairs to and from her bedroom, she needed to use a chairlift attached to the banister. Fenny described her condition, half-humorously, by saying, "Her 'get-up-and-go' has got up and went!"

A woman of extremely strong character and strong will and a certain eccentricity, Kitty seemed to take the effects of her advanced age with intermittent good humor, delivering sharp-tongued observations on politics, religion, and people, as if she had always spoken her mind with impunity. A dog lover, she doted on two noisy, ill-tempered Chihuahua puppies that were in the process of being housebroken—if they were not settled in her lap, they were settled on newspapers.

In the country, Fenny was the gentleman farmer. He spent a good part of the day driving a tractor with a straw hat on his head to protect him from the hot sun—raking the hay into rows to dry and for the baling machine to pick up. I spent much of my time taking long walks with Henry and his wife, Mary, on trails through family property, going on picnics with them, or chatting with Kitty by the fire. At five o'clock, a formal high tea was laid out in the living room, and family and friends and visitors to the village dropped in as a matter of course, some of them staying on for drinks. The tea, which was served every day, was something of a village institution.

One evening, I had dinner with Katherine and Bill Cary at their modest farmhouse. All the family was gathered there and we ate sitting in the garden, with Linn and Katrina helping their mother serve the food. (Although Linn was dating Hans-Peter, he wasn't there.) Bill was quite weak—he was recuperating after extensive chemotherapy treatment in New York—but he did not allow that to interfere in any way with the conviviality of the party.

My most haunting memory of Linn in Cooperstown, however, is not at the dinner but in a field where Henry and I happened to encounter her fortuitously. She was astride a bay mare named Nimrodel—whom she'd named after an elf princess in Tolkien's "Lord of the Rings"—and she was crying. I recall that I reached up to her and she reached down to me and we sort of hugged.

Henry asked Linn what the matter was.

"My parents don't like Hans-Peter. They are doing everything they can to make me break up with him."

Abruptly she rode away.

I wondered aloud why that was. Hans-Peter seemed eminently presentable. He was fluent in English, had a good education, and was in Washington, D.C., doing a Ph.D. Henry said that Bill and Katherine probably wanted Linn to marry someone of their background.

"What exactly does 'background' mean in this country?" I asked.

"Someone whose family is well-connected and is known to them—basically, an old, prominent family."

"That sounds so old-fashioned. I can see that in Katherine, but why Bill?"

"When it comes to the girls, Bill yields to Katherine, and Katherine thinks that Linn and Katrina would be happiest if they married into families like theirs. Anyway, Bill doesn't feel that Hans-Peter is intellectually up to Linn."

IT WAS A couple of years after my visit to Cooperstown that I asked Linn to "Heat and Dust." Within a week of that, just when I was getting to know her in a new context, I was forced to fly off, first to Chicago in connection with a MacArthur fellowship I had been awarded some months earlier, and from there to Boston in order to make a keynote speech at a dinner of the Signet Society at Harvard, to which I'd once belonged. Our separation so soon after getting together seemed ominous to me. My anxiety was intensified when, one evening, I couldn't reach her on the telephone. I eventually learned from her roommate that she had gone to Washington, and that confirmed my worst fear—that she had gone to see Hans-Peter. Although they had officially broken up, they were still in close touch—indeed, he still wanted to marry her. I fretted that in my absence she had gone back to him. A couple of my previous relationships had dissolved at the reappearance of an old boyfriend. The ghosts of those heartbreaks still mocked me in my dreams. I now cursed myself for not having learned to stay clear of a woman who still had to resolve the issues of her old relationship before she was free to move on. Indeed, I feared that I might have already lost Linn before our relationship had even taken root.

When I got back to the city and saw Linn, she told me that she had gone to Washington only to say goodbye to Hans-Peter. I was not, however, completely reassured. I started seeing her intensively and, within a few days, I pressed my apartment keys into her hand, telling her that I wanted her to come and go as she liked. Even though I realized that I was putting her in an awkward position, I couldn't help myself. One reason might have been that, when I was growing up in India, marriages had been arranged, almost without exception; yet, having lived in America and England since I was fifteen, I had, perforce, been practicing the Western rites of courtship and romantic love. As a result, I often acted as if I were torn between the two systems. I certainly rushed things, as if getting to know a woman as a person were less important than tying the marriage knot; on the other hand, when in love I lost all sense of self-esteem. How could I ask a woman to marry me when I felt unworthy of even kissing her?

Just weeks before I put my keys into Linn's hand, I had had my forty-ninth birthday and I still had not quite resolved my conflicts about love and marriage. A less perceptive woman might have spurned the keys—might have run in the opposite direction—but Linn took them, if shyly, as if she instinctively understood that they were a sign of my commitment and hope.

I was just relishing Linn's acceptance of the keys when she said, teasingly, "A few months before my father died, he warned me against getting involved with you."

Despite her lighthearted tone, her recollection gave me a turn. All the years I had known her, she seemed much closer to her father than to her mother, identifying, for instance, with his scholarly interests and simple living. If he disapproved of me for her, she was ultimately unlikely to go against his wishes, I felt—the wishes, too, of his last days.

"I wonder why he said such a thing," I said. "At the time, there was nothing between us."

"I think he'd heard that you'd had some young girlfriends before and worried about me."

"Of course, I have been seen around town with women younger than I was, but Bill couldn't have known about my private life. I never discussed that with anyone."

I explained that talking about my private life to anyone had been hard for me, perhaps because, initially, the American high-school kids I was thrown in with were so different from me that there seemed to be no way to bridge the gulf. Later, as I tried to assimilate myself into the Western and sighted worlds I was embarrassed by my Indian past and my blindness, and that made honest, open communication difficult. Whatever the reason, I kept everything to myself, rationalizing that it was best to stick to the rule "Never apologize, never explain." But my silence had come at the cost of years of loneliness. I told Linn that recently I had undergone deep psychoanalysis, itself prompted by heartbreak, and learned, among other things, that what I had considered embarrassing and shameful was instead common human experience. In time, I said, I was able to trust people with confidences, even discuss the fact of my psycho-analysis with friends, something I had kept secret while I was going through it. And that it was also what had helped me to mine a rich autobiographical vein in my writing. I further explained to Linn that her father's opinion of my previous rela-tionships could have been formed only from hearsay—some-thing I never worried about because there was no way of controlling people's gossip— and that if he were around now, and I could talk to him about my past, he might feel differently.

"But I'd like to think that he would approve of us," I added.

"He did like you very much. He looked forward to his lunches with you at the club and your coming to our house."

I suddenly felt that, through her, his benevolence was smiling on me. I told her that I would always remember the last time I saw him. That was just before he died. After Linn had accompanied me to her parents' bedroom door, I had gone in alone. Infirm and spent, he had struggled to sit up in his bed, had taken my hand, and had kissed me, something he had never done before. At that moment I had felt like a member of his family.

HENRY AND I lunched once a week. That habit went back some twenty years, to our early days at the magazine. At the first opportunity, I told him over lunch about my involvement with Linn. I fully expected him to excoriate me and accuse me of base conduct. (There was a touch of the Victorian in all the Coopers, as well as the expectation of it transmitted by the Raj to me.) I told him that I felt guilty, that the fact that Linn was an adult and thus aware of what she was doing—in fact, had encouraged me—was no excuse. I should have made myself unavailable to her—that's what my friendship with him and his family called for.

Henry listened to me with growing incredulity. He tried to stop me, I thought because he was angry, but in fact the opposite was the case.

"But that's great!" he exclaimed. "I am very happy for Linn."

"Happy for her!" I exclaimed.

"Happy for both of you!"

He brushed aside my apologies, qualms, and reservations, as if they were beneath the notice of any intelligent person. But now it was my turn to be incredulous. I had been so indoctrinated in the Indian view that blindness was a bar to my ever getting married that I was bedevilled by the thought of how I would feel if a daughter of mine got involved with a blind person—or, for that matter, any handicapped person. I would hope that I would support my daughter in her choice of whomever she loved, but such was the trauma of blindness, reinforced by experiences of rejection and condescension, that I could not be sure that I would, in fact, live up to that expectation. Such was the severity of the trauma that I had a tendency to have contempt sometimes for other people in my circumstance, and, therefore, by extension, contempt for myself— otherwise, why would I think that my blindness was such a huge impediment that love could not rise above it? It was as if I believed that love could conquer everything except blindness. Rationally, I realized that people were damaged in all sorts of ways and that some of that damage was worse than my blindness, but emotionally that realization seemed to make little difference.

"You can't mean it," I said to Henry. "I think you wouldn't want one of your daughters to be involved with a blind person. Truthfully, I don't think I would want that, either."

He was genuinely confused by my reaction.

"You are very generous and kind," I finally said.

"Nonsense," he said.

"I am sure Katherine won't take your point of view," I said. "If she didn't find Hans-Peter suitable for Linn, how is she going to find me suitable? Anyway, I think I should go and confess to her straight away."

"You talk as if your falling in love with Linn is a crime."

"Isn't that the way her mother would see it?"

"That's her problem—not yours. Anyway, disabled people the world over do get married."

"Let's say for the sake of argument I take your rosy view on that subject. On top of it, I am a writer."

"What does that have to do with anything?"

"Well, let me give you an example. I have these friends. Their daughter fell in love with a poet who also happened to be Jewish. They were so outraged by the fact she had chosen someone impoverished and not of her background that they banned her from coming home, even for Christmas. As far as they were concerned, she would not be part of the family until she gave up the poet. This she eventually did, after two whole years of family pressure and campaign. And the father himself is an artist!"

"What kind of an artist?" Henry asked.

"A sculptor who does commissions for the Catholic Church and big businesses. He makes a thousand times more money than the poet ever would make."

Even as I was telling the story, I realized the hypocrisy of my friends' attitude—and, by analogy, of mine too, in that I could condone my love for Linn and my attempt to win her, but couldn't quite condone my hypothetical daughter's ever marrying a blind man.

Henry scolded me for holding unenlightened, self-destructive views. At the end of lunch, he said to me, "The natural thing would be for Linn to talk to Katherine, as things develop. But there's no need for you, yourself, to say anything to her."

As a person, Linn was independent and headstrong, but when I later brought up the subject with her, she seemed as frightened as I was about Katherine's reaction. Linn didn't want to tackle her mother directly. She said that in time Katherine would guess and, eventually, whatever her private feelings, would have to come around. In the meantime, she counselled me to stay calm.

ONE EVENING, A few weeks into our relationship, I was regaling Linn with my adventures and misadventures with the land in Maine.

"I heard something about your land from Doda"—her father she meant; the name was pronounced "Dooda." When Linn was two, she had come out with a little poem for him: "Doda the clown / is coming to town." She and, later, Katrina (she was two and a half years younger than Linn) both called their father Doda.

I said, "He knew perfectly well that it was on a faraway, hard-to-reach island. Still, he used to gloss over my folly and say it would one day turn out to be like East Hampton property." I didn't want to tell her that she had turned up in my life just as I had decided to perhaps abandon building a house there—even perhaps to sell the land. In fact, I suddenly had an urge to show her the land while I still had it, not only because the island had occupied me for so long and I wanted to share that past with her but also because I wanted to impress upon her that, in my own way, I had a stake, however tenuous, in the world of the gentry.

"I'd like to show you the land," I went on. "But it would involve a day's trek up and a day's trek down."

She was not deterred by the travel, or even by the problem of whether or where to stay on the island, saying that we could camp out on the beach. We decided to go to Dark Harbor over the approaching Memorial Day weekend.

LINN AND I were at LaGuardia airport to catch a plane to Portland, Maine, on the way to the island for the long weekend. We had never travelled anywhere together—indeed, we had been seeing each other for barely two months. I remember approaching the revolving door at the terminal with her, hand in hand, then letting her go ahead of me and, as soon as I emerged, discovering that she had dashed ahead to the ticket counter, as if she didn't grasp that I needed her hand to guide me through the crowd.

A wave of hopelessness swept over me. Pessimistic by temperament and touchy about blindness, I was prone to exaggerate any sign of inattentiveness from the woman I was with. I wanted her both to accept me as if I could see yet to help me when I needed her to help me because I couldn't see, but I was never able to say this directly to her in so many words. If I were disappointed even slightly, I would despair of anything ever coming of our relationship. In fact, my moods would fluctuate depending on the degree to which a woman instinctively grasped my need for independence and dependence. But now I rebuked myself for my overreaction and stood to one side of the revolving door, patiently waiting for her and thinking that, given that we were still in the early stages of our relationship, things were going as well as I could have expected.

Linn came running back to me as if she'd realized I needed her and took my hand. I felt happy at once.

ON THE ISLAND, we stayed not in a tent on the beach but at a large, old house with thirteen bedrooms on the east shore, belonging to Bob and Maureen Rothschild, acquaintances who summered in Dark Harbor but were not going to be using their house that weekend. Rothschild, a self-effacing man, who always pointed out that he was not one of the famous Rothschilds but had made his money in furniture, had heard about our visit from a common friend and insisted that we should stay there, saying that the house would otherwise just be sitting vacant. He had said that there was a caretaker, whose wife cooked for them, and that the couple would look after us. I said we would go to Dark Harbor just for the day and stay on the mainland in an inn, as I generally did when I visited my land. But he then said to me, "It's different now— you're going on a romantic trip." My relationship with Linn was still so tentative that I was superstitious about verbalizing it to myself in quite those terms, but my friends and acquaintances had reached their own conclusions. Anyway, I did think it would be romantic for her to have her initial experience of the island in a large house, much as I had had in Annette's house. There would, however, be differences between the two experiences. Annette's house had been on the western shore and so was known for its cocktail-hour sunsets behind the Camden Hills, across the sheltered sea-lane. The Rothschild house was on the eastern shore and was known for its early morning sunrises and wilder waters; it looked out onto other islands and the open sea beyond them. Still, I felt that staying at the Rothschilds' would be a better introduction for Linn to my land, since it was also on the eastern shore. I gratefully accepted Bob Rothschild's offer.

By the time we reached Dark Harbor, it was almost night. Linn's only impression was one of surprise at how isolated and lonely the island was. It was so late, and we were so exhausted by the travelling, we did little more than have dinner, prepared by Maxine Nelson, the wife of the caretaker, Lars, and go to bed.

Early the next morning, I suggested to Linn that, instead of driving to my land in our rented car, we bike there. I wanted to prove to her that I was able to do things a seeing person could do, and so was worthy of her—indeed, I wanted to court her with such energy and verve that she would be over-whelmed. I expected her to demur, however; she had never seen me ride a bicycle and, even if I could convince her that I could manage it, she might not want to ride with me on a public road. But she greeted my suggestion excitedly.

She seems to be free of the usual prejudices about the hand-icapped, I thought.

I asked Lars if I could borrow a couple of Rothschild's bikes. He was aghast at the idea of my bicycling, but agreed to lend them to me. Linn grabbed a couple of large towels and packed a picnic, and we walked the bikes up the drive.

We set out for the two-and-a-half-mile ride to my land, cycling mostly on the town road, Linn leading the way and I fol-lowing her, as Samuel and I had done many years earlier. Unlike Samuel, however, she was perfectly at ease, and we kept up a steady stream of conversation so that I never lost my bearings.

I felt giddy. I had feared that the Rothschilds would have those awful American bikes with foot brakes that stop the bike dead as soon as one backpedals. But their bikes, like the English ones I had grown up with, had hand brakes with a chain and freewheel. Moreover, the seat was set just right for my height. I remember stopping suddenly but keeping myself upright by tipping the bicycle and putting my foot down.

Linn was struck by how narrow the island was, with the water visible on both sides from the road in so many places. She was also struck by how flat it was. I remember once thinking that if I had had her in mind when I was looking at the Crane land, I would have passed it up for something in the mountains; she liked climbing, hiking, and skiing. Still, she was a good sport about being by the ocean—she remarked on the island's great beauty.

Intoxicated with the idea of riding bikes with her—like anybody else—and of introducing her to an island she didn't know, at times I rode furiously, almost racing her and pulling abreast of her. Most people hadn't yet come up for the summer, so cars went by infrequently. Whenever I heard one coming, I dropped behind and hugged the shoulder of the road. Once, I veered so close to the shoulder that I took a spill and scraped my shins. From childhood, I had constantly bruised my shins and they were perhaps the most traumatized part of my body. My shinbones were so tender that if I banged them against a coffee table, I would nearly double over with pain. The skin there was so paper-thin that with just a scrape against anything hard it would begin bleeding. I now pressed a handkerchief against the scrapes to stanch the blood and dull the excruciating pain.

Fleetingly, I wanted Linn to pamper me, as if to acknowledge my hurt and my effort to please her. She showed evident concern but didn't fuss, as if, being an athlete, she regarded minor injuries as routine.

We were soon back on our bikes and talking and laughing as before.

ONCE ON MY land, we got off the bikes and left them on the grass up near the town road. We walked down the dirt road to the beach and then started back up to Barnes's building site through the clearing that had in the meantime been cut to create his architectural room. Even since Jack Leach had done the cutting, a few months before, new growth and foliage had sprouted up, so that we had to duck under and elbow aside branches here and there. Occasionally, we also had to step over wind-felled trees.

"What do you think about my piece of ground?" I asked.

"I like it—it's wild and pristine," she said.

When we arrived at the site, I was distressed to realize that the new growth had already blocked the view of the water so that the site seemed as if it were in a glade.

"This site is going to require a lot more cutting, and I wonder if it would keep for long the shape of the architectural room that Ed envisages," I said.

Linn wanted to see Zimmerman's original building site, so we clambered our way down there and I showed her the abandoned driveway.

"From this site, I can hear the waves of the bay all the time, whereas from up there I would scarcely be able to hear them, unless the land is opened up a lot," I said. "But then, that's the way I like it."

"But you do get a much greater vista of the water from where Barnes has situated the house than you do from here," she said. "Or, rather, you will, once more trees are cleared away. That's a shame—I don't like cutting trees."

"Neither do I. But now that we've begun clearing, there is not enough brush and dead trees to prop up the living ones." I explained to her that the ledge, the shelf of sedimentary rock, under a thin covering of soil, was a common feature of the island, and told her that, because of the ledge, the root structure of the trees was not very deep. "Anyway, the birches don't have many roots. I am afraid that the trees will fall by themselves as soon as there's a storm."

We tromped through the forest, at one point searching for what sounded like a running brook, which could be heard but not seen. We couldn't discover the source of the water but eventually found its runoff, under a thick cover of brush and felled trees. It trickled out from somewhere and had no specific channel, and so created the marshland. The land seemed as if it had never had a chance to dry out, as if the rays of the sun had never reached it.

We squelched our way back to the beach, our shoes and legs covered with mud.

Linn threw off her clothes and jumped into the icy water and swam for a good ten minutes while I sat on the rock and gingerly washed off the mud as best as I could. The water was so cold that, every time I came into contact with it, the top of my head shivered from the shock.

We gathered some sticks and scraps of wood and made a fire on the beach, warmed ourselves, toasted some marshmallows on sticks, and ate our picnic sandwiches. We spent the rest of the day sitting on the beach or exploring. We hiked through the upper part of the land and walked to the southern tip of the island, about three-quarters of a mile away. Finally, we biked back to the Rothschilds'.

Maxine was eager to cook us dinner, but I didn't want to impose on the Rothschilds' hospitality any more than we already had, and so we drove to the only restaurant on the island, the Blue Heron, which had just opened for the summer.

All during the day, I had been looking for the right moment to ask Linn to marry me. Having suffered losses of one kind or another—from the loss of my eyesight in early childhood to abandonment by a fiancée in later life—I didn't want to lose any time in proposing to her. I was sure I loved her, and I certainly had all the telltale signs of being in love; when we were not together, I constantly thought of her, wondered what she was doing, called her, waited for her calls, felt that I had never known anyone like her and that we were destined to be together. But every time I thought of asking her, my heart would race; I feared again that I was being too hasty and was setting myself up for rejection. I was all too aware that if I were in her shoes, I would find myself totally unsuitable. I was twenty-one years older and a writer whose income was unpredictable from year to year. I had so little confidence in the marketability of my writing that I imagined that if the editor of *The New Yorker*, William Shawn, who had bought and edited practically all of my work, ever left the magazine, I would be out on the street. Yet I was determined to let Linn know that I wanted to marry her, and drew encouragement from the signs of her affection for me, like her coming with me to Maine.

Somehow, I had lately got it fixed in my mind that the most propitious place to ask her was on the island and on my land. I knew I had done everything backward—bought the land and started planning the house before I had a wife. I now wanted to put things right by consecrating, as it were, both our relationship and, before I parted from it, the land—a sort of stand-in for the more appropriate home we might later build together.

Night was fast approaching, and the next day we would have to start back for the city. I suggested that, after dinner, we drive back to my beach, and she eagerly embraced the idea.

We drove in the dark to my land and down to the beach. The island had no streetlighting, and the only relief from the darkness was from our own headlights, those of an occasional car, or the light from an occupied house.

I had suffered so many heartbreaks that I could leave nothing to chance, so I had brought along a ring—a ring as inappropriate for Linn as I was. It was an antique, fragile item, with a portrait of a demure Georgian lady who bore as little resemblance to sporty Linn as Victorian housewives did to female executives or suffragettes. Yet I didn't think that I could propose to her without a token of my love in hand. Even now I am embarrassed to write that, moreover, I had acquired the ring with another woman in mind, and had it still only because she had returned it after leaving me and I couldn't bear to throw it away. I came up with the strategy of giving Linn the Georgian ring as a surrogate until, together, we could shop for a new, appropriate one for her. That was, of course, if she accepted me.

We stood at the water's edge, so close to it that a couple of times we had to step back in order to avoid getting drenched by the rising tide.

I was fingering the ring in my pocket without knowing how I could bring it out delicately. I was still worried about frightening her with the intensity of my feeling and the swiftness of my proposal.

"Isn't this beach romantic?" I didn't know how else to begin.

"The beach is completely unspoiled—almost primitive."

"Yes. The first time I came here, the friend who was with me said that this is what you'd imagine the world must have been like when Adam and Eve were created."

"It's amazing that you found it."

I decided that was my cue and I seized it.

I stumbled through my proposal, even as I apologized for being too old.

"I'm overwhelmed—you are not too old, but I am too young," she said simply.

I brought out the ring and said, as offhandedly as I could, that it was just a memento.

I thought she might flinch, but she took it.

She was horrified at the portrait, but, much to my relief, she didn't ask any questions about how or where I had got the ring—if she had, I would have had to tell her. Instead, she wondered aloud how anyone in bygone days could have worn the ring and washed dishes.

"They didn't," I said. "The maids did that. Like at your grandparents' house."

She laughed, tried it on and took it off, but kept it. I told myself that her answer was more yes than no, that she naturally needed time to think, but that that was enough.

EARLY IN JULY, a few weekends after our trip to Maine, I went with Linn for a weekend to Massachusetts, to Stockbridge in the Berkshires, to visit her aunt Josephine, her father's only surviving sibling, Auntie Do, pronounced "Doe," who had Alzheimer's and was in a nursing home there. The place had a depressing atmosphere—for hours on end, patients were left sitting in front of a blaring television in the lounge. The only respite they seemed to get from their mechanical pacifier was when they were given meals or baths or put to bed. They seemed either to be drugged into a continuous stupor or to doze off into a perpetual torpor. Auntie Do was in such an advanced stage of the disease that although she had a strong constitution, she couldn't talk, and the only sign of recognition she gave Linn was a weak smile.

Afterward, as if to cheer us up, Linn proposed a climb on Monument Mountain, which she said her father used to go up and come down every morning when he was in Stockbridge visiting his sister.

"Go up a whole mountain!" I said, aghast.

"It's not much more than seventeen hundred feet high. I think the trail to the peak is only one and a half miles long."

I realized that I was thinking of Monument Mountain in terms of the Himalayas—that, possibly, Monument Mountain was nothing more than a large hill.

"I think I can manage it," I said, mastering my anxiety.

"Doda could get up there in forty minutes."

That's amazing, I thought. The last time he made the climb, he must have been over seventy.

"How long does it take you?" I asked.

"Twenty minutes."

"Gosh, you are like a gazelle."

Eager to impress her with my physical prowess, I set off on the climb at a great pace. Halfway up the mountain, I was so short of breath and my heart was thumping so fast that I was sure I was going to have a heart attack on the spot, but, ignoring Linn's counsel to take a short rest, I pressed on. When we were about three-quarters of the way up, my legs went limp, and I imagined my heart was about to give out—that if

I didn't stop I would never come down from the wretched mountain. I sat down just where I was.

I could tell that Linn was disappointed, not so much by my lack of physical stamina as by the thought that she would have to stay with me and forgo the chance to reach the top. She pursued all her physical goals with the determination of an athlete.

I insisted that she go on and told her that I would be happy waiting for her there. She dashed off.

After she was out of earshot, I listened for any sound, but I couldn't hear so much as the chirp of a cricket or the footstep of a person. It was just like being on the island the time Annette hadn't shown up.

The silence of the mountain began to tell. I remembered hearing about ferocious wild animals in the foothills of the Himalayas, and began to worry that I might be attacked by one here. Since I wouldn't be able to see it coming, I wouldn't be able to defend myself, or, rather, even if I were to hear it coming, I wouldn't know which way to jump. I hardly knew which way was up and which way was down. I sat there paralyzed, with my ears cocked and my mouth dry. I should never have told her to go to the top by herself, I thought. She must have known that I didn't mean for her to leave me. I then wondered angrily what kind of girl she was, to abandon me on an unfamiliar mountain with God knew how many precipices and falls.

I heard a rustling and crunching of leaves to my right, in the direction Linn had run up—then four distinct, even sounds, one after the other among the fallen leaves, as if a huge animal were slowly but surely creeping up on me. I was certain that a bear was looking me over and was about to pounce. I instinctively put up my hands to shield myself from the blow. Then I fancied I heard something between a growl and a snort.

I am going to die just so that she can make it to the mountaintop, I thought. What would she have sacrificed by passing up going to the top for the umpteenth time? That made me reflect, in my panic, that an Indian woman would not have looked to her own pleasures. Instead, brought up with the ideals of sacrifice and renunciation and of selfless devotion to her man, she would have been solicitous of me, certainly would never have forsaken me on an isolated, frightening mountainside.

My heart began practically galloping. I felt limp all over. I screamed, but, as in a bad dream, no sound came out.

Then I heard some loping steps just above my head.

God, I thought, there are not one but two bears.

As it turned out, the overhead sound was Linn running down to me.

"Do you see the bear?" I asked.

"What bear?"

I laughed to cover up my embarrassment, but confided to her the nightmare I had lived through. She laughed, but not cruelly. She told me that my fears were groundless.

HAVING SCARCELY BEEN away for summer weekends since the time when Annette owned her house in Dark Harbor, I was now regularly skipping out of New York, this time for Cooperstown, where I had a long-standing invitation from Fenny. In 1982—a couple of years after he had done my head and a year before Linn and I had started seeing each other—he had found that his speech and hearing had markedly deteriorated, with one side of his face becoming paralyzed. He was immediately operated upon, and found to have a tumor in the brain stem which could be only partially removed. The tumor was a recurrence of a rare disease of the nervous system called von Recklinghausen's syndrome, which causes benign fibrous tumors. In fact, he was first diagnosed with the disease as a young man training to be a surgeon, when he suddenly had trouble using his left forearm. A tumor in his elbow was discovered and removed, and he regained full use of his arm. But after the operation on the brain tumor, some fifty years later, there was only temporary improvement in his speech or hearing.

Soon after we returned from Stockbridge, Linn and I visited Fenny in Cooperstown, where he was recuperating. She stayed with her mother and I with Fenny and Kitty, but Linn, like the other members of the family, was in and out of Heathcote most of the time. Also, as it happened, I had that weekend to read and correct the *New Yorker* proofs of a series of articles about my childhood, and Linn and I spent long stretches in the library working on them. She would read them to me, making suggestions for improvements along the way. I was mesmerized by her voice; that it was my writing she was reading—and writing about my early years—gave her reading additional poignancy.

Fenny was mentally alert and seemed to sense that Linn and I were profoundly involved. I remember that once, as I was coming down from my room and passing his study, I overheard him saying something to Henry. Fenny's speech impediment was such that his words came out half-formed and I didn't realize that he was talking about Linn and me until I was almost down the stairs and thought back on what I had heard.

"I dreamt that Linn had eloped with Ved and Katherine was mad as a hornet," Fenny had said.

"That's not just a dream, Daddy," Henry had said. "That could really happen."

The exchange gave me the shivers. Linn's apprehensions about Katherine's reaction were shared even by Katherine's father. I myself had no doubt that Katherine was aware of everything—she knew that we had gone to Dark Harbor and Stockbridge and she had seen us going around together in New York. But she didn't so much as acknowledge that there was anything between us, as if, by not admitting it, she could wish it away. My position was made more awkward because Linn still had not told her mother about my proposal, though that was perfectly understandable, since she hadn't accepted it.

While Linn and I were driving back from Cooperstown, we stopped by to see Pat and Liz Moynihan at their upstate farm. They guessed right away that we were deeply in love, and asked why we didn't go ahead and get married.

Linn had never said yes in so many words to my proposal, and she confided now to the Moynihans that her father had recently died and that she didn't want to upset her mother.

Pat offered to perform the ceremony on the spot, saying that he was a justice of the peace, that Liz and he had a lot of champagne on hand, and that there was never a better time and place to get married than on a summer day in the country.

I was horrified, even though Pat had floated the idea half in jest. I couldn't imagine that Katherine would ever forgive us for depriving her of a role in our wedding, and I was old enough to know that, once the ceremony was over, there was a long life ahead in which it would be important for her and me to be on good terms. But Linn seemed almost tempted. There is a certain rebellious, adventurous streak in her that can be easily excited.

We had a swim in the Moynihans' pool, a bibulous lunch, and went back to New York, laughing whenever we thought of how easy it would have been for us to have got married. But my laughter was more nervous than genuine—actual marriage for me remained as elusive as ever.

I invited Linn to come with me to India, where I was going at the end of the summer for a couple of weeks to visit my family. My family members in India did not have the money to travel to America to see me, so I generally went home, often on an assignment, to see them. Moreover, my father, who was the same age as Fenny, had long been a heart patient. Although Linn had briefly met my parents when she had been in India for the Ford Foundation, I wanted her to get to know them and for them to get to know her. She was thrilled at the suggestion, and we got our plane tickets.

When we told Katherine about it, she gave Linn a letter to an old family friend who lived in New Delhi. She asked Linn to look it over, and Linn later remarked that in the letter

Katherine had neither said that we were travelling together nor mentioned me at all.

With any girl other than Linn, I might have worried about how she would fit into my family, how she would adapt, how she would react to the modest circumstances in which my family lived. Although by Indian standards all my relatives were well-placed, after the Partition many of them were not as well-off as they had been before. Also, the Indian way of life tended to be simpler and more basic than the lifestyle of people in comparable positions in America and England. Although otherwise extremely proud of how well my family had managed, I did feel ashamed of how they—and, by extension, all Indians—were forced to live compared with the affluent way her family lived. Even those Indians who were well-to-do were not as preoccupied with material symbols of well-being as their counterparts in the consumer society of the West.

I remember wondering how Linn would react, for instance, to my father's house having no paintings in it, just family photographs on the wall of the living room, along with posters that he had picked up from museums on his travels. I couldn't gloss over the fact that her mother's and grandparents' apartments and their country places were filled with paintings, even portraits of their ancestors and children. Indeed, in her mother's living room in New York there was a painting of Linn herself, for which she had sat when she was an undergraduate at Oxford. As part of my assimilation into the sighted world and Western society, I surrounded myself with nice things, fancying that if I lived well people would not pity me. Thus, the walls of my apartment were hung with paintings and drawings, which I had slowly acquired. Although they invariably had a special association for me and were by painters I knew or were drawings that had appeared as illustrations for my articles—including three marvellous drawings by Saul Steinberg—the fact remained that I couldn't see them, only imagine them, often from the descriptions of the artists themselves. But my anxiety on this count had more to do with me than with Linn. The truth was that in temperament she was a scholar, who didn't notice her surroundings. Indeed, she was above caring how she looked and what she wore, and maybe that's why she didn't mind that I couldn't see her.

Her simplicity was evident to everyone at home the moment Linn stepped off the plane. She fit into our family as if she were one of us, and my mother kept on repeating to me in Punjabi, "She doesn't seem like a foreigner."

They say that in love one sees one's own reflection, and, certainly, while travelling in India, I began to see in Linn certain of my own characteristics. She was flexible and adaptable but—unlike me—extremely forgiving. At one point I took her to Kathmandu in Nepal for three days so that she could indulge her passion for mountain climbing. I had arranged for us to go on a mountain hike. Instead, because of some bureaucratic bungling, we were taken for a ceremonial walk around the local botanical garden. Some other girl would have complained and pouted, but Linn laughed it off as an experience.

We celebrated her twenty-eighth birthday in India. Not long after, we were in a hotel room in Bombay. Linn was at the desk writing a letter, and I was reading a book on tape with an earpiece. She looked up from the desk and said, as if we were in the middle of a conversation, "Yes, I will marry you."

I yanked out my earpiece, jumped up, and ran to her. "You really mean it?"

"I do."

"What if your mother refuses her consent?"

"She won't like it, but she won't be able to do anything about it."

I remember thinking about the disparity between where I had proposed to her and where she had finally accepted me. I had chosen according to my lights the most remote, the most romantic, the most upper-crust island in my reach, feeling that would impress her. But she had accepted me in a city that an Oxford poet friend of mine, Dom Moraes, called a "forked island," teeming with tenements, slums, and homeless people, though throbbing with energy, excitement, and possibilities. The venues were a mismatch, and they indicated that, as people, we had already unconsciously adopted each other's cultures. But that couldn't make me forget the basic differences between where she was in her life and where I was in mine, between her family and mine. We would have to work to bridge that chasm, through our love, our friendship, our mutual interest in things of the heart and the mind.

"I want to do it fast," I said. My impatience was getting the better of me. I felt that if I waited any longer for reasons of propriety, I might be jeopardizing my own future happiness.

"Anytime you like," she said.

"Maybe in Oxford on our way back. We could ask your mother to fly over."

"Sure," she said.

"But I seem to remember that to get married in an Oxford college one has to get permission from the Archbishop of Canterbury, and that'll really complicate things."

"Then we can get married in America."

"You have no doubts?"

"None."

In London, we picked up for Linn an antique engagement ring—a sapphire in a carved setting decorated with small diamonds—and an antique wedding band with the inscription, in eighteenth-century script, "God aboue increse our loue."

We announced our decision to Katherine, and she accepted it with a dignified silence. For the sake of her and of our friends, we decided to be married in New York, and set the date a few months from then, on December 17th. In accordance with tradition, Katherine made the wedding arrangements. She felt that a wedding lunch or wedding dinner would unnecessarily add to the cost. We had no trouble with that; in any case, given my age, I felt that a reception with drinks, hors d'oeuvres, and a cake, which is what Katherine wanted, would be sufficient.

Everyone agreed that the reception should be held at the Century Club. Katherine felt, however, that we should serve

New York State sparkling wine rather than French champagne. For Linn, one champagne was the same as another, and I reconciled myself to Katherine's decision, but then Henry stepped in and said that he must have his friend and his niece married in style, with French champagne, and that he would foot the bill. Finally, Katherine did not want any children at the wedding or the reception—she felt they would be disruptive. I felt sad about that. In India children are the soul of weddings, and the children of my few Indian relatives and friends settled in America or Canada could not understand why they were excluded. Still, a couple of parents did come with their children, and we were glad to have them there.

In deference to Katherine's wishes, we agreed to get married in the St. James Chapel of the Cathedral Church of St. John the Divine, by the Very Reverend James Morton, Dean of the Cathedral. Since I had been born a Hindu and was agnostic, I felt a little hypocritical. Still, it was easier to acquiesce than to make waves. Anyway, given Linn's Christian background and the fact that I was living in America, the church ceremony seemed appropriate, especially since Dean Morton was ecumenical in his outlook. Also, I found Katherine's choice of the cathedral poignant—ten months earlier, I had attended there the funeral services for her husband, Linn's father.

For the night before the wedding, Fenny and Kitty arranged a dinner in their apartment for their extended family and those few members of my family who were coming to the wedding. Fenny was excited that Linn was being so adventurous by marrying someone from a whole different part of the world and, in her own way, living up to the intrepid example set by his brother Linn. He wanted me to suggest for the evening an Indian touch that would make my relatives feel at home, and at the same time introduce the members of his family to the traditions of my world. It so happened a close friend, Indrani Rahman, one of the renowned exponents of classical Indian dance, had been asking me if there was any part of my wedding when she could dance, as her "offering" to Linn and me. There seemed no place for a Hindu dance at my Christian wedding until Fenny suggested the dinner. Even though I thought that Indrani's dancing at one of the most intimate moments of my life was somewhat bizarre, because I could appreciate it only with my imagination, I mentioned her offer to Fenny; he was immediately taken with the idea—as, indeed, was Indrani.

On the evening of this dinner, Indrani arrived a little early and as the guests gathered, she retreated to a room to get ready for her dance. While she painted the palms of her hands and the soles of her feet red, put up her long hair and decorated it with a profusion of flowers, adjusted her huge earrings, lined her eyes with black kohl, fixed her temple sari (heavy South Indian silk with gold brocade), and tied on her ankle bells, I stood around handing her things as she asked for them, something an acolyte would do as a matter of course if she were doing a performance on stage. She explained to me that she was going to perform the Shiva dance in honor of my wedding: how with her hands and face—a sort of sign language of the dance—she was going to conjure up Shiva approaching his consort Parvati, with his swaying, matted hair, his blazing third eye, and his necklaces of serpents with their hoods flared.

"How will you specifically evoke, say, the hoods?" I asked.

"I'll cup my hand," she said.

"And your love of Parvati?"

"With my large dancer's eyes that God gave me."

"Will it be hard not to have music or tabla accompanying you?"

"I'll pound out the rhythm of my dance with my heels and my ankle bells will give me nice music like this." She pounded her foot, making her ankle bells ring lightly and rhythmically.

Her entrance in the foyer was electrifying. Her father had been an Indian and her mother an American, and she had the voluptuous body of an Indian and the delicate features of a Westerner, combining in her person my East and Linn's West. As a young woman, she had been selected as Miss India. Everybody was mesmerized by her beauty, and I heard Fenny say that, if he were in better health, he would have liked to have her sit for him.

We all made ourselves comfortable in front of the marble staircase of the Cooper, Sr.s' duplex while Indrani danced with great intensity in the foyer near the door, dramatizing Shiva's seduction of Parvati.

The dinner that followed, with Linn's grandparents, their children and grandchildren, my older brother Om, his family, our nieces, and their children all seated around well-appointed tables, had a jolly, festive air. Katherine seemed so relaxed and outgoing that I thought I was discovering a new, gentle side of her.

THE WEDDING ITSELF is a blur. There were the vows, perhaps the most poetic sentences in any language. And then there was the music: Monteverdi, Bach, and Purcell—pieces Linn had chosen with considerable care. The echo in the cathedral was so all-encompassing that the music took on an eerie, supernatural resonance.

The apparent incongruity of our match was exemplified by the guests at the reception: childhood friends and well-connected families on Linn's side, and a motley crew of foreigners, writers, and editors on mine. At one point, two bag ladies were discovered sitting on a sofa in the corner of the public room of the club, feasting on hors d'oeuvres and quaffing champagne as fast as they could. At first they were taken for my guests, but their behavior was so brazen that the maître d' eventually summoned Henry.

"Whose guests are you?" Henry asked them over the dance music.

"The bride's," said one.

"What's her name?" he asked.

"No, the bridegroom's," said the other.

"What's his name?" he asked.

"Are you from the newspaper?" the first asked.

"Don't tell him—he's trying to insult us," the second said.

"We don't want to be anywhere we are not welcome," said the first.

They got up and haughtily sailed out.

WE WENT TO a lavish resort in Antigua for our honeymoon. From the outset, Linn was embarrassed to be there. She didn't like the fact that the place had gates and guards. But, like our wedding, the trip had an eccentric flavor. When Linn wasn't swimming and I wading in the sea, we spent our time sitting on the beach reading Aristotle's "Poetics," De Quincey's "Confessions of an English Opium Eater," and Kafka's "The Metamorphosis"—all for a paper Linn was writing for a postgraduate evening class she was taking at New York University. The other guests in the club couldn't stop gaping at us—we were such an odd sight in that milieu. Then, after three days on our own, Katherine and Katrina joined us. It was their first Christmas without Bill and they wanted their small family to be together. At first, I was alarmed at the prospect of sharing my honeymoon—or "wedding trip," as my mother-in-law insisted I call it (she thought "honeymoon" sounded middle class)—with them. But then I rationalized that I had lived alone all my adult life and should take pleasure in being surrounded by a whole new family—and I did.

VII

BUILDING

A ROUND THE TIME OF THE WEDDING, I GOT A CALL from Ed Barnes saying that the bid documents were ready, that Henry Myerberg had canvassed all the possible contractors in the area, and that he was now only waiting for word from me to get going. That evening, I mentioned Ed's call to Linn. In the months of our courtship, there wasn't much that I did from which I shut her out. She took an interest in my friends and in whatever I was writing; it was therefore natural that she should come to know everything about the house. After all, aside from books, it was the most important project that I'd ever undertaken. After her visit to my land, Linn had grown attached to the idea of my building a house there. Indeed, every time she came to my apartment, she saw a model of the house sitting on the mantelpiece of my living room. She and I had gone over Henry's working drawings together; she had also got to know the Barneses—we sometimes saw them for a drink or for tea.

"Why would Ed have to call you to get your go-ahead?" she asked. "I thought the house was all set."

"I'm sure he knows money is a big stumbling block for me."

Money was one thing we scarcely ever talked about.

"Oh," she said. "So what are you going to do?"

"I suppose go ahead with the bidding process. What have I got to lose? It would be helpful to know what the damn house is going to cost."

She laughed, no doubt thinking I was cursing the house because the process was so slow and tedious.

The next morning, I gave the nod to Ed, and soon after we left on our wedding trip Henry sent the bid documents to Yeaton and to Wallace Leach, another building contractor on the island and half a dozen mainland contractors, soliciting bids by January 27, 1984, or a month after the documents were mailed. In due course, he received formal bids, but only from Yeaton and Leach. All along, there had been a general feeling in Ed's office that it was advisable to use an island contractor. As Ed had put it, "you wake up in the middle of the night and you find there's no water in the house or a pipe has sprung a leak. If you have a relationship with the local plumber, he'll come and fix your problem. If you don't have that relationship, you'll be stuck with an off-island plumber, who might not be able to take care of the problem in a timely fashion, or who might be reluctant to come at all for fear of antagonizing his fellow-plumber. In any island community, there's a tight-knit trade group, all of whose members support one another and jealously guard their territory."

Leach didn't want to commit himself to a firm contract price. That left us with only Yeaton's bid, which came in at two hundred thousand dollars, a shocking seventy-five thousand dollars above what Ed had estimated. As if that weren't scary enough, I received from Barnes's office, together with Yeaton's bid, a draft of the Independent Contractor Agreement, with a note from Ed saying I should get it reviewed by a lawyer before signing it. The agreement was far more complicated than the

Abbreviated Form of Agreement Between Owner and Architect, but there was no ambiguity about one point: once I put my signature to it, I would be legally bound to come up with an installment of twenty or thirty thousand dollars every month to pay Yeaton for material and labor, overhead and profit, depending on how much work he had completed. I got the shakes. Right or wrong, I was through with the house, the island—the whole state of Maine.

I already knew that I would miss being in regular touch with Ed and his office. The act of writing was so gruelling that I had looked forward to his office's interruptions. They had provided me with a diversion and had made me feel I was doing something real out in the world, in contrast to writing, which was cerebral and sedentary—something like dreaming all day.

But if I went ahead with the house in Maine, I would have to liquidate all my savings—my cushion against accidents or emergencies—and take a construction loan. Even if I were able to do that, I would have trouble meeting the interest payments. I called Ed and told him that there was no way I could come up with the money. As so often, I was about to tell him that I was through with the project, but when it came down to it I couldn't get the words out. Instead, I stalled and asked him how he could explain the discrepancy between his initial estimate and Yeaton's bid.

"Well, Yeaton's including in his price the cost of the septic system, the well, the garage under the house, and electrical installation—he has to bring power to the house."

"I would have thought such items would have been included in your original estimate."

"We did include them, but it seems we didn't price them according to the island's trades. Everything there turns out to be that much more expensive. Since it was our miscalculation, we'll base our fifteen-per-cent architectural fee on the estimate we gave you. If it were just me, I'd waive it altogether, but my office is involved."

His offer succeeded only in confusing me. I did not want

to accept a favor from a man whom I had hired to be my architect; I still had not got over the fact that Annette had deeded her half of the parcel of land to me. Yet his generous gesture once again stopped me from telling him that going ahead with the house was out of the question.

"I think it's only fair to warn you that, along the way, there are bound to be cost overruns," Ed added.

"I thought two hundred thousand dollars was Yeaton's firm contract price."

"But in all building projects there are cost overruns. No matter how good the drawings are, during construction all kinds of things come up that generate change orders. Each change order is priced separately and added to the contract price and, in my experience, cost overruns end up being about twenty per cent over and above the contract price."

"Why is that?" As so often before, my intellectual curiosity about architectural details seemed to override my good sense.

"There are always things you want to improve during construction."

"What if a client uses self-discipline and simply decides not to make any changes?"

"That's never practicable. The deck might look fine in a drawing, but when it's built, it might not look right. You might want to raise or lower the railing or whatnot."

I calculated that a twenty-per-cent cost overrun on top of two hundred thousand dollars would come to two hundred and forty thousand dollars. And Ed's reduced architectural fee on top of that would take me to nearly two hundred and sixty thousand dollars. No doubt, there would be additional expenses of twenty or thirty thousand dollars for an architect to visit the construction site. And even that was not all. I was already out of pocket seven thousand two hundred and seventy-nine dollars for land-development expenses, and sixteen thousand two hundred and twenty-two dollars for sundry architectural expenses. (In addition to the expenses for all the trips I had made with Ed and Henry to the site, there had been the fees and expenses for Zimmerman and my young New York architect friend Patrick.) I was frightened out of my wits, but I was still at a loss about how I could back out of the project gracefully.

"How can you make sure that the contractor is following your drawings?" I asked. Stalling while talking to Ed was becoming all too easy for me.

"You basically have to trust your contractor. If you were really rich, you could have a clerk of works sitting there monitoring all the supplies and materials coming in and supervising the work. As it is, Henry will be going up for monthly visits and will pick up any obvious deviations or defects."

Ed explained that since the architect was the liaison between the owner and the contractor, as well as the arbiter in case of disputes, Henry would visit the site regularly and check on Yeaton's work. After each visit, he would issue a field report to the contractor, architect, and owner outlining what part of the construction had been completed, along with a requisition for payment setting out what I owed Yeaton that month.

As Ed was talking, I was getting more deeply involved every minute, even thinking ahead, like an incorrigible dreamer, to what it would cost to bear the additional expenses for Henry's monthly visit and, later, to furnish and landscape the completed house.

"When I originally bought the land, I was just thinking of putting up a little cabin," I said tentatively.

"People often don't know what kind of house they want right away. Before they settle on a house, they're apt to have all kinds of ideas. My son John, who is an architect, owns some land in Deer Isle. He's just going to put up a platform tent and live there for a few summers, walk around until he discovers the perfect site, and then he'll decide on a house."

"The option of my putting up a platform tent has long gone, hasn't it?" I said. "For me to pull out now would be like jumping off a speeding train, wouldn't it?"

Ed laughed, as if not grasping the fact that that's what I

really wanted to do. So I came right out and said, "There's no way I can swing building a house at Yeaton's contract price. I simply don't have the money for it or the capacity to earn it. I'm going to put the land on the market."

"That's perfectly understandable," he said. "I've enjoyed working with you."

I was overwhelmed by the way he took the bad news. Another architect might have launched into a torrent of recriminations. Indeed, an architect billing on an hourly basis, as Zimmerman had, would already have totted up billing hours to the tune of thirty or forty thousand dollars.

"I can't tell you how bad I feel having strung you along for so long," I said.

"There's no reason to feel bad," Ed said. "I don't think one should be sentimental about a business decision."

"Has this ever happened to you before?"

"Clients often abandon projects before construction gets under way."

"Is there any way I can compensate all the people involved?"

"I think you might be out of pocket some money to my office and to Yeaton as a 'breakage fee,' but you might recoup that and more by selling the drawings."

"I don't understand."

"You own the drawings. When you sell the land, you might be able to sell the drawings with it. Many custom houses have a lot of fussy things owners want, like extra dressings rooms and powder rooms and bay windows. Your house is clean and pure. Anyone buying your land might be happy to build from our drawings."

WHEN I TOLD my friends that I was pulling out of Maine, they started telling me that I was making a mistake. They were unanimous in their opinion that real estate was the best hedge against the rampant inflation of the time and pointed to the staggering rise in the prices of coöperative apartments in New York. Indeed, many of them had bought and sold apartments in the rising New York market of the nineteen-seventies and the early nineteen-eighties and thereby increased their net worth many times. In fact, I, too, might have participated in the same real-estate boom. In 1963, I had bought an apartment at the Dakota, one of the oldest and grandest buildings in Manhattan, for nineteen thousand five hundred dollars. But then Milton Greenstein, the *New Yorker* lawyer who informally advised all of us writers on financial matters, told me that it was a terrible mistake for people whose income at the best of times was uncertain to own a co-op apartment. One in essence leased it, he said, from a non-profit corporation that owned the apartment building, and assumed the obligation to pay rent, he went on, or a monthly maintenance charge, to cover the cost of the building's mortgage, taxes, staff, utilities, and insurance; on top of that, one was liable for sudden assessments for repairs and refurbishments of the building. Buying a co-op apartment, therefore, was nothing more than buying a lease. One merely owned shares in the corporation, and if one couldn't pay the maintenance for two or three months, one risked forfeiting the investment, along with the apartment. Milton, who had cut his teeth in the Depression, was full of stories of owners' not being able to pay the maintenance and so losing their apartments, whereupon, to save the building, the corporation would frantically offer the shares and the apartment nearly gratis to anyone who could assume the co-op obligations.

Fearing that my writing would dry up and that I would not be able to pay my apartment's monthly maintenance of three hundred and seventy-two dollars—almost half of my eight-hundred-dollar monthly advance from *The New Yorker*—I sold the apartment two years later for the same price I had paid for it. For the next fourteen years, thinking I was being prudent, I lived in a small rented apartment on Fifth Avenue. During that time, the price of the shares of my former co-op apartment appreciated to over a million dollars. I told myself that in leaving the Dakota I had been penny-wise and pound-foolish. I joked with my friends that, if I had stayed there all those years guzzling champagne and gorging on caviar and then sold the apartment, I would have done better financially than I had done by going to work every day.

In any event, when I told Linn that I was putting the land, along with the working drawings, up for sale, she was disturbed. She liked the thought of our building a house together. Even more important, she thought that the land had a special place in our marriage.

"How can you think of doing that?" she asked.

"I was on the verge of selling the land before you ever saw it," I said. "I'm convinced it's the only practical thing to do."

"That's not something you should decide by yourself," she said. "As your wife, shouldn't I have a say?"

At the time of this conversation, we were at dinner. She had cooked filet of sole. First she got up to get extra lemon for me, then to fetch tartar sauce, and then vinegar for the salad dressing. Our dinners were often interrupted by her getting up and sitting down. As a feminist, she would have liked for me at least to share in the work, but I wasn't any good in the kitchen. We were in the early days of our marriage, trying to adjust to each other.

When we settled down for coffee, we picked up our interrupted conversation.

"There's no way I can afford to build a house," I said.

"What if we build the house together?" she asked. "I could draw some money out of my trust."

Bill had inherited from his father, a lawyer in Columbus, Ohio, shares in a small company in that state called Newark Telephone. He had held onto them for years. Around 1980, the telephone company had been sold. He had cashed in his shares and as a result was able to leave both his daughters some money, which was held in trusts *per stirpes* for them. The trustees were a couple of his friends at his law firm, and I told her that I didn't think that they would approve of her taking some of the money from her reserves to build a summer house on some remote island. She said that the trustees would honor her wishes. I was reluctant for her to approach them, until she mentioned how Adolph and Beatrice Berle, close friends of the family—indeed, Bill had succeeded Adolph Berle as Dwight Professor of Law at Columbia University Law School—had bought a farmhouse in Stockbridge and developed the land around it together. They had enjoyed gathering their family and friends there.

I might still have been resistant to Linn's idea if it weren't for the fact that, together with my personal life, my financial situation, for the first time, was improving. Between 1976 and 1984, I had sold many long New Yorker articles and four books. Most important financially, I had got a chance to rectify to some degree my mistake in selling my Dakota apartment. The rental building in which I had been living since 1965 had become a coöperative in 1979, and I was able to buy my apartment at a special, insider price of twenty-three thousand dollars and then turn around and sell it for a hundred and seventeen thousand five hundred dollars, after broker's commissions. At the same time, I found a much better apartment three blocks up Fifth Avenue, which I was able to buy for a hundred and thirty-five thousand dollars, because the owner was anxious to sell. In the time I had lived in that apartment, it had almost tripled in value. Also, in July of 1982, a couple of months before I met Ed Barnes, I was awarded, out of the blue, a MacArthur prize fellowship. (One could not apply for a MacArthur but was nominated anonymously for it.) Thereafter, every month for five years, four thousand dollars was deposited tax-free into my bank account. It meant that, for the first time in my life, I didn't have to scrimp and save. Indeed, before the fellowship, whenever I thought of getting married, although I would tell myself that two could live as cheaply as one when in love, there would still be nagging fears about being a breadwinner and about my future. But, with the prospect of finding the MacArthur golden egg in my basket every month, I fancied that I could do almost anything.

Eventually, Linn and I discussed the subject of our building the house together with her trustees, who, by now, were my friends, too. They said that real estate had proved to be the best investment that they themselves had ever made and recommended that Linn go ahead with the property in Maine. They worked out an arrangement whereby I deeded half of my land to Linn and she agreed to assume half the construction cost of the house. Liquidating my savings to come up with my half was a wrench, but soon my trepidations about money and construction were overtaken by a feeling of exhilaration at my new circumstances. I realized that, thanks to my marriage, I was much more financially secure than I had ever been before.

In retrospect, March, 1984, the month I celebrated my fiftieth birthday, was a turning point in our life together: that month, we jointly signed the construction contract with Yeaton, and the same month Linn became pregnant with our first child. As we were going through various stages of her pregnancy, viewing the sonograms, waiting for the heartbeat, hearing the heartbeat, feeling the first kick of the baby, we were also building the house and dreaming of having our city child spend summers in Maine, nourished by the memories of sea and beach, rocks and trees.

MARCH 23, 1984

Yeaton was known to be one of the smartest men on the island. He had served as the principal of the Islesboro school, where he was known for running a "tight ship" and for being a great disciplinarian—generally for being unyielding and fierce. He gave the impression of being able to hold his own with anyone. He was certainly not intimidated by working with a New York architect.

"Your well came out dry," he said gruffly in his first call to me. "You have the option under the contract to drop the whole project or you can give me permission to drill a second well. That will set you back thirteen hundred dollars."

"What assurances are there that you would hit water with the second well?" I asked.

"I don't have a water-divining rod, but we got a trickle in the first well. If we drill a few yards away from it, we might get a good rate of flow."

"Why so close?" I asked. "Is that how water is usually found?"

"You're on an island," he said. "There's water everywhere. It's just a matter of hitting a vein."

I gave my permission. The site of the well—or, rather, soon, the wells—was near the site of the house, and it made sense to keep to that area.

MARCH 28TH

Another call from Yeaton. "I don't think you're going to find the second well satisfactory. The rate of the flow is only three gallons per minute. The contract says it should be at least five. Do you want me to drill a third well or you want to pull out of the project?"

"Is drilling a third well going to cost another thirteen hundred dollars?" I asked.

"Yup."

"I'll check with Ed and call you back."

When I called Ed, he said he had hoped that the rate of flow would be more than that, especially since we might end up having a lot of lawn that we'd like to water. Still, since it was a summer house it would probably not be in use for more than two or three months of the year, and therefore he thought I should make do with the second well and continue with the project. Until then, I had labored under a fantasy that I was building the year-round house of a householder rather than a beach house on a resort island. But I now accepted that reality, together with the unpredictable nature of construction. Anyway, I conveyed Ed's view to Yeaton.

"Yeaton says he barely started digging for the foundation when he hit the ledge," Ed told me over the phone. When Ed was originally siting the house, he'd asked Yeaton if he thought we would hit it. Yeaton had thought not. In fact, he had subsequently bored a random hole without encountering the ledge. "He says he'll have to blast it with dynamite."

"That would add a lot to the expense. Besides, I don't want the basement to be too far below-grade. I always thought you wanted the house to be flooded with light."

"But without sinking the house deeper, it will loom too tall in relation to the trees," Ed said.

"Then wouldn't a better course be to make the house flatter and broader?"

"To do that, we would have to draw a whole new house and lose the months we spent making the working drawings."

The time to have thought about making a sort of ranch house would have been when I gave my original approval to the rough drawings, I reflected. But at the time I didn't even know what a ledge was. All this is part of my ongoing architectural education.

"Are there any hazards in blasting?" I asked.

"Yeaton says you can open up seams in veins which can turn into little springs. But any fissures in the ledge would be sealed by a concrete foundation slab three or four inches thick."

"Oh," I said. I must have sounded a little sad because Ed said, "You're going to get yourself an elegant house with a tall, impressive stair tower. Maybe I can get my friends at Haystack to design a really beautiful handrail for it."

May 7th
Field visit with Henry Myerberg

Henry told Yeaton that the house was skewed a little to the north and did not line up with the center of the clearing. Yeaton retorted that it lined up exactly with the stakes as they

Groundwork, 1984

had been hammered in at Ed's direction the previous August. He thought it was simpler now to reshape the clearing than to reorient the house, and Henry yielded. Henry's accommodating nature seemed to be no match for Yeaton's will.

Stepping along the service road, which ran between the path to the house, on the west, and a bank that dropped down into the woods, on the east, I observed that it was almost as steep as the driveway at the abandoned house site.

"It can't be," Yeaton said. Henry checked it against the drawings and established that the top of the slope, where the service road began, was two feet higher than indicated. Yeaton said, rather curtly, that he would adjust the grade. I urged him to use the shale from the old driveway. He countered that the expense of digging up the old shale would be more than that of using new shale.

"But the abandoned site is ugly," I said. "I was hoping to return it to nature."

"If you want to pay extra for it, I'll do it," he said. "Otherwise, I'll adjust the grade with new shale."

I wasn't convinced by Yeaton's argument, but, realizing that he was due extra payment for anything above and beyond the contract, I gave in. Then, pacing the top of the service road, I discovered that there was no way a car could turn around there. It would have to back up a hundred and twenty feet from the garage to the so-called parking area near the dirt road. Henry readily admitted that he had neglected to provide for a turnaround, and Yeaton said he would be glad to price one, after he got a sketch. Then he would need a change order, an amendment to the contract.

Henry studied the elevation of the foundation wall and observed, "Despite the blasting, the house is still going to end up too tall in relation to the spruce tree Ed used to site it and surrounding trees. Ed won't like that."

"Ed shouldn't be surprised," Yeaton said. "You people drew a two-story house and then some."

"But Ed envisioned a sort of tree house tucked away in the woods," Henry said.

"For a mere tree house, it's got a lot of finishes," Yeaton said.

"Actually, I wondered all along if the house isn't too citi-fied for rustic Maine," I said to Henry.

"The island you're on is not rustic, Ved," Henry said. "It has mansions to rival those in Newport."

"What do you want to do about the height of the house, then?" Yeaton asked.

"Ed will have to see it for himself and decide what to do," Henry said.

With Yeaton, Henry went over some drawings of cabinetwork and instructed him that, before proceeding with fabrication and installation, Yeaton should submit all shop draw-ings and samples of material to him in New York for approval.

A little later, Yeaton wanted to know how high the con-crete retaining wall should be. The wall, which separated the path and the service road near the house, was drawn but not yet staked or poured. Now Henry decided that, actually, a dry retaining wall, made out of the shards of rock blasted from the ledge, would look prettier than the concrete wall as drawn. He instructed Yeaton to make the change and told him to let him know in due course what the credit for forgoing the concrete work would be.

In later years, we found that the stone wall, though pret-tier, did not prevent water from coming down to the service road, as a concrete wall might have. During the winter, snow would accumulate against the top of the western basement wall, abutting the hillside, and the northern side of the house. When the snow melted or when it rained, the water would seep through or go over the retaining wall, especially from the northwest corner, where the hill was steepest. We tried several remedies, like an underground culvert, but the gradient near the door of the garage was so steep that there seemed to be no way to divert all the water to the east over the bank down into the woods. The water would sometimes find its way into the garage, and although there was a floor drain there, it could not handle all the overflow, leaving us with the problem of the water migrating further into the house. We had to rely on a caretaker to check the house whenever the weather conditions warranted it and to manually pump out any standing water. At the outset, I had imagined that because we had a modern house, we could get along without the services of a caretaker—caretaking, together with trapping lobsters, was one way the islanders earned money in the off-season—but in this, as in so much else about the island and the house, I was mistaken.

One day, long after the house was built, I met up with Walter Lamont, a drainage expert and woodsman from the mainland, who was doing some work on the island. He took one look at the service road and said he could fix it for me in no time. Half an hour later, he returned astride a bulldozer. He sped down the service road without pausing and drove so close to the house that Linn and our girls (we have two daughters), watching from the kitchen window, were sure that he was about to swipe the building. They shouted for him to stop, but the bulldozer made so much racket that he could not hear them. In a matter of minutes, he changed the grade of the service road and cut a swale in the bank, near the garage door. The moment he stopped, we all ran to him and told him that he'd almost cut the electrical and water lines running under the service road. He wryly said that he'd been electrocuted many times and been resurrected. After his bulldozer escapade, in any event, we never had the problem of water in the garage again.

JUNE 1ST–3RD
FIELD VISIT WITH ED AND HENRY

As soon as we had parked the car in the parking area, Ed indicated a spot above the service road where the car turnaround should be situated and directed Henry to send Yeaton a sketch for pricing. Then he went down the service road and clambered over the stone retaining wall and around to the front of the house. Despite the creation of the architectural room and its reshaping as Henry had indicated in our last field visit, there had been so much spring foliage in the clearing that the sea was all but invisible. Ed said that sometime during the day we should all go down to the cove and mark additional trees to be cut. I worried aloud about the expense of more cutting and asked why the problem hadn't been fully anticipated when we had done the original clearing. He said there was no way of anticipating how much cutting would eventually be needed, because each year we would find new trees we would want to take down, depending on which vistas and angles of the sea and the distant islands we wanted.

Oh God, I thought. Cutting is going to be an endless process that will require regular checking and thought. As someone who couldn't see the bloody water, I had imagined Ed would design the perfect architectural room and I could then forget about the whole cutting business. But now, it seemed, I would always be fretting about how much or how little cutting we should do—how much was tasteful and would look right. If I had not been obsessed with how things looked, and if Linn had been interested in such matters, I might have left the task to her, but, as it was, I couldn't let up.

Ed walked back toward the sea and looked up at the trees around the foundation site. By experience, he seemed to be able to estimate how tall the house would be once it was erected. Then he walked around and looked at the top of the spruce and other trees from different angles and agreed with Henry that the house was indeed going to be too tall. As it happened, the weather since the first field visit had been so bad that the concrete for the foundation had not yet been poured—only the footings were in place—so Ed was able to lower the house by lowering the foundation itself. He asked Yeaton to depress the concrete slab in the garage by a foot and an inch, replace the beams over the basement door openings with flush wood framings, correspondingly adjust the height of the concrete piers under the deck, and replace the concrete steps that were to lead from the basement to the deck with wooden ones, the height of which could be eventually adjusted. All these impromptu measures, devised on the fly, probably reduced the height of the house no more than eight or ten inches—but Ed felt it was a significant improvement. Ed asked Henry to detail the revisions in the drawings for Yeaton and to issue a change order.

At the time, it never occurred to me that we ran any risk of compromising the structure of the house by lowering it. It seemed to me a purely aesthetic judgment, and, as so often, I was grateful to have Ed's eye to rely upon. In later years, however, I think all of us regretted the change. The slab was lowered and covered with sheets of polyethylene to prevent underground vapors from infiltrating the basement. But the perimeter drains at the footings, which had already been set in concrete, were not, apparently, lowered. In any case, these drains did not carry water from rain or snow away from the back of the house. Even if we managed to keep the garage dry, the back walls of the stair tower and the rest of the basement—given over to a bedroom and bathroom—would remain damp or sometimes, at the base, get soaked with water. No matter what measures we took, like installing a noisy dehumidifier, an additional southern basement window to let some more sun into the bedroom, or an electrical-fan system to circulate the trapped air, the Sheetrock in the basement remained moldy. Also, from the very first day, the basement bathroom was infested with sow, or potato, bugs. Every time they were cleaned out, new ones would appear overnight—and not just a few but a lot, crawling and wriggling on the floor. No one could explain why or how a new house could have such a problem. I'd always been afraid of bugs. At home, I'd sometimes been stung by them, and the fact that I couldn't see them, even to identify what they were, added to my fear, which had only been heightened by my experience with the yellow jackets during that first stay at Annette's.

In 1996, eleven years after the house was completed, we dug up the entire foundation slab, retrofitted the basement with new perimeter drains, poured a new slab, covered it with new polyethylene sheets to serve as a vapor barrier, and installed new wood floors. That still made little difference, making us wonder whether the culprit had ever been those drains, as we'd thought all along, or simply the decision to build the house below-grade. There seemed to be so much underground water at the spot that for all we knew, blasting through the ledge had opened up fissures and produced springs—or an underground lake—on which the house sat. Whether the concrete slab was old or new or protected with a vapor barrier, it would always be moisture-ridden. In 2000, we reconstructed the basement all over again and took additional measures like putting radiant heating under the wooden floors of the basement bedroom and hallway. We also replaced the expensive electric heating system throughout the house with a less expensive oil one. That enabled us to leave the heat on in the house all year round. With that, finally, fifteen years after completing the original construction, we had a dry house from top to bottom.

What was especially discouraging was that the whole issue of the house versus the trees, which had preoccupied us so much at the time of design and construction, turned out to be moot. Since the soil on the island was so shallow that the root structure of the trees was precarious, once the supporting dead trees and brush were cleared for the architectural room (it kept evolving every year, just as Ed had said), a gust of wind was enough to fell even the strongest pine or spruce, and many of the downed trees were lovely, delicate birches. In September of 1985, Hurricane Gloria seemed to slice through only our piece of ground on the island and brought down no fewer than sixty trees on the property, leaving us with the task not only of repairing the scarred land but also of clearing the so-called blowdowns. The island contractors, while billing an hourly rate for labor and renting their chainsaw, seemed to make little distinction between salvaging a tree for firewood and disposing of one that was only good for pulp. In either case, it ended up costing about seventy-five dollars to remove just one felled tree. Still, the longer we owned the house, the more we wanted to clear away brush and dead trees in order to open up the dark woods—to let in some sunlight and dry out the marshland. Even the robust spruce tree, which had provided Ed with the site of the house, eventually contracted a fungal disease. Despite years of effort by an arborist to save it, it died.

AT ONE POINT during the April field visit, Ed said to me that he wished he hadn't changed the windows, which had been an issue between us from the beginning. I liked old-fashioned double-hung, or "guillotine," windows, with upper and lower sashes and well-proportioned lights. He liked single-pane, so-called awning windows, hinged at the top. I had given in to his preference. But he had also wanted custom mahogany-framed windows from Duratherm, a Maine company famous for its windows and spiral stairs, made to order in any size or shape. We had already decided upon mahogany-framed glass sliding doors from Duratherm, so I balked at the extra expense for the windows. "After all, it's just a summer house, Ed," I had said. "Ten months of the year, it will be sitting vacant and deteriorating in the wind, snow, and rain." He had revised the drawings and replaced the Duratherm windows with off-the-shelf pine sliding and awning windows from Pella.

I now said to Ed gently, "I thought we'd arrived at a good compromise about the windows."

"Windows are like a face to a person, and now that I'm looking at the drawings at the site, I think the face of your house doesn't quite come together. I wonder if by resorting to Pella windows, we might not have compromised the aesthetic integrity of the house."

His use of the word "integrity" gave me pause. My insisting on those windows would be rather like an editor's changing my copy by fiat, I thought.

"It's your house, Ed," I said quickly. "If Duratherm windows are what you like, that's what we should have."

Allée, 1985

"No, it's your house and your pocketbook," he said. "But I'd like your house to be perfect."

His use of the word "perfect" reminded me of the time I had once gone shopping with Vanessa, an old girlfriend. I had tried on a turtleneck shirt with my blazer and asked her, "How does it look?" She had said, "It's great, but not perfect."

I had said, "Can you be more specific?" She had said, "It doesn't have front interest." I had asked, "What do you mean?" From a nearby counter, she had picked up a brass chain with a medal stamped with the relief of some tribal deity's head and had put it around my neck and said, "Now, that looks perfect." I had said, "But, Vanessa, I couldn't go around wearing a tribal medal around my neck. It's not me." She had said, "But it's exciting. You can't wear a turtleneck with a blazer without some front interest." I had decided to forgo the turtleneck shirt, but, in that instance, it had been a question of what suited me. In respect to the windows, it was a question of what suited the house, and of that, I felt, Ed was the best judge.

I asked Yeaton how much it would cost to change to the Duratherm windows, and he said that he thought the add-on would be about sixteen thousand dollars, but since the drawings would have to be revised and the windows ordered, custom-built, and shipped by Duratherm, the construction schedule would be set back by at least a month.

"Luckily, I haven't bought the Pella windows yet," Yeaton said. "So if you want to spend some more of your money, you can still do it."

There was an edge to his remark—I had been leaning on him to hold down the cost—but I disregarded it.

I was preoccupied with the thought of whether I should hedge on the question of the windows. But I reasoned that, unlike a writer, an architect was not fully in control of his handiwork. In fact, he ultimately lacked control over how the house was designed or how it was used. If Linn and I had been a different kind of owner, we could have insisted that he install, for instance, asphalt shingles on the roof, an

Spruce used for siting the house, 1984

anathema to him, rather than cedar shingles, and he would
have had no choice but to give in. In contrast, people might
skim a book of mine, misread it, or never read it at all, but the
book would exist the way I wrote it. It was in this spirit that I
checked with Linn and gave our approval for the Duratherm
windows.

I wondered if, in return, I could get Ed to concede on our
different views about the bedrooms. I understood that symmetry was a hallmark of Ed's architecture, and the house had
been drawn with three parallel bays, the outside dimensions of
each being fourteen by twenty-two feet. The two outer bays
contained the living room and kitchen on the first floor and
two spacious bedrooms with cathedral ceilings on the second,
and the central bay contained the dining room, together with
the inset and part of the entry hall on the first floor, and bathrooms and closets and a bedroom hallway above that on the
second. On top of the central bay was the single nest of an attic,
also with a cathedral ceiling. Linn and I, however, had always
wanted more than two bedrooms on the second floor, while Ed
felt that that would spoil the pleasing symmetry of the house.
I now suggested to Ed cutting one of the bedrooms into two
smaller ones and, indeed, converting one of two facing closets
on the third floor into a bathroom, so that the top room could
also be used as a bedroom. (It was one of the oddities of the
house that the three rooms downstairs were smaller than what
we needed but the two bedrooms upstairs were much bigger.)

"There is a certain balance in having the master and the
second bedroom on the second floor mirroring each other," Ed
said. "As for the top floor, I'd imagined the room would be
your writing studio. It will have a big window and the best
view of the sea through the birches."

"But we plan to have a couple of children, and I remember,
when I was small, how much it meant to me to have a room to
myself, the little time I had it," I said. "As for the view on the
top floor, no doubt it's wonderful and my assistant would enjoy
looking out at the sea, but I don't know any good writer who

cares a fig about a view when he's writing. Anyway, I would probably end up writing in a corner of the living room."

"Then your whole house will be nothing but bedrooms," he said with a laugh.

I joined in the merriment but said, "People in the country don't spend much time in their bedrooms, I think. They just go to sleep there."

He allowed that that was true and agreed to divide up the north bedroom into two. In later years, I had second thoughts about my intervention, at least in respect to the second floor. The two small bedrooms there were poky, with hardly any room for more than a bed and a night table. Still, our first daughter, Sage, and later her sister, Natasha, who was born in 1987, did enjoy having rooms of their own. On Linn's inspiration, the space above the little bedroom hallway was not closed up with Sheetrock. Instead, accessible from the top landing, it was equipped with a floor and a railing and became a small play area under the slope of the ceiling. Sage and Natasha soon dubbed it a "mouse house." The bathroom on the third floor was an unalloyed success. It was as trim and compact as a bathroom on a boat, and whenever Katherine or other guests came to visit we put them up on that floor. The room not only had the best view, as Ed had said, but was snug and self-contained.

JULY 10TH
FIELD VISIT WITH HENRY

As we were driving to the site, I asked Henry if the field visits might be cut down from once a month to once every two months; the expenses for such trips added nearly a thousand dollars to the cost of the house each time. He said that if he had his druthers he'd make still more frequent visits, because, however routine the contract work seemed or however competent and conscientious the contractor was, an architect's eye always picked up oversights in design or flaws in construction that, when remedied, ultimately improved the house. Indeed, once the floors and walls were closed up, many of the defects visible to a trained eye would be hidden, and, when discovered, could be corrected only at great expense. I grasped that it was better to spare no expense now than to risk being stuck with a shoddy house later. After that, I tried harder to resist the temptation to save money, even though the project seemed like a behemoth with an insatiable appetite.

At the site, Henry sat in the car and watched Yeaton use an electric saw to cut down and adjust a length of strut for the deck. "It's unusual to find a contractor working as a carpenter on the job himself," Henry said. "As an owner, you should be pleased to have a contractor who is a hands-on presence."

Since we'd last been there, all the foundation walls had been completed and the carpenters were now busy nailing the frame to them—indeed, they had already built the inset and most of the deck, bordered on three sides by a bench and a railing that formed its back. A leaching field had been prepared and the septic tank was ready for the architect's inspection. Scrambling around the site, Henry picked out a number of items requiring attention: the flues for woodstoves for the basement and master bedrooms needed to be straightened and cleaned, the vapor barrier between the ground and the slab had to be made continuous, the drainage line around the stair tower had to be kept as low as practicable, and so on. He then reviewed with Yeaton and his plumbing subcontractor the revised schedule for installing pipes and fixtures and the exact location of the vents in the bathrooms. Afterward, Henry huddled with Yeaton to review the complicated drawing of the stair tower, which Yeaton had found hard to follow. Apparently, the two had been in touch about it on the telephone, because Henry came equipped with a model and axonometric drawings. While the two were busy, I was able to stumble around the site by myself and get an impression of the footprint of the house. Excluding the bulge for the stair tower at the center of the back, it was forty-five feet wide and twenty feet deep.

West elevation, 1984

Back in New York, Henry got Linn and me to accompany him to the warehouse of a shop in order to choose bathroom fixtures—sinks, bathtubs, toilets, and tap handles. We didn't know one kind of toilet from another. I got impatient, and Linn retreated from the whole expedition and stood by the door, as if she'd been corralled there against her will, leaving me to field Henry's questions. He wanted to know if we would like a Jacuzzi.

"That's vulgar," I said.

"Any special request for the bathrooms, then?"

"I can't imagine what that would be."

"Do you want one handle for hot and cold water?" he asked. "It's more streamlined."

"No, I want the traditional two handles. Whenever I use a one-handled faucet in a hotel, I don't know which way to turn it, and I always end up scalding myself."

I was as impatient as Linn to get out of the shop, but later, year after year, we would regret not having taken the expedition more seriously. The bathtubs on the second floor (the basement bathroom had only a shower) were so small that even Linn, who is five foot four, couldn't comfortably stretch out in them. Although there was plenty of space for longer bathtubs, now there was no way, short of taking down the walls of the bathrooms, to take the old tubs out or put new tubs in. The toilets, in their own way, were also unsatisfactory. They were the low, silent variety, and they never flushed properly. The medicine cabinets were so small and shallow, with thin, frameless mirrors for doors, that we didn't have room for even the most basic things. And the soap dishes in the bathrooms were so poorly designed that, every time we took a shower, water accumulated in them and melted the soap. Moreover, they had been mounted shoulder-high so they were hard to reach when sitting in the bathtub. The tile man was afraid to remove them or drill holes in them for fear they would break and we would end up having to retile the bathrooms. Such complaints seem petty, and ordinarily we would have adapted

East elevation, 1984

to whichever house we found ourselves in, but the maddening thing was that all these mistakes were a result of our own inattention. Years later, we came across more sensible soap dishes, small wire baskets, in a hotel in Europe. I located the manufacturer, bought several of them, carried them to New York, and the next time we were in Maine, had them installed in every bathroom as a supplementary soap dish.

AUGUST 6TH

FIELD VISIT WITH ED, HENRY, AND LINN

After a morning's work, we sat on the deck bench drinking tea we had picked up from the Dark Harbor Shop. We were facing the inset with our backs to the sea. Ed looked up and noticed that one of the corner windows in what would be the baby's bedroom looked straight into the bathroom of the master bedroom.

"Oh my God, Henry, how did we make that mistake?" he asked.

"I think we must have been concentrating on the arrangement of the windows rather than what they looked into."

The Freudian slip, as we thought of it, gave us all some amusement. (In time, the mistake was rectified by putting a translucent windowpane in the bedroom.)

Ed paced along the deck and looked into the three rooms "lined up like the stripes of the French flag," as he was wont to say. He suddenly said, "The inset has more of a feeling of the outdoors than the indoors. I think it would look more like an extension of the indoors if it weren't shingled." Ed asked Yeaton to give us a price for replacing the already installed cedar shingles with vertical sidings and soffits.

"Goodness me, the house has just been framed, and we're already redoing it," I said.

"When you use a house and live in it, you're always thinking of improvements," Ed said. "That's the fun of owning a house."

Despite the regular shocks at the cost of the house being

ratcheted up, I still went on thinking that it was an object, like a writing desk—once paid for, that was the end of it—forgetting that a house is not an inert thing but has a life of its own, with thousands of parts and details that will constantly require rethinking and redoing, every change undoubtedly requiring additional expense.

"The house is like your baby," Henry said, touching off all kinds of associations in my head. When construction started, Linn's pregnancy had just been confirmed, and we used to joke that there was a race between the arrival of the baby and the completion of the house. We even told ourselves that, like the baby, the house would be a source of continuous joy and comfort, that it would be something we shared and had built together. But now I could scarcely think of the house without mounting anxiety. Linn was in the sixth month of her pregnancy, and we had just learned that Duratherm would be two months behind in delivering the windows. Then, while Ed and Henry were checking and rechecking various items, they decided that electrical and telephone cables aboveground should be buried, so that the house would appear completely freestanding, without any telltale encumbrance. That would result in another delay while we negotiated easements with the utility companies. Given all the problems, Henry now calculated that the baby would be at least six months old before the house was ready. I felt that as long as the contract was running and the extra expenses were piling up, my head was in a noose. I couldn't wait to get free of it. Of course, a certain amount of anxiety was inescapable. I even had some trepidations about the impending arrival of the baby—about how good a father I would be and whether my disability would interfere with bringing up the child. But it was one thing to nurse a child through the years and see it grow and develop; quite another to attend to an inanimate object year after year.

"You look very pensive," Linn said to me. "What are you thinking?"

"It's all so unbelievably complicated," I said.

"What is? Building a house?" she asked.

"Yes," I said. I remembered how my father had grown up in a village where they had only mustard-oil lamps, and I wondered what he would make of Linn and my having to negotiate easements with Central Maine Power, the local utility company.

"This is a happy moment," Ed said. "Just think—you're having your first tea party in your new house." He added with a laugh, "Next time, we should be sure to bring some Leachburgers with us."

It was one of our standing jokes that everything on the island seemed to be named Leach. There was Leach's Market, Leach's Earth Work & Materials, Leach's Express (which was actually Jack's truck, used for hauling produce, supplies, beds, furniture, or anything else to the island). Indeed, a food stand at the ferry dock sold hamburgers called Leachburgers. The idea of sitting around on the deck eating Leachburgers made us all laugh. My anxieties dissolved as I listened to the happy sounds of our spontaneous tea party and the gentle lapping of the sea, and breathed in the air itself, so fragrant with spruce and pine, together with freshly cut timber—so pure that it was almost an intoxicant.

AUGUST 28TH–30TH
FIELD VISIT WITH HENRY AND LINN

I was struck by the keen interest Linn was taking as we trooped behind Henry and Yeaton when they walked the building site, inspecting the millwork for the stair treads, balusters, and handrails for the stair tower, and also for the kitchen cabinets and their doors. As they continued their round, they stopped now and again to review items such as the adjustment of grading and flashing of the brick chimney, the positioning of boulders at the deck stairs, the selection and placement of the woodstoves.

I led Linn away from the construction and down toward the beach where I had proposed to her the Memorial Day

Entry hall, 1984

weekend of the year before. She followed me reluctantly, saying, "I should have had some say in designing the house."

"But you never evinced any interest when we were here earlier this month," I said.

"It was all so new to me," she said.

"But you didn't say anything to me later, either."

"That's because you took over everything to do with the house, as if it were your baby and I had nothing to do with it."

"That's not fair." I must have had an edge to my voice, but I was averse to acknowledge it. I half expected her to drop the subject, but she continued to press her point.

"You talk to Ed and Henry all the time. Whenever there's some decision to be made, they talk to you, not to me."

It was the first of many times when I had to remind myself that, perhaps because I was much older than Linn was, I tended to take charge and not give her views the weight that they deserved and that, in doing so, I was perhaps repeating the pattern of my parents. My father, who was thirteen years older than my mother, tended to treat her like a child. And my mother, as an Indian and a Hindu woman, was deferential to men—she thought of my father as her lord and master. Unlike my mother, Linn was well-educated. Anyway, as an American woman she didn't think of herself as subservient to me. I told myself I'd better watch how I conducted myself with her or I was going to be in trouble.

"Actually, I myself haven't had much say in designing the house, either," I said. "I've always thought of us as ideal clients who give the architect his head and who don't interfere."

"But my concerns and tastes have been ignored," she said.

She was right. Fancying that she was more brainy than visual, I did not rely on her eye. In fact, I had been a little leery of trusting her judgment ever since we fixed up our apartment soon after our marriage. She had wanted to tear down a wonderful old kitchen closet with plaster walls and an old, panelled door, in order to enlarge the eating area so that she could have a kitchen like her mother's in the country. I had set myself

Top, left to right: Paul Pendleton and Michael McCorison (electrician); bottom, left to right: Rodney Leach and Yeaton Randlett, 1984

against the change. I thought that the closet was not only elegant and in character with the rest of the apartment, but also essential for storing household supplies. I had prevailed, but the disagreement hadn't been forgotten. In any event, there were certain people whose eye I instinctively trusted, assuming from my relationship and experience with them that their taste would be like mine if I could see. Rarely was I led astray, although I had been when I let a European princess, who was one of the most elegant women in town, choose for me a couple of nineteenth-century glass oil lamps, which I planned to turn into bedside lamps, only to discover that, once they were fitted, they were clunky and heavy-looking. Certainly, in the case of something as major as the house I thought it was best for me to rely on the eye not of Linn but of Ed and Henry. After all, they were trained to visualize how a concept or a drawing would look as a finished building.

"What would you have done differently?" I now asked.

"I don't know, but I should have been consulted at least in the designing of the kitchen and the kitchen cabinets."

"Maybe I didn't get you involved because I thought that, like me, you'd want such matters left to experts."

"But Henry isn't going to use the kitchen. I'm going to use it."

Again, I had to remind myself that I was married to someone who couldn't be beguiled like my mother. At the same time, I recalled how soothing and yielding my mother's nature was, how reassuring her domestic activities. I heard in my mind the clicking of her knitting needles, the rattling of her embroidery frame, the whirr of her sewing machine, the bubble and splash of her washing clothes in an outdoor tub. Just thinking about that made me momentarily sad about being with Linn, and I found myself reflecting on a sociological study of Indian immigrants in the West, which I had read some time before, which argued that, however Westernized and intellectually sophisticated they became, they remained emotionally bound to their Indian upbringing: when the time for marriage came, many of them asked their parents to find them a good Indian wife, as if their character had indeed been set by the age of five and were impossible to modify, irrespective of subsequent influences, no matter how powerful.

Now, thinking only to change the subject from the house, I said, "You know what an Indian girl is supposed to do when she gets pregnant?" Linn would soon be in the seventh month of her pregnancy. "She's supposed to spend all her time listening to beautiful music, smelling beautiful flowers, and thinking pleasant thoughts. All that is good for the baby."

"Then you married the wrong kind of woman." In tone she was joking, but her remark was not without meaning.

I was wondering how to douse the flames of our smoldering disagreement before it got out of hand when she announced, as if a mysterious force had asserted itself and preempted our marital tiff, "Chickadee is kicking." The nickname "Chickadee" went so counter to my exalted notion of a baby that I was never comfortable with it, but Linn, perhaps because she liked thinking of the baby as a diminutive being, persisted in using it.

"Wait until I tell our baby what you called it," I said.

"Isn't that what the baby really is?" Linn asked.

"No, it's a person. It now has a heartbeat and it kicks."

When we got married, Linn had not believed she would get pregnant right away. "Why not?" I had asked, and she had said, "I'm athletic." I had said, "Many athletic women get pregnant." She had said, "But I didn't start menstruating until I was almost twenty." I had said, "That could have had to do with your diet or a number of other things. Anyway, you grew up like a nun. I certainly don't know a more chaste and puritan family than yours." She had said, "But I don't want to get pregnant. I want to work— to get my Ph.D. and teach." There was no denying that the cares of motherhood had been as far away from her as the cares of books would have been from my mother. But I had said, "You can combine motherhood with a career. Many women do." She teased me that I was being disingenuous. I thought she had a point.

After we'd been married for a couple of months, I wagered that she would be pregnant by the time I was fifty. When I celebrated my birthday a few weeks later and, around the same time, her pregnancy was confirmed, to my great delight she accepted it as if she were born to it, even if she continually made light of her condition. She went on referring to the baby developing inside her as Chickadee, as if it had no dramatic bearing on her life. But then that was not different from the way I sometimes made light of the new responsibilities of the house that was going up every day, as if of its own will. Indeed, her uncertainty about her impending motherhood had an echo in my own uncertainty: in our different ways, we were both anxious about the changes that had already been wrought in our lives and the more dramatic changes that still awaited us, as inchoate as they were unpredictable.

SEPTEMBER 10TH
FIELD VISIT, HENRY BY HIMSELF

I had asked Henry on the telephone if there was anything special on the agenda for the field visit this time.

"I need to get up to speed on all the change orders," he said. "I also need to review the locations of switches and thermostats, receptacles and telephone jacks."

"If you don't mind, I'll pass up the visit," I said. With the approach of the baby's due date, Linn was not supposed to fly, and the demands of the house were receding from my consciousness.

Linn and I had just found out, without wanting to, that we were going to have a daughter. Linn was the last person to pay any attention to having a pink décor for a girl's room, but, as if in spite of herself, she was busy accumulating pink caps, pink frocks, tiny pink knitted booties, pink sweaters and blankets, many of them gifts from family and friends. For my part, whenever I met young people, I would wonder if they were married; if not, why not; and if they were married, why they weren't starting a family. Indeed, as the baby inside Linn became more real to me I became obsessed with such questions. Even though I'd known Henry now for over eighteen months, I had never thought to ask him anything about his private life. I didn't even know where he lived—in the city or the suburbs— or what he did when he wasn't in the office. I now asked him directly, without any preliminaries, "Are you married?"

He seemed to be surprised by the question but, obliging as always, said yes.

"Do you have children?"

"Oh, no," he said. "Karen and I are just approaching our second anniversary. I need to get established before we can think of having a family."

His preoccupation with his work struck a sympathetic chord in me. But I said, "Don't wait too long or you'll end up being as old as I am when you have your first child."

He laughed.

SEPTEMBER 30TH–OCTOBER 1ST
FIELD VISIT WITH HENRY

There were no workers or subcontractors on the site, and it had a forlorn air about it. "Yeaton, nothing significant has been done to the house since I was last here!" I exclaimed. "We're six months into construction, and it isn't even half done."

"It's Duratherm's fault," Yeaton said. "I can't do anything until the windows are delivered."

"When will that be?" I asked.

"They're now promising them for October fifth, but I won't resume work on the house unless all the pricings for the changes have been approved and the change orders processed."

For some months now, Yeaton and I had been having a dispute over his pricings. He was giving us high prices for add-ons, like the dynamiting of the ledge, but giving us low credits for deletions, like the elimination of the substantial concrete work. I had therefore held off giving my approval to the pricings, with the result that there was now a backlog of unprocessed change orders. Our contract with Yeaton had been drafted by the American Institute of Architects, and it designated the architect, the ostensibly disinterested third party, as the arbiter of disputes between owner and contractor. Since, as the project architect, Henry was in charge of processing change orders and issuing requisitions, along with new sketches and drawings, I had appealed to him to tackle the contractor about the pricings on our behalf. Henry was less than half the age of Yeaton, eager to please, and was just starting out in his career. Still, several times, he had gently broached the subject. Yeaton, however, had proved to be as unyielding as a rock. I now decided there was nothing to be gained by getting into a fight with Yeaton and further delaying or, indeed, jeopardizing the project. My priorities were shifting, and anyway I wasn't sure if my objections to the pricings were a matter of perception or reality. With the changes, the cost of the house had been increasing so fast, and I was so nervous about it, that I wasn't completely confident about my judgment. I gave Henry the signal that I was prepared to sign all the accumulated change orders.

By prior arrangement, Susan Hatch, the landscape designer on the island, appeared. A personable young woman, she was full of ideas and plans. To dampen her enthusiasm, I told her that the house was already way over budget, and we wanted as little money spent on landscaping as we could possibly get away with.

"I understand, but at the very minimum you'll have to mow a path down the hill from the deck to the beach, so that you can get down there from your house without going the long way around by the dirt road," she said. "Also, near your deck the land falls away steeply, so you'll need steps. They can be framed in wood, which is cheaper, or made of stone, which would be more expensive but will really dress up the head of the path." She proposed building a bridge at the bottom of the path over the marshland near the shore and then a removable set of steps for the drop to the beach. The bridge raised the old spectre of boardwalks and honky-tonk. I recalled that the mere mention of a boardwalk had made me disengage myself from the architectural services of Patrick, but I told myself a small bridge was different.

"The steps would have to be taken up each fall and put back in the spring," she said, explaining that the sea on the eastern shore was so wild in the winter that it inundated the beach and the adjacent land, sweeping away anything on or around the shore. "That's why practically no one on the east side can have a year-round dock," she added.

I had very strong feelings about what would look right in the interior of the house, but I was uncertain about the exterior, perhaps because one was circumscribed and easier to imagine and control, the other vast and difficult to comprehend and tame. I suddenly felt the need for Linn's eye.

"I really think we must wait on all these questions until my wife, Linn, is here," I said.

"But in the meantime do you want me to work out some alternative proposals?" Susan asked.

"Sure, but I can't emphasize enough that Linn likes the natural, rustic look of Maine. She is natural and simple, herself, and that's the way she would want our grounds to look."

"I fancy, then, that she'd like logs rather than pressurized wood for the bridge."

"I'd like to put off the final decision until the two of you can meet and perhaps Mr. Barnes, our architect, is here, too. He has strong views about landscaping."

"But the best time for landscaping work is in the fall or winter, when people on the island are looking for employment. They get busy in the spring and summer. Then it's almost impossible to get any help."

"We'll just have to take our chances."

"When do you think I'd be able to meet your wife?"

"I really can't say. She's expecting in November."

"So am I," she said excitedly. "Maybe we'll have our babies at the same time."

Her interest in getting our landscape work seemed to shift abruptly. She wanted to know more about Linn. As she continued to talk, I remember thinking that perhaps she and Linn would become friends, and perhaps our children would, too, as they grew up.

OCTOBER 29TH–30TH
FIELD VISIT, HENRY BY HIMSELF

When Henry got back to New York, he telephoned me. With less than a month remaining until Linn's due date, there had been no way I could be parted from her.

"Things are looking up," he said. "Many of the Duratherm windows are installed and so are many of the house's sliding glass doors. The masonry work on the chimney is nearly complete. The installation of the cedar shingles on the outside walls is well under way, and I chose the paint for them and for the plywood in the inset."

"Did any pressing issues come up?"

"Yeaton wants a six-month extension to the contract time for finishing the house." Under the contract, Yeaton was required to finish the house on April 1st, or a year to the day after he first broke ground. "He says he lost three months on the windows. He implied that if you didn't let him off the hook the house could be in trouble."

"There's still half a year to run on his contract time, and you just said he's made such good progress. Why does he need an extension? Has he got involved in building another house?"

"I heard such a rumor, but I have no way of checking it."

"Give him what he wants."

"You're sure you don't have any second thoughts?"

"No. This is not the time for me to pick a fight with Yeaton."

NOVEMBER 27TH
FIELD VISIT, HENRY BY HIMSELF

Our daughter, whom we had named Sage, was hardly a week old when Henry came back from Maine, and I scarcely took in his report of all that he had seen or directed, approved or disapproved of in Maine. I did, however, understand this much—that the work of painting the exterior of the house was about to get under way and was to continue as long as it was dry and the temperature was above forty degrees Fahrenheit. I also registered that the process of installing Sheetrock in the house had finally begun. This meant that perhaps the next time we went up, Linn would be looking at interior walls instead of exposed studs. I even fancied the house might be so snug that we would be able to sit around on the floor and play with our baby, perhaps in front of a fire.

JANUARY 11, 1985
FIELD VISIT, HENRY WITH KATHERINE CARY AND
THISTLE BROWN

I asked my mother-in-law if she could go in my stead. I did not want to leave Sage, just seven weeks old, and didn't like the thought of being bounced around in a small plane in the turbulent Maine sky with my little family on the ground. She said that she had been longing to see the house her daughter was building—she sometimes talked as if Linn and I were not a couple—and that she would go in Linn's place with her friend Thistle. When she got back, she took Linn aside and told her all the add-ons she wanted in the house, like a second set of steps on the deck, an extra closet in the master bedroom, and a replacement of the translucent glass in the child's bedroom with a curtain and sash. Then Henry called. I asked him how he had got on with Katherine and Thistle. He was extremely circumspect, but indicated that they had been quite vocal in their opinions. He had clearly found the two women, whom he referred to as my "representatives," formidable.

"What did you think of the add-ons they wanted?"

He didn't want to express an opinion but eventually allowed that the women's changes were more practical than aesthetic, and that Ed would find them detrimental to the design of the house.

"What would you like me to do?" he asked.

"Stay the course," I said.

I asked him how the house was getting along. He said he had reviewed samples of wood stains for the oak floors, stair treads, and risers, and settled on flat-, glossy-, and satin-finished paints for the walls and trims. He had also noticed that the spackling where the wallboard joints had been taped was messy and that there were deviations from the drawings, as in the case of a few of the kitchen shelves, which were supposed to be open and accessible but had been made with sliding doors. Yeaton had agreed to remedy those problems.

MARCH 21ST–25TH
FIELD VISIT WITH ED, HENRY, LINN, AND SAGE

The visit fell on my fifty-first birthday. As we pulled up in the parking area at the top of the hill, people in the car admired the house—the clearing of the winding path to it had opened up the view. They said it looked like a jewel box set in its little valley. I remember thinking that if my life hadn't taken the tortuous romantic turns it had, I would have become a householder twenty-five years earlier, as my siblings had done. In fact, now, as dictated by the Hindu stages of life, I would have been getting ready to disengage myself from worldly cares in order to devote myself to community service. Even as I thought this, I realized that the new house bore no resemblance to the traditional Indian house of my childhood in Lahore. That house, made of brick and cement, had been designed before I was born by my father's civil-engineer brother, Romesh, with a view to maximizing the space of a few hundred square yards so that our whole family could fit into it, with servants and a milk cow, and at the same time have a garage and inner courtyard and additional space on the terrace roof for everyone to sleep on during hot nights. Indeed, one of

Southeast elevation, 1985

my earliest memories was of being woken up on the roof by the rain, dragging my cot into the rain shelter, and falling asleep listening to the pitter-patter of the rain and the gurgle of the water travelling down the tin drainpipe. In contrast, my new house was in a New England shingled style, set on fifteen wooded acres and designed by an eminent architect. Even though I had been involved in every step of its design and construction, it just now felt so alien that I could scarcely imagine us living in it.

As we got out of the car, we were joined by Susan Hatch and her baby—a son, Daniel, who had been born on the same day as Sage. The two women, both mothers for the first time, took to each other, just as I had imagined. They fell back as Ed, Henry, and I started walking down the winding path through the woods to the house. I noticed that every time I took a step, something clung to the sole of my shoe. I asked Ed about it, and he said he had directed the path to be dressed with wood chips, which a recent rain must have turned into a mulch.

"Ed, we can't possibly live with this path," I said.

"It's awfully pretty," Ed said. "The chips give a sylvan look to the path. The sun will soon dry it out."

"But they're sticky and squelch underfoot!" I cried.

"Now and again, you'll have to clear away the rotted chips and replace them with fresh wood chips," Ed said. "Whatever path you have, it will require a certain amount of renewal and maintenance."

"I'd always hoped to keep the maintenance costs low," I said.

Linn and Susan caught up with us. "Every time it rains, we'll all be tracking mulch into the house and messing up the floors," Linn said. Susan agreed and suggested that we sweep the wood chips into the woods and dress the path, as well as the service road, with peastones. Ed reluctantly went along, saying that the path would look a little cold and suburban and would entail some extra expense, but that he couldn't deny that it was more practical. To soften the effect of the peastones, Ed and Susan decided on planting ferns along the borders of the path.

West elevation, 1985

Susan then pointed out that the path was so narrow that in the dark guests could lose their footing and tumble into the woods. She and Ed came up with the idea of installing path lights on posts, with a switch in a little laundry area just off the kitchen. (When the lights were put in, the electrical subcontractor failed to use wire insulated for use underground. Within the year, all the lights had shorted and had to be dug up and rewired, at still more expense.)

Ed noticed that, during the construction, the trees alongside the path that had screened the service road below had been damaged and removed. "If you are walking down to the house through the woods and you see the service road, it takes the romance out of the approach," Ed said. Susan said she would work up the cost of planting new trees to camouflage the service road.

"Do you think it's really necessary?" I asked Ed.

"I think so," he said. "I always imagined that the guests coming to your house wouldn't know about the garage under the house. That's a little suburban."

Linn and I approved the idea of the new planting, but I asked Ed, "Where else could we have put the garage?"

"It could have been in a separate building," he said. "Some people in the country put their cars in a barn."

"I guess we could have opted for a barn, too, if we had wanted to spend the money," I said.

We clambered to the service road and dropped down into the woods to examine the leaching field that, from the beginning, had formed an unsightly bump in the lawn just beyond the deck. At every field visit, it seemed, Henry had suggested a fill-and-grading treatment, but the bump, as if it were a primeval feature of the land, would not be disguised or rubbed out. Susan said she could try to prettify the bump by planting lupin and other wildflowers all around it in the shape of a crescent. Ed reviewed her landscape plan of combining a path, a bridge, and a set of steps to the shore. He thought the bridge made out of rough logs would look much prettier and more countrylike than one made out of pressurized wood. I didn't like to take on yet another maintenance problem—periodically replacing logs—but then I reasoned that there were so many fallen trees on the property that cutting them into logs might not be so expensive.

Susan said her contract price for doing the landscaping would be seven thousand dollars. Although Linn and I thought that it would be much less anywhere but on the island, we felt we had no choice but to go forward with it—Ed's house required some landscaping, however minimal. She left, with Daniel in her arms, and we started for the house.

The painting of the exterior had made little progress, and Yeaton blamed the delay on the weather, but said that now that spring was here, the painting should go fast. In contrast, the inside of the house was so far along that Linn and I almost thought we could move in. When she had last been to the site, seven months earlier, the house had had no windows, no wall-boards, not even roughed-in plumbing. It had lacked clear form and presence, but now it was as palpable as Sage herself. In fact, it was a pleasure to walk with Linn and the baby in and out of rooms and to go up and down the stair tower. Every-where, there was the smell of glue and unprimed wood, of sandpaper dust and paint. In the kitchen, a carpenter was ham-mering in the cabinets. In a bathroom, the plumber was grunting as he tightened the joints of pipes under a vanity. In another bathroom, the tile man was finishing up the tiling with a grouting knife. Indeed, everywhere was the thrum and clack of an engine getting ready to start up.

We had hardly been in the house for half an hour when our initial good cheer was overtaken by new anxieties. I had been so preoccupied with my family in recent months that I had not registered, for instance, Ed's decision to paint all the solid-oak cabinets in the kitchen white—no doubt, he thought that looked elegant. Linn felt it looked antiseptic, but, as in so many things, that came down to personal taste. (Years later, the film actor John Travolta bought an old Islesboro property that had a lot of old, carved oak in it. He had everything painted white, because he thought it looked clean, light, and modern.) Ed now had second thoughts about the kitchen and agreed with Linn, but to strip the cabinets would have been not only expensive but also ineffective, since, the workmen said, the oak could never regain its original lustre.

Surprisingly, Henry had chosen gray paint for the side wall of the stair tower from basement to top floor, and for the underside of the oak landings. Everyone now said that the stair tower looked dingy. That, however, could be remedied by repainting it white. Yeaton thought that job would require several coats of white paint, and the cost of repainting would be twenty-five hundred dollars. Ed thought the expense was well worth the gain in brightness, but Linn and I had already spent too much money to satisfy Ed's aesthetic considerations, so this time we held fast, stiffened by our changing priorities and the thought of Sage's future needs.

Then, leaning over the railing, I noticed that the balusters were frighteningly far apart. "Ed," I cried. "Sage could fall through the balusters and kill herself."

"They're nine inches apart—that's according to code," he said, and added, with a little laugh, "In fact, my original idea was to have no balusters, just a handrail held up by corner posts so you would just see these treads going up and up and up into space." He was clearly trying to make me feel better by making light of the subject, but I wasn't having it.

"Whatever the code, Ed, I waited years to get married and have a child. I'm not going to run any risks with her."

"But while she's small she'll be watched," Ed said.

"But even a five- or six-year-old child could slip through the gap and fall."

Ed talked about the stair tower being a significant aesthetic element in the house, but for once I resisted him, perhaps because I was taken over by an image of Sage crawling up or bumping down the stairs, much as I had done when I was small and probably Ed had done, too.

"It looks beautiful the way it is," Ed said, getting flustered. "If you look at this house as a painting, the staircase looks so dramatic."

"But stairs in a painting are one thing. Stairs in a house are quite another," I said. "For you, the house might be a work of art, but we have to live in it." It was the first time during our long association that he and I had had anything approaching a serious disagreement.

When Ed grasped that I was not about to yield and that Linn felt the same way as I did, he asked Henry, "What about using a rope? It will look like a sailing motif."

Yeaton produced a coil of rope from his truck, and Henry and Ed improvised first by fashioning a makeshift baluster between the wooden ones and then by threading the rope between them.

"Didn't you say you don't like to introduce too many materials in the house?" I asked. "Now you would not only have wood balusters and steel posts, but also rope decorations. Anyway, couldn't a child push through the rope?" I realized that I was needling him. Fortunately, Henry and he soon arrived at the conclusion that, regardless of the sailing motif, the rope was impractical.

We had barely begun tackling the baluster problem when I began to worry about the gaps between the treads, between the floor of the deck and the underside of the bench, and between the seat of the bench and the top of its back—respectively, six, eleven, and thirteen inches. I was especially alarmed by the back of the bench, because it also served as the railing for the deck.

"And a child running along the bench could easily topple over the back and fall a whole story down to the basement level," I said.

"You'll have to have a rule that children stay off the bench," Ed said.

"But, Ed, as soon as you tell children about a rule, they start thinking about how to break it," I said. "I'm sure that Sage would find the temptation to run along the bench irresistible."

It was clear that Ed, for all his usual good humor, was getting increasingly irritated, and Linn and I felt guilty about going counter to his judgment. We temporarily dropped the subject.

Once Ed was back in his office, however, he came up with perfect solutions to the problems of the stairs and the deck. He doubled the number of balusters throughout the stair tower, inserted a single steel bar between the treads and two steel bars between the deck floor and bench, and designed a simple steel fretwork a couple of feet high to be mounted atop the back of the bench. The cost of these modifications was considerable, because, for instance, the handrails had to be disassembled and reassembled, and the carriage of the treads made ready for the bars. Still, for once, Linn and I did not begrudge the expense. We were happy with the results and equally grateful for the peace of mind they promised.

APRIL 24TH

FIELD VISIT, HENRY BY HIMSELF

After Henry got back, he telephoned me. "Yeaton has substantially completed the house and therefore his part of the contract," Henry said. "I tested all the appliances and electrical equipment. They're all in good order. The faucets, showers, and garbage disposal are working. The windows operate smoothly. The interior is clean and free of debris. I've submitted to Yeaton an initial punch list of items he still needs to attend to before you accept the house for occupancy." He read out the items from his punch list: "Extend the peastone surface on the service road all the way to the garage. Provide a stepping stone, preferably a piece of granite, at the entry porch. Install a medicine cabinet in the basement bathroom. Install towel bars in all the bathrooms as indicated by the architect. Paint the concrete floor of the basement bedroom black. Paint the base of the dishwasher white. Locate kitchen counter light as per contract drawings. Adjust all sliding and pocket

Stair tower, 1987

doors to operate more easily. Clean the blue chalk line from the concrete finishing wall." Henry's litany continued. It must have consisted of forty items.

"It sounds like Yeaton will be on the job for some time," I said.

"I think he'll be done in a month. He's eager to get his final payment and complete the contract. After that, you'll have to make a separate agreement with him for any additional work you want him to do for you."

"Is this, then, your last field visit?"

"No, I think I'll have to make two more trips. More punch-list items are bound to come up, and there are sure to be postconstruction issues."

Now that the house was nearly finished, many of my deep anxieties, which had been kept in check while my energies were channelled into the construction, bubbled up. What would we do with all the empty rooms—the basement bedroom, the living room, the dining room, the kitchen, the three bedrooms above it, and still another room above that? How would we furnish them and make them habitable? How would the furniture look in them? When and how much time would we find to go and live there? Once on the island, what would we do all day? Without even a cinema or a pub, where would we go to amuse ourselves? Linn and I had always thrived in the cloistered community of colleges where we stepped out onto the quadrangle and campus streets and serendipitously bumped into people. Even in Manhattan, at the Ford Foundation where she worked, there was a lot of daily contact among people. And the New Yorker offices functioned like a little college, each person doing his or her own thing but all of us working together in a small, confined community. Whenever we got stuck, or simply wanted to take a break, we stepped out of our offices and hung around the water cooler, the social center of our floor. On the island, the Dark Harbor Shop was the closest thing to it, but the store was not in easy walking distance and, once there, whom would we socialize with? In all the time we had been planning and building the house, we'd met only contractors and subcontractors, architects and the like.

I could read or write in our house, I thought, but immediately recalled that for that I would need a reader and an amanuensis. Such amenities could be found in big cities or college towns, but were, I thought, unheard-of on the island. Linn could perhaps lose herself in country pursuits—play tennis or swim—but she wasn't an especially keen tennis player and the Maine water was notorious for being so cold that people said it practically had ice cubes floating in it. The mere thought of it made me shiver. I tried to recall what Annette had done all day. She had had a houseful of guests or had gone to other, uninhabited islands. But then she had had at her disposal a staff, a private yacht, a private jet, and heaps of money to entertain with and to create her own world within the confines of the island. At best, Linn and I could afford only a mother's helper. And I was so unused to the country that I didn't even like to carry firewood; once, when I had done so at Annette's, I couldn't tell if the wood had blackened my hands so they would soil anything I touched—Annette's sofa, my clothes, or indeed, my own face. I had had to check with her maid and, after washing, recheck to make sure that I had scrubbed off all the soot. And then there was the fear of the outdoors, of its tooth and claw, of the hidden ground nest of yellow jackets I could unwittingly step into.

MAY 17TH
FIELD VISIT, HENRY BY HIMSELF

Henry reported that Yeaton had finished the house and wished to be paid and released from all legal obligations under the contract. I asked if the punch-list items had been resolved. Henry said they had, with the exception of one or two items for which Yeaton was awaiting delivery of a part. I immediately dispatched the final payment to Yeaton.

We all flew together to Portland and drove in a rented car to the ferry slip. It was still early in the season, so there was no wait to get our car onto the ferry. We deposited our luggage at the Islesboro Inn, a house with fourteen bedrooms, where Ed, Henry, and I had often stayed in recent months to maximize our time on the island. After that, we rushed to the house.

Linn and I had not been there since March, and I was eager for her impressions. But she seemed to be so preoccupied with Sage that she did little more than walk through the rooms. Most of the time, she sat on the steps on the deck and let Sage suckle. We were bringing her up according to the prevailing child-rearing theory that babies should be fed on demand. Sage took full advantage of it and seemed to cry often until she was attached. Then she clutched Linn's hair, had her fill, made happy gurgling sounds, and fell asleep. In my own way, I, too, was preoccupied with her. I felt that I would be able to take the complete measure of the house only when Linn and I came to stay there. Anyway, with Henry and Yeaton standing around, I think both of us felt self-conscious about being new owners of what the islanders were now referring to as "the Mehta estate."

At one point, I tried to get into the house to get a glass of water and found that all the sliding screen doors were stuck and I could scarcely budge them. I called Yeaton and he came over. I showed him the screen door.

"They got warped because of the recent wet weather," Yeaton said. "Once you get some sun in the summer, they should dry out and shrink a bit."

I didn't know what exactly I expected him to do: to take down all the screen doors; to plane, sand, and paint their top and bottom edges; and eventually to reinstall them, as if he were still working for me? My rational side told me that I had had a terrific contractor, that his work had been carefully super-vised by a topflight New York architectural firm, that every bit

of that work had been documented and governed by meticulous drawings. Yet my irrational side seemed to assume that
everywhere there must be hidden faults, and I had best find out
what they were while the house was still under the standard
warranty of one year. But I fancied the warranty covered only
big problems, like a leak in the roof, not small daily irritations
like jammed screen doors.

"Do you mean to say, Yeaton, that every year the weather
will make these screen doors inoperable?" I asked, trying to
control my annoyance.

"Your architect ordered the screen doors from Duratherm.
I only installed them. If you have problems with them, you'll
have to talk to the company. Excuse me, I will be going now."
He walked away.

"I thought once the doors were primed and painted, the
sealant protected them from the weather," I said to Henry.

"But the Maine weather is severe," he said.

Henry examined the doors closely and noticed that they
had small wheels at the bottom. He said he'd get Duratherm
to send down a man who would plane down the top of the
doors and adjust the wheels to give them more room to slide.
But he said we should be careful not to have the doors planed
down too much, because when the doors shrank in the
summer, they might pop out of their housings, fall, and
damage the screens. (In due course, a Duratherm man did
make the necessary adjustments and the doors became more
easily operable. But he advised us to take them down in the
winter and stack them flat in the basement. As it turned out,
there was so much moisture there that all the doors warped
anyhow, and eventually we had to buy new ones. We had
barely got over the problem of the sliding screen doors when
all the swinging screen doors in the house warped, apparently
because Yeaton had used lightweight, standard, off-the-shelf
models in place of the heavier Duratherm ones. I commissioned Duratherm to make new screen doors, but they warped
as well, because the local painter neglected to paint and seal

the edges, forcing us to the expense of yet another lot of swinging doors.)

I asked Henry if it wouldn't have made more sense to have stable metal frames. He said that metal frames would have looked unattractive. I said I couldn't understand why—after all, the mesh of all the window and door screens was copper. He said, still, the metal frames would have looked discordant against the wooden housing and the shingles. As it was, all the wood would age and acquire a nice, weathered look.

I suddenly felt tired, so I just sat next to Linn and Sage on the steps and dreamt about being back in New York in our apartment, which dated from the nineteen-twenties and had long since had its construction wrinkles ironed out.

In time, we accepted such problems as part of the house's growing pains. As for Maine's weather, we came to love it—rain, chill, fog, and all.

SOME YEARS EARLIER, I had helped make a documentary film, in connection with which I had travelled to India with a production crew of six for a month. We had lived and gone around like a family. When the location work was finished, the members of the crew had scattered to work on their other respective projects, and the producer had taken the raw footage to Boston for editing, while I had returned to my solitary work as a writer in New York. Without the excitement of working with other people, I felt bereft, and I had a similar feeling of loss now. I wondered what I would do without the weekly or sometimes daily conversations with Ed or Henry—or, for that matter, with Yeaton. Then Ed introduced us to Toshiko Mori, a young, thoughtful, and refined Japanese woman who was an architect in her own right and was helping Mary furnish the buildings Ed designed. He suggested that she might help us furnish our house. At first, I was resistant. I felt that designing the interior of a house, like choosing one's clothes, should reflect one's own taste and personality. Yet, what with Linn's scholarly asceticism and my reliance on an expert eye, we quickly came around to Ed's proposal. We thought it would save us a lot of stress and anxiety. Besides, we both liked the idea of having the house furnished in a way that would make Ed proud.

Ed had us to lunch with Toshiko. We took to one another right away. She said that, because of her association with Ed's office, she would forgo the customary decorator's markup of thirty to forty per cent on the wholesale price of everything she bought for the house and would bill us only fifty dollars an hour for her time. We happily agreed to the arrangement but warned Ed and Toshiko that Linn's mother had already set aside some furniture for our house. Katherine and her siblings had just emptied their parents' Park Avenue apartment in New York, and the family was also getting some furniture from Linn's aunt's house in Stockbridge—both places had been sold. We told Ed and Toshiko that although all the good pieces had been picked over and divided up, Katherine wanted to truck whatever was left to Islesboro. The furniture was Victorian and heavy-looking and would not show a modern house to advantage. Still, we couldn't gainsay Katherine, especially since we were stretched to our limits in building the house and had scarcely any allowance to furnish it. I could sense the pall my explanation cast on them, but they were equally polite and courteous, and the most they would allow themselves to say was that how we furnished our house was ultimately our choice.

"But Ed, you must be pained that we are not going to furnish the house in a style in keeping with your architecture," I said.

"But it's your house," he said equably.

"Still, if you get an owner who has bad taste, what then?" I asked.

"I choose my owners carefully," Ed said with a laugh.

I resolved then and there that as time went on, despite Linn's preference for family furniture, I would gradually clear away the Victorian clutter and get beautiful modern pieces and try to perpetuate Ed's design and vision. But it was not easy to keep to the resolve. As it turned out, the best modern furniture was as expensive as some antique pieces, and although we did splurge and buy solid mahogany outdoor furniture for the inset, for the inside we settled for simple oak-veneered and imitation wicker furniture. In time we did acquire a few elegant cherry tables and chairs.

THERE WAS SOME delay before Katherine could truck the furniture up to Maine. One broken-down rush-bottom kitchen chair had been accidentally thrown out as the Park Avenue apartment was being emptied, and, because the chair was part of a set, she spent quite some time trying to locate it, only to discover it had long since been taken to the dump. In her barn in Cooperstown, she turned up two D-shaped hall tables that had once stood in Otsego Hall, the house of James Fenimore Cooper, and I spent some time looking for a leaf to connect them so that they could serve as a dining table. Then, as the shipment was being readied for Maine, I turned down some of the items, like brass beds and mattresses that had come from the maids' rooms, and it took time to separate them out. Just around the time the shipment reached Maine, Toshiko had had delivered to the house some of the new things she had bought for us—beds, chests of drawers, and a kitchen table—and we decided to go to our house and try it out for a few nights.

One autumn afternoon, we flew up, rented a car, and drove to our house without even informing Paul Pendleton, who had been working first as our eyes and ears during construction and then as our caretaker, that we were coming. We coasted down the service road, parked the car in the garage, and slipped into the house through the basement. All around, there was a cloying, heavy smell of urethane and fresh paint. Upstairs, the rooms, though small, felt cavernous, cold, and forlorn. Our voices, bouncing against the glass of windows and sliders, sounded brittle and raspy. Ed had made a counter and an opening, furnished with a sliding Plexiglas window, in the wall between the dining room and the entry hall so that one could see from the dining room the stair tower, with its risers climbing into space up the tower and, alternatively, from the entry hall the inset, the deck, the allée, the water and, on a clear day, the islands beyond. Ed fancied that the counter would be a perfect place for Linn to put a nice vase with fresh-cut flowers to welcome visitors, or to drop her car keys as she came through the front door. (Because of the orientation of the house to the sea, the front door was situated in the northwest corner of the house.) The opening would also give those visitors a glimpse of the dramatic orientation of the house. But the opening's unintended effect was to make the house noisy. From the dining room, even with the window shut, our voices carried straight up the tower to the bedrooms above. It seemed that despite Ed's genuine wish to design for me a soundproof house, he, like other contemporary architects, had favored natural light and air over quiet and pleasant acoustics. For instance, the large, fixed half-moon window in the stair tower, while flooding it with light, made house sounds harsher—glass is a notoriously poor acoustical material. Also, because the stairs were open, like a ladder, rather than closed up and carpeted as in old houses, even the shuffle of shoes in the basement carried all the way to the top of the house. It was as if with modern materials and a preoccupation with light and air a contemporary architect could not build a house whose main objective was soundproofing without making unacceptable aesthetic compromises. In any event, there was nothing to soften the sounds of our speech or movement owing to the absence of upholstered furniture, dhurries, and curtains—still on order. And without a single picture or poster on the wall to arrest the eye or to give the space a personal touch, the house seemed not only uninhabited but uninhabitable.

Sage, now ten months old and starting to walk, whimpered and spat up. Linn wiped her face with a bib, and we went upstairs to the bedrooms.

"We should have picked up pots, pans, and dishes on the mainland before we arrived," Linn said. "We don't even have a garbage pail for Sage's diapers. We'll have to drive over to the mainland tomorrow to do our shopping."

I asked Linn to start making a list of the basic things we needed in the house, but realized we didn't have so much as a pencil or paper. I took off my jacket and was irritated to discover there wasn't a hook or a peg anywhere to hang it on.

"Why did Henry forget to put up hooks or hanging rods?" I cried.

"No doubt he was busy thinking about punch-list items," Linn said.

I called Yeaton and asked if he could install a few hooks for us when he had some time.

"I'm out of the contract," he said flatly.

"But we can't live in a house without hooks," I said.

"For me to come back to the job and do all that work would cost you five hundred dollars," he said.

"You're not serious!" I cried. "Isn't it just a matter of putting in some screws or hammering in some nails?"

"If you think it's that simple, you should do it yourself," he said.

"But I can't," I said. "I don't even have a nail or a hammer."

"It's just as well, because if you were to hammer a nail into Sheetrock, it wouldn't grip. The first time you hung something on it, it would fall off and leave a hole. And then you'd want someone to come and patch it up and paint it."

"Then how does one hang anything?" I asked.

"You'd get a stud finder, which tells you where there are studs so you can hammer a nail through the Sheetrock into the stud so that the nail will hold."

Oh, God, the wretched Sheetrock, I thought. If we had had plaster walls, I could have hammered a nail anywhere I pleased. Even with a stud finder, a carpenter could have done the job for probably a hundred dollars, but I wasn't sure how I would go about finding the carpenter who had worked on the house and

West side, 1987

what the proprieties were for approaching him on my own. Anyway, I wanted the job to be done while we were there, and so, in desperation, I agreed to Yeaton's price, reasoning that having already paid a total of five hundred thousand dollars for the land and the house, what was another five hundred dollars?

"What kind of hooks would you like?" he asked.

"What are the choices?" I asked, getting interested.

"There are many kinds of brass hooks, and you could also have straight wooden pegs," he said.

"What would look right in the house?"

"For that, you have to ask Mr. Barnes," he said. In his Maine accent, "Barnes" came out sounding like "Baahnes." I must have heard him pronounce "r"s like that hundreds of times, but this time it really got me worked up. I felt like shouting at him, "You can't even pronounce 'r' and you want five hundred dollars for some hanging rods and pegs?" But I said on the telephone, "I don't want to trouble Mr. Barnes. Can you give me your opinion?"

"I'm not an architect, but I reckon wood is more country, brass is more city."

"Let's go with wood, then," I said.

When I had gone to wash my hands earlier, I had been annoyed to find that the taps in the bathroom did not all turn counter-clockwise, as in our apartment in New York, and that some of the silicone was coming out of the join between the sink and the wall. And when I examined the bathtub, silicone was also coming out of the join there.

"You know the house is under warranty for a year," I said now, thinking I would get him to come fix the taps and the silicone problem under the warranty if it killed me.

"Yeah. What's the problem?" he asked.

I told him.

"The handles in the bathrooms turn the way they're supposed to—hot counter-clockwise and cold clockwise," he replied. "If they turn differently in New York, and they bother you, then you should get them fixed there."

I was speechless. Finally, I brought out, "What about the silicone?"

"It has nothing to do with the seals of the joins. Just take a washcloth and rub it off."

A realization began to dawn on me that someone more handy than Linn or I would have bought the necessary materials and tools and attended to the problems himself rather than appealing to a house builder—that in fact neither of us was really suited to living on an island where, in order to survive, one had to learn to do everything oneself or pay dearly. I marvelled how my attitude toward money had undergone a change in the building of a house. From being careful with my money, I had now adopted a rich person's attitude—perhaps Annette's—toward money.

I hung up and mimicked for Linn Yeaton's accent.

She laughed.

"We'll be paying for this house until I die," I said.

"But remember, I am paying half of everything," she said.

"But we are going to be left owning a white elephant slowly weathering and deteriorating hundreds of miles from New York. I believe there's a law of physics that everything starts to run down the moment it is created."

"You're just feeling anxious because of the newness of everything."

"All the time we were building, I never realized how fragile a modern house is. It's all just glass. I don't think I'd feel safe sleeping here even one night. Anyone could throw a rock and break in. I'm not one of those strongmen who could defend you and Sage."

"But you're talking as if the house is in New York City. In the country, people never lock their doors. We didn't in Cooperstown."

"Let's go and check into the inn."

"Calm down. We came here for an adventure, and we're going to stay here for a few nights."

❧

IN THE MORNING, the curtains for all the windows and sliders arrived from Toshiko. To save us money, she had had them made in New York. At the same time, a curtain-hanging man arrived in a truck from the mainland. After he unpacked and started hanging the curtains, he discovered that some were too short, some too long, some too wide.

I called up Toshiko, almost in tears.

"The measurement discrepancies must have crept up because the New York fabricator made certain assumptions about installation that were not shared by the Maine installer," she said. "You see, to save you money, I had split the job between companies in New York and Maine, and no two people in a trade do things in the same way. They all have their own idiosyncrasies. But there's no point in laying blame on anyone now. I'm coming to Maine in a few days. I'll bring my sewing machine and adjust the curtains myself."

I was touched by her kindness. But I was sure that, even if she were a magician, she could not fix them. Still, I didn't want to hurt her feelings, so I said, "But you'll need a helper to hang the curtains."

"I'll adjust them. The curtain man can hang them later."

As it turned out, she did come up and labor the whole day with her sewing machine, opening up and restitching the curtains. But unlike the hanging rods or pegs, which Yeaton remedied relatively easily, she wasn't able to put the curtains quite right. What had gone wrong with her measurements in the first place remained a mystery, at least to me—the work of a gremlin who seems to surface now and again during the building of any house. In time, we found a local man in Camden and somehow, by fiddling with the locations of the curtain rods, he was able to fix the curtains. But, as he said, they were only "ninety per cent perfect. To be a hundred per cent perfect, you would have to start off from scratch."

VIII

ADDITIONS

W E FOUND THAT WE COULD SCARCELY GET AWAY TO
Maine for more than a few weeks a year. We had
trouble uprooting Linn's mother's helper and my
amanuensis from the city in the summer. Even when
we did find competent temporary people who were prepared to come to the island and live with us, there were
other complications. One mother's helper, an English
au pair, got homesick and, without any island activities, developed such cabin fever that we had to ship her home. Another
turned out to have an intense relationship with a boyfriend, who
visited her and us every weekend, which made for a difficult
ménage. As for an amanuensis, it was almost impossible to find a
temporary person to do the job. The truth was, we were not the
kind of people who could pick up and go away just like that. Perhaps we could have worked out some kind of weekend summer
life if we had had a house within reasonable driving distance—
say, in the Hamptons. But a faraway island seemed hopelessly
impractical, possible only for people with enormous private

means and unlimited leisure. In any case, for us, the house was proving to be a continual financial drain.

Until Maine, I'd always prided myself on being immensely practical, so now I set about trying to rent our house. Within months of its completion, I got hold of the island telephone directory. Except for those people who had worked for us, I recognized only a few names in it, but I sent them each a letter, addressing them as "Dear Neighbor" and telling them about our house and our difficulty in using it in the foreseeable future. I asked them if they knew of any prospective tenant who might be interested in renting the house for the summer—or, indeed, all year round. (Unlike most of the other summer houses, our house was fully winterized.) I was dispirited when I didn't get a single response; my friends who owned houses in the Hamptons had no dearth of prospective tenants.

In time, I discovered the ineptitude of my approach. The summer residents of Dark Harbor included such luminaries as Douglas Dillon, a former Ambassador to France and Secretary of the Treasury whose family owned Château Haut-Brion, one of the five first growths of Bordeaux Cru; the four daughters and the son of the late Winthrop Aldrich, who was a former Ambassador to the Court of St. James, and whose sister had been married to John D. Rockefeller, Jr., and so was the mother of Nelson and David; and other socially prominent people from Boston, New York, and Philadelphia. Indeed, many of their cottages, of the fifteen-room variety, were still known by the names of the even older families who had once built and lived in them. The "old money" formed an intricate, self-contained society linked by marriages and family traditions. They would have regarded even Annette's stepfather as nouveau riche. They certainly would not have taken kindly to being addressed as "Dear Neighbor" and being solicited for leads that, in normal course, should have come from a real-estate broker. Every time I thought of my blunder, my face turned red. Indeed, in those early days, whenever we were on the island, we were aware of a certain social chill. I naturally ascribed it to my blindness, to my Indian-ness, even to my being a writer—the English tradition of honoring and quoting writers was not the island style. Linn, however, could lay claim to the credentials of the island's upper class. After all, Cooperstown was named after her family. Yet her reception seemed to be no warmer. In any event, within two years of completing the house, we thought about selling it.

To gauge the house's market prospects, I got in touch with Sotheby's International Realty. One of their appraisers, George C. Ballantyne, who had an M.A. in architectural history from Columbia and an M.B.A. from Boston University, made a special trip to Dark Harbor to look over our property. "Your Islesboro residence is the most striking contemporary house I have inspected on the Maine coast during the past nine years," he wrote to me on July 7, 1987. "The quality of construction is also the finest I have seen in any contemporary residence during the same period." Mentioning that he had done his thesis on the residential architecture of Frank Lloyd Wright and that, in the course of it, he had interviewed many of Wright's clients across the country, he said that with few exceptions the cost of construction of their houses had always greatly exceeded the budget. If the owners of any of these houses had turned around and sold them as soon as they were built—as we were thinking of doing—they would have inevitably sustained a big loss. In any event, he didn't think that we could recoup our investment in the present market, explaining:

> At any given time, all currently available Maine and New England oceanfront properties compete for the same group of prospective buyers. As prices increase, the number of financially qualified purchasers decreases. Properties that the market perceives as most competitively priced sell while others remain on the market. A prospective Maine purchaser in the $500,000 range may currently choose from a number of oceanfront properties. If your Islesboro residence were to be offered for sale in the $700,000 range, it would

not appear competitive with other properties. If you have the flexibility, we would encourage you to enjoy your exceptional residence for another year or two and allow Maine residential prices to catch up with the value of your Islesboro property.

Within the next two years, we anticipate there will be many Maine sales in the one million dollar plus range. Boston based buyers are beginning to seek alternatives to Cape Cod. To date, this group of potential purchasers have not been a strong force on Islesboro or north of Camden. Rapidly appreciating prices in southern Maine, however, will encourage these buyers to go further north. This competition among purchasers should ensure rapid price appreciation of both your Islesboro residence and more remote properties.

It is an extraordinary residence and I am delighted you commissioned Edward Larrabee Barnes for it. If all clients during the past centuries had only been concerned with cutting costs, it is unlikely that "East Brick" in Nantucket, "Falling Water" in Mill Run, Pennsylvania, or your Islesboro residence would ever have been built.

We decided to shelve the question of selling our property indefinitely and to enjoy the house, just as Ballantyne counselled.

Almost from the outset, Ed had suggested building a swimming pool, but Linn and I didn't think that we could justify the investment. Now, encouraged by further conversations with Ballantyne, who thought that a pool would make the house more desirable for a prospective buyer, and bolstered by a windfall we had had in the stock market, we decided to go ahead and build one.

At the end of the summer of 1987, Ed and Mary stopped to see us in Dark Harbor—they were driving to their own summer house in Somesville. I told Ed about the decision, and he got excited.

East side, 1987

"I'd always thought you'd ask me to design you a pool," he said. "Now that the house is settled into the land, this is a good time to get started."

Ed drew up a chair at the kitchen table and immediately started sketching a pool while Mary went out for a walk to enjoy the view. It was an unusually clear day, and the islands seemed to be arranged like a sculpture out in the sea, as if to dazzle her eye.

Ed sketched two alternative designs for the pool—one a perfect circle, the other shaped like a kidney. I had imagined Ed would situate the pool on the south side of the house, where Linn could easily watch Sage and her friends from the living-room window, but he dismissed that as suburban. Instead, he suggested building the pool at the old abandoned house site, about a hundred and fifty feet northeast of the septic tank—between the hill to the west of the ill-fated driveway and the embankment to the east, just above the sea. He thought that would give it more of a country feeling and would also be stunning, in that one body of water would seem to be delicately poised on the other. Linn and I embraced the idea.

He then went on to sketch a glassed-in gazebo with a generous deck, saying, "The gazebo would have a practical function. It would allow swimmers to come in, dry off, and warm up, to get out of the rain or sun, to leave their clothes and picnic baskets, or just to think and meditate by the sea. The deck will be big enough for you to have a good-sized table with one of those umbrellas, under which people could sit and sip tea or wine in the late afternoon. We could make it out of bluestone, which can be cut to any size or shape we want. On a sunny day, the stone would heat up and be wonderful for bathers to lie on."

As Ed talked, he filled in the gazebo with almost a whole wall of glass sliders looking out to the pool and the sea in front and a shower looking into the woods in back. Finally, he blocked off the north side near the woods for a pump house, a small, concrete, bunkerlike structure that he said could be painted green to melt in with its surroundings.

"Gosh, Ed. We would be building a whole complex," I said. "It's going to cost two or three times the money we were planning to spend on it."

"You don't have to do it all at once," Ed said. "You can first do the pool and then build the gazebo when you have the money. Most clients start with a country hideaway, and before they know it, they're building a barn, a gazebo, a pool, a pool house, and even tennis courts. It's the old impulse people have to create little empires."

"But we don't have such grand ideas," I said.

"Try thinking of your house as a succession of experiences," he said. "There's the path to the house. The house itself. The inset and the deck. The allée. The woods. And the beach. Each of these serves as a marker in your progress through the site. The complex would be a continuation of these little experiences."

A couple of weeks later, when Ed and Mary stopped by on their way back to New York, we had a preliminary meeting on the island with Tom Carbonella, a smooth-talking representative of a pool company in New Hampshire—there were apparently no pool companies in Maine that had the equipment to put in a long-lasting gunite pool. We walked down with him to the site to stake it out. Within minutes, he was trying to wean us away from the kidney-shaped pool we'd all but settled on, to a rectangular pool, which he said we had to have in order to accommodate a mechanical pool cover.

"Covers are great," he said. "They prevent your chemicals from evaporating. They keep leaves and other crud from falling into the water and clogging up your drains. Best of all, they keep the water heat trapped in the pool. That's a real advantage in Maine, where it can be cold, clammy, and foggy. With a kidney-shaped pool, you'll be stuck with a manual cover, which will require two men to get it on and get it off. And you'll need to find two men who won't mind getting soaking wet, because, boy, when you take off that cover, it's really drenched. A mechanical cover is wired electrically, and you can open and close it at the touch of a button."

"But Ved and Linn would like a pool which would be aesthetically more interesting than a rectangle. Is there any way a mechanical cover could be designed for a pool with an interesting geometric shape?" Ed asked.

"Not with our present technology," Carbonella said. He explained that the cover travelled in a straight line by means of wheels on a track mounted inside the pool, so that the cover could rest on the water, and that therefore the apparatus could work only on a rectangular pool.

We were so naïve about pools that the argument for having a mechanical cover seemed, to us, unassailable. Still, we wanted to know if it had any drawbacks.

"For years, I've been selling mechanical covers to pool owners from California to Maine," Carbonella said. "I've not had any complaints. Anyway, if you don't have a cover, the authorities will require you to have a fence and a gate, and that will look ugly in the beautiful setting you've chosen here for the pool."

Ed reluctantly agreed to a standard twenty-by-forty-foot pool, and he and Carbonella immediately staked it out. But no sooner had Linn and I agreed to a price of seven thousand dollars for the mechanical cover, excluding installation, than Carbonella started pressing on us other add-ons. One was a Turbo Clean system on the pool floor, which constantly circulated the water and deposited any fallen leaves, bugs, and detritus in skimmer baskets, obviating the need for a dredging net or a vacuum cleaner. Another was Chemtrol, a sort of computer "brain" that automatically regulated the water's chemical balance, making manual testing unnecessary. Still another was Water Witch, which automatically maintained the water level. Indeed, the gadgets supposedly freed the owner from all responsibilities of day-to-day maintenance of the pool, his only onus being to empty the Turbo Clean skimmer baskets regularly and replenish the chemicals.

Some time earlier, Paul Pendleton had retired as our care-taker and had even stopped doing any part-time work for us. Since then, we'd had trouble finding anyone on the island to help us for reasonable pay. So it was not difficult for Car-bonella to entice us with his gadgetry. We rationalized that the pool was like a baby. When Linn first got pregnant with Sage, we had given scarcely a thought to a crib, a changing table, a high chair, toys, picture books—all of which we had since acquired, one by one. Similarly, our decision to have a pool naturally would require more than just putting in a gunite shell. And, of course, like a growing child, who con-stantly adds to one's enjoyment, the pool, we trusted, would do the same.

When we were all back in New York, Ed wrote to us that he would like his son, John, who was doing a job for him in Frenchboro, Maine, to take over our pool project, suggesting that John could combine trips there with trips to Islesboro and represent him for the preliminary work on the complex. John was the Barneses' only child; he was thirty-six and an architect; and he had recently moved to New York from San Francisco. He had joined Ed's firm with the idea of, perhaps, eventually succeeding his father, who was seventy-two. Although Ed was enlisting John's help, there was clearly no diminution in his own interest in the project, for in the letter he wrote:

> Now, about the design. I enclose a first sketch which I propose to finish and send to Yeaton for coordination with the pool company. The grassy terrace around the pool is eye-shaped so that the grades at each side will taper softly back to a natural grade. The embankment on the upper and lower sides of the terrace would be heavily planted; spruce on the upside, ferns on the downside. A gazebo would be added on the uphill side of the pool so that reflections on the water would throw dappled sunlight on the ceiling. As for overall landscaping, it seems to me we should start little spruce

trees in the sideburns at each side of the septic tank, and clear slightly below the pool so that there are glimpses of the ocean from the pool house.

After you and Linn have glanced at this rough sketch, please give me a ring.

Yours,

Ed

Over the next few months, as we worked with John and Ed, the complex underwent many changes. The idea of a concrete pump house was dropped, because it could not accommodate Carbonella's elaborate pool equipment. In its place, a whole new building was designed, with space for housing the pump and the other equipment on one side and, on the other, first a room for changing and then a sauna. For some time, we had held out against a sauna. It seemed a sybaritic indulgence, like the Jacuzzi we had long ago rejected. But we finally agreed to it when John impressed upon us that, even in the summer, Maine could be foggy and chilly for days at a time. In any case, a separate changing room became irrelevant because that purpose would be served by the "gazebo," which itself went through several transformations, from a sort of Quonset hut to a whole separate house. Initially, Ed thought—and we agreed—that we should have a toilet in addition to a shower there, because the pool was so far away from the house. That had required an underground pumping station to pump the effluent uphill to the distant septic tank. Once there was plumbing, it seemed only a small step to make the gazebo into a self-contained little pool house, and before we knew it we had added a fireplace, a kitchenette, and a small utility room. We even thought of adding a couple of bedrooms and making it into a proper guesthouse. The cost of doing so was minimal, since the groundwork would already be done and the structure would already be in place. But we quickly came up against, first, a constraint of the site, which was defined by the hill to the west and a precipitous slope falling away from the edge of the pool to the sea in front, and then by a constraint of architectural aesthetics, which dictated that the optimum size of the house be a cube twenty feet in length, width, and height, that being the width of the pool, or half of its length. Ed thought that if the house were any wider it would obstruct the view of the upper landscape from the pool. If it were any taller, it would cast a shadow onto the pool in the afternoon. And if it were any deeper it would interfere with the back drainage area between the pool house and the hill. Certainly, during snowmelt and rain, water would come down from the hill and flood the area. We spent many months pulling and tugging, as it were, to enlarge the cube and come up with a house with a bedroom wing or two, but, as Ed had foreseen, we could not escape the rigidity of those constraints. We even debated moving this house to a different location, but there was no clear place where the complex wouldn't stand out as an intrusive, alien element. Some other architect might have bulldozed or levelled an area to accommodate a complex of any size, but it was a hallmark of Ed's architecture that a building should fit its natural site rather than the site's being reshaped to fit the building.

In the spring of 1988, as we reached the stage of preliminary drawings, John decided that he didn't want to live in New York—that he was going back to San Francisco. That must have thrown Ed, although he never mentioned his feelings to us. But, soon after, he decided that he could not see us through the construction of the complex. Instead, he found for us a local Maine architect to take it on, at the same time assuring us that he would continue to be involved in a supervisory way. Thoughtful as always, he arranged for all of us to meet to stake the pool house in September, almost a year to the day since he had started sketching a pool on our kitchen table. But the local architect was not up to Ed's standards, and the pool house ended up being saddled with no fewer than five architects: in addition to John and Ed, Henry Myerberg and not one but two local architects. It was a replay of what I'd gone through with Zimmerman and Patrick when I was first thinking of what to do with my virgin land, but much worse. Those two architects had gone without laying a hand on what we now called the main house, while all five architects on the complex, in one way or another, became entangled in the pool-house construction. Moreover, the cost overruns set us back nearly fifty thousand dollars more than the initial estimate of eighty thousand dollars, and when the cost of the pool and its accompanying gadgetry was added, the cost of the complex was staggering. Still, we were delighted with it. The pool house had sliding doors that opened toward the pool and the ocean, a cathedral ceiling, and in the back, a row of three casement windows. It had the same molding, window, and door details as the main house. It also had a skylight window above a little loft where small children could play or sleep. Built around the chimney, the loft could be reached by a hidden ladder from the utility room at the back of the fireplace. Above all, it was wonderful to play in the pool with Sage and her little sister, Natasha, and then to shepherd them into the pool house and sauna to warm up.

CONSTRUCTION HAS A way of snowballing. The more we did to our property, the more we wanted to do. As the girls grew older, the main house seemed too small, and, as Ed never stopped reminding me, he had initially designed a house for a bachelor, and we had become a family of four. I started thinking of adding to the house and of making it more comfortable, imagining the girls could enjoy it long after I was gone, in the spirit of my father, who had built and expanded his house in Lahore back in the nineteen-thirties, as his family grew. Then, too, the house seemed incomplete without the addition, and I had the kind of temperament that not only liked to finish things but also to finish them to perfection. If I encountered difficulties with, say, a manuscript, I might spend years tinkering and shaping it and would not let go of it until I imagined it was flawless. The building project was no different. All the same, I would have steered clear of further building if my

Swimming pool, 1989

feelings about money had not undergone a subtle, but significant, shift. With Linn at my side, I had conquered my old fear that I might not be able to write because I wouldn't be able to pay my readers and amanuenses—indeed, that I might be out of house and home, the way we had been after the Partition.

In any event, the dining room of our house had always felt like half a room. Its size was reduced not only by the inset but also by a pair of built-in floor-to-ceiling bookcases on its western wall. Ed had liked the thought of our eating in a room with books. After all, the house was for a writer, as he had conceived of it. Indeed, the bookcases had been elegantly designed, with the two units separated by the counter and the square opening to the entry hall. They were a nice architectural detail, but they jutted into the room by a foot, which in concept seemed a small encroachment of floor space but, given the size of the room—eleven feet deep and thirteen and half feet wide—turned out to be substantial. In fact, not only could the dining room scarcely accommodate a table for six but there was no space for a sideboard or a serving table. Similarly, the living room had space only for sofas and easy chairs around the fireplace, and not much additional space for a desk or a computer, a stereo system or a television set, or, indeed, for the children to run around and play. Linn felt sad that there was no place in the house for a piano; she enjoyed singing lieder and arias. Unlike many old houses that had a lot of wasted and empty space, our new house was so tight that every inch seemed already to be allotted. It seemed that one couldn't just introduce an item like a piano without having planned for it at the drawing stage, and we were belatedly realizing that neither of us had become at all used to conceptualizing space from architectural drawings.

One day, in New York, I sat down in Ed's office to talk over the whole space problem.

"When we designed the house, I could have predicted that you would need at least another room," Ed said, as soon as I broached the subject. "At the time, we were not only working against your budgetary constraints but also against the expense of building on an island. I think someday you'll have to build an addition."

My immediate thought was that we should do an addition while Ed was still working—he was now seventy-five. His involvement would insure that the addition would be in the same architectural style as the house. Anyway, I couldn't imagine any other distinguished architect extending himself to us the way Ed had. Still, the idea of starting another construction project when we had just come out of building the pool complex was unsettling.

"Wouldn't an addition cost a lot?" I asked.

"Everything on your island seems to bust the budget," he said.

"Just suppose we did do the addition—would you be able to help us?"

He thought for a moment and then said, "I think only we should do the addition to the original house."

"Do you really think you would have the time?"

"The office is feeling the pinch of the recession just now, like everyone else. If you were interested, we could just do some schematic drawings to give you an idea of what the addition might look like."

"How much would that cost?"

"Not very much, if we just kept it to schematics. If I had to put a figure on it, I would say thirty-six hundred dollars, maximum."

All of a sudden, I took alarm. The addition, instead of being a distant vision, seemed to be taking shape even as we were mulling over the idea. I fancied the contractor bills were already tumbling out of the mailbox, like ice out of an ice machine.

"I'll talk it over with Linn," I said, "but I'm sure she'll tell me to stay clear of any more architectural adventures."

Ed laughed.

WHEN I GOT home, instead of talking to Linn, I immediately called Ballantyne of Sotheby's and asked him if the house would be more salable if it were somewhat bigger; the idea of holding onto the house for us or for the children was fast evaporating. "As you know, we've now invested in a pool and pool complex," I said. "Wouldn't someone who was interested in a pool also want a more generous house?"

"He certainly would," he said. "People who have the kind of money to buy a house like yours need a lot of space. They are likely to have guests staying over or perhaps be on their second or third marriage, with children and stepchildren. Anyway, such people like their second homes to be as grand as their primary residences."

"How much bigger does the house have to be to attract those kinds of client?"

"You could certainly do with a nice-sized formal dining room and another living room. As far as sleeping arrangements go, your pool house could probably take the overflow."

"How much more valuable would the bigger house be?"

"All I can tell you is that any big, elegant house on the coast moves much faster than a small, elegant house on the coast."

"Suppose the addition cost half as much again as the original house?" I persisted. "Will I lose money or make money?"

"I think you'll make money, but it would of course depend on market conditions."

That evening, I discussed with Linn my conversations with Ed and Ballantyne.

"You must be crazy to think of more construction," she said.

"I know," I said. "But I think of our house as Ed's house—as a memento of his work. Who knows how long he'll be active? Let's at least get the schematics done while he is around and interested."

"Even those will be expensive," Linn said.

I reflected that when I was about to pull out of building the original house, she had prevailed upon me to persevere. Now our roles were reversed. She didn't want to build the addition, and I had to convince her that it would be advantageous both for our family and for the ultimate value of the house.

"I know what you mean," I said. "Whenever I do or buy something expensive, I initially feel depressed, but later, if the investment works out, I'm in clover."

I mentioned the subject of a third child, which we had both been hoping to have for some time. Linn had grown up in a small family, of two girls, and she didn't want to repeat that pattern in her own family. As it was, we not only had two girls but they were two and a half years apart in age, just like Linn and Katrina. Linn wanted to have one more child, at the very least. Since giving birth to Natasha, she had become pregnant several times, but, sadly, the pregnancies were unsuccessful, and we had agreed to go on trying until I reached the age of sixty, in 1994, when she would be thirty-nine. We still had three years left.

After this conversation, I started joking about having a new house addition for a new family addition. That, as much as anything, eventually brought her around. A couple of months later, in January of 1991, I went with Linn to Ed's office and gave him the go-ahead for the schematic drawings. Ed deputized David Wallance to work with him in developing them. (Henry had left Ed's office in 1986, to set up on his own, even though he continued to work on the pool house as a consultant.) Ed said that David had been with his office since 1985 and that he'd had experience in designing residential projects. He was in his late thirties and was as considerate and reserved as Henry had been brisk and outgoing.

Trying to think small and keep a control on expenses, I said we were really interested in having only one additional room.

"You'd be surprised how much just one additional room can change the feel of a house—what would you like that room to be?" Ed asked.

"I don't know. Something that could accommodate a piano and all the things our present living room cannot. Oh, yes— also, in order to make the dining room more usable, we would like to move the bookcases into the new room and wall in the opening between the entry hall and the dining room."

Ed and David took note of our wishes, and after they had

worked on the addition for two or three weeks, Ed almost danced into our apartment one evening with the schematics. As we studied them with Ed's help, we were enthralled. The addition seemed to transform the house, not only giving us more room but also making the house architecturally more interesting, while not altering its essentially compact character. Moreover, the addition's placement was inspired. We knew the main house could not be conveniently expanded eastward; that would have required taking down some beautiful trees and dealing with the problem of the lower elevation. Similarly, expansion northward would have interfered with the winding wooded path to the house and the service road. So Ed and David had attached the addition to the rear and side of the house, extending it from the bulge of the stair tower southward about thirty-two feet. While the original house had been formal and symmetrical, or, as the architects liked to say, "axial," like the human body—the left and the right sides mirroring each other—the addition was freer: it created a new outdoor space and changed the roof-line from symmetrical to asymmetrical, suggesting the roof-line of a traditional New England saltbox house. The apex of the addition, essentially one big room, went up two and a half stories, right up to the roof-line of the old house. The roof-line of the new addition extended from the stair tower southward, and the eaves came down so low so that one could almost touch them from the ground. As a result, the whole house seemed to engage better with the land and to be more on a human scale, so addressing, once again, the problem of the house's seeming too tall. The addition also had its own view of the sea. The proportions, the balance, the volume all seemed just right, and once the addition had been sketched, Ed and David's placement of it seemed the only natural one.

Entered from the northwest corner of the old living room, the addition contained a thirteen-by-eighteen-foot "stage area" that was almost as big as the old living room. The near half of the stage area was given over to a bar. The far half of the stage area was reserved for a grand piano and, along the north wall next to it, tall bookcases. There was a triangular window on the west wall near the spot where Ed imagined the pianist would sit. Three broad steps down from the stage area was the main, eighteen-and-a-half-foot-square room, planned as the new living room, which, besides its very high ceiling, had three "points of interest": one was the bar, so designed that one could serve guests in the living room from the stage side and also equipped with cabinets ample enough to hold everything from liquor bottles through a television and a stereo system to children's games. Another was a fireplace in the south wall. The third was a huge, seven-by-seven-foot glass pocket door in the east wall, which faced a small, rectangular window in the west wall near the fireplace and looked out toward the sea.

We wholeheartedly approved the schematics, but for days we debated whether to go ahead and commission Ed and David to proceed with working drawings. Still, in a way, our decision to go ahead was a foregone conclusion when I wrote to Ed that, while we were at it, we should add another bedroom—that, as it was, if we used the attic room as Linn's study and the basement as a guest room, we had use of only three bedrooms on the second floor: the master bedroom for us, and two small bedrooms for the girls. I said that we still hoped to have a third child, and that it would be helpful if we could somehow build a second story inside the addition and add a bedroom, so the whole family could be together on one floor. Ed had long teased me for trying to squeeze more bedrooms out of the structure's envelope, so he was not surprised. Before long, he came up with an idea for a child's bedroom, a sort of open box above the near end of the stage area, with an entrance upstairs, opposite the master bedroom, where the addition would be attached to the original structure. This child's bedroom had a second triangular window in its west wall, with its apex pointing in the opposite direction from that of the triangular window below it. To lighten the effect of a small room, he also indicated a little interior window in the south wall, a sort of lookout from where a child could see down into the new living room. (Unlike the Freudian slip of the bathroom, the lookout was a conscious architectural flourish.) Similarly, people in the living room could look up into the child's bedroom and, above it, to a sort of balcony to the east, accessible from the top landing, just under the line where the original house and the addition would meet. We dubbed the balcony a pirate's perch, because one could look down from it into the child's room without being seen.

Linn remained opposed to the addition, but I thought that an extra bedroom and a new living room would make such a difference to our enjoyment of the house that, whether we built or not, we should ask Ed's office to go ahead with the working drawings. Ed established a ceiling of eighteen thousand dollars, not only for preparing the working drawings but also for seeing us through the bidding process, if it came to that. At one time, before I became a house builder, the figure would have shocked me, but since then the house had become a sort of indigent relative whom we were committed to supporting and caring for, however outrageous the demands.

As the working drawings progressed, we began focussing on the addition's finer points. For instance, we asked Ed to take some floor space, along with a window, from the master bedroom, and to design a half-bathroom for the child's bedroom. The master bedroom was on such a generous scale that I thought we could easily afford to lose the space. Ed gently protested that I was turning the interior of the second floor into a rabbit warren, but allowed that a child's bedroom would be more usable with a half-bath.

Ed and David were still refining the drawings into August, seven months after the idea for an addition was first floated. As soon as we received the finished prints, I was so taken with the addition that I wanted to embark on construction right away. Yet I was all too aware of certain realities. Linn had still not become successfully pregnant, and since the building of the original house my whole writing career had been put in jeopardy. Beginning in 1961, most of my writing income had come from publishing in *The New Yorker,* but in 1985, the magazine, which had been a family enterprise for sixty years, had been acquired by the publishing empire of Samuel Newhouse and his younger brother, Donald. Then, in less than two years, Newhouse fired William Shawn, who had been the magazine's editor-in-chief for thirty-five years and, for twenty-seven of those years, my mentor, and it was clear that it would not be long until a lot of us "old-timers," as we were already being referred to, would also be let go. (That is what happened.) Simultaneously, my income from books—I'd been publishing them every couple of years since 1957—was also drying up, as commercial books elbowed aside serious writing. Despite every reason to be cautious, I decided to build the addition, as much to enhance the value of the house as to pay homage to Ed. Since Linn remained opposed to the idea, I told her I would bear the full cost of it myself. The stock market was going up, our investments were going up, and although I didn't think, like some brokers, that that tree would grow to the sky, I thought that the market would have a long, good run—and that is what happened.

It took a couple of months for the bids to come in, and they ranged from a hundred and ten thousand dollars to a hundred and sixty thousand dollars. In the end, Robert Clayton, Yeaton's top carpenter, who had inherited the business after his boss retired, and who had come in with the lowest bid, proved to be the only suitable candidate. He got the job; I nailed down some profits in the market and also secured a construction loan; and he began building in January, 1992. It took him a year and a half, or twice the time he had anticipated, to finish the addition.

THE MOMENT WE first walked into the new room, we were thrilled by its height and spaciousness and its striking view of the bay. But I, for one, was unnerved to discover that the two triangular windows had no trim of any kind, nor any provision for a curtain. Yet I was hard pressed to imagine not having something in the window to keep the sun out. As if to compound the confusion, the lookout in the child's bedroom, like the rectangular window next to the fireplace, had neither a recess in the wall for a shade nor so much as a rod or bracket for a curtain. Yet how could a child be expected to sleep without a shade blacking out the living-room lights below, I wondered. Had Ed gone in for a sensational architectural touch, a little in the manner of Philip Johnson, who had built himself a much-publicized glass house? I realized that I should have thought of the problem when the lookout was first sketched, but at the time I hadn't focussed on its practicality.

I rang up David and said that perhaps it was dramatic to have no trims or curtains and to have just clean white walls, but that windows without any kind of shade seemed utterly impractical.

"It's true that Ed thought that, in many instances, you might be able to get along without any shades or curtains on an island," David said. "Still, as you will have noticed, the triangular windows have been set deep in the wall, in recesses. In them, there are slots for special kinds of shades. But, as you know, designing the appropriate window treatment is really up to Toshiko." Luckily, Toshiko Mori had agreed to help us to furnish the addition, on the same terms as before.

When I got in touch with Toshiko, she said, "I've been trying to make arrangements to have triangular shades made for you, but I've been having a lot of trouble. There are only two companies in New York—MechoShade and American Draperies—that have the experience to make shades for architects. I've been in touch with both of them, and neither one wants to bid for the job—they say it's too small and too far away."

"Wait a minute. You mean, there's no company in Maine that can make the shades? Isn't it just a matter of cutting out the shapes?"

"It's not that simple," she said with a laugh. "For a start, there are many kinds of triangular windows, with apices on the sides or in the middle. That also determines the placement of winches, pulls, and mountings. There might be someone in Maine or Massachusetts who would take on the job and, after three or four tries, make something passable, but you really need someone who has had a lot of experience. I'm still hoping that Ed's office will be able to prevail upon American Draperies to reconsider bidding on your job. Ed gives the company a lot of work, so he has a lot of influence with the people there. If they decide to do it, they would have to send someone up to your house to measure the windows."

"You can't mean it!" I cried. "Can't they take the measurements off the architectural drawings?"

"Buildings are never built exactly to the specifications of the drawings. Do you remember the problems we had with the curtains to your house? If the measurements are an eighth of an inch off, the triangular shades won't work. If the American Draperies people agree to do the shades, they will have to do the installation themselves."

"You mean, we'll have to pay someone to go up to Maine twice? Surely, a local contractor can do the installation."

"If the American Draperies people don't install the shades, they can't take responsibility for their working properly."

"I wonder if we could have done without triangular windows," I said. "Their shades are bound to be exorbitant."

"But the triangular windows look very nice. It's a new geometric form in your house."

"I know," I said and told myself the addition was already built, and the time for objecting to the triangular windows had long since passed. "But what about the treatment for the lookout and the rectangular window?" I asked.

"They will both need a pull-up shade."

"I've never heard of them—what are they?"

"You see them in doctors' offices. They're installed in the floor and are often used to black out part of the window for privacy, while letting natural light come in through the top of the window." She paused, as if she was looking at some notes. "The big glass pocket door will need two overlapping curtains—one sheer, which could be drawn in the daytime as a partial protection of furniture from the sun, the other opaque, to be drawn at nighttime."

Eventually, Ed and Toshiko were able to get American Draperies to bid on the shades and curtains. Their bid for the job was eleven thousand six hundred dollars—thirty-eight hundred dollars for two triangular shades; eighteen hundred dollars for two pull-up shades; thirty-nine hundred dollars for panel-lined drapes, panel sheers, and decorative brass rods with rings; and twenty-one hundred dollars for measuring, travel, and installation. Toshiko thought that we were getting a bargain—travel expenses and travel time alone could have been three or four thousand dollars, she said. I was anything but consoled. Then, when the shades were eventually installed, the triangular ones left one and a half inches of the windowpane exposed on one edge, and the roller mechanism for the pull-up shades was mounted haphazardly on the baseboard, so that it stuck out as an extra element instead of seeming an integral part of the window. On top of it, all the shades were made of such flimsy material that after a week or two of use, they began to fray and tear. American Draperies was obliged to remake all the shades in a heavier material and reinforce the edges, so they wouldn't rip. The company's people had to come back and reinstall all the shades, at the same time cutting and removing a section of the baseboard and reinstalling the roller mechanism for the pull-up shades in the newly cut recess. Before the shade ordeal was over, we also had to put in heavier eyelets and heavier pulls and make still other adjustments. The company absorbed the expense of the extra work and, as it happened, was able to offset the cost of the travel because it coincided with a job at the University of Maine in Orono.

When I asked the owner of American Draperies why some of these problems hadn't been anticipated, he said reflectively, "Every custom shade has its own individual idiosyncrasy."

Furnishing the new living room had its own individual idiosyncrasies. The fireplace on the west side of the room was disproportionately small. It seemed to compete with both the big glass pocket door and the bar as the focus of the room—and by extension, as the spot where people could gather and mix. There seemed to be no way of having one seating arrangement for general conversation—it seemed to call for two or three. That, in turn, required more rugs and more furniture.

But the problems of the shades and the furnishings seemed to pale in significance compared with the problem of the pocket door, which continued to vex us long after the room was furnished. It took the combined strength of Linn and me to budge the door, when—in theory—it should have rolled along its track with the touch of a finger. As if that weren't bad enough, the moment there was any wind, air would whistle through the room from under the door and mysteriously migrate upstairs, leaking out of the cracks of the built-in closet and drawers in the new child's room. There was such a strong draft everywhere that, no matter how high we turned up the thermostat, the new rooms remained ice-cold. And whenever we tried to start a fire in the new fireplace we couldn't get it established without filling the whole house with smoke and setting off smoke alarms. Even the original house, once snug and warm, became chilly.

Ed said that he could not understand the reasons for the problems we were having with the door. He felt he could do little about it from New York. For once, he seemed to lose patience with us and the house and counselled us to consult the people on the scene. Duratherm, the manufacturer, sent representatives to examine the door. They certified that there was nothing wrong with its construction and traced part of the problem to the uneven track. Robert Clayton, for his part, contended that the architects had poorly designed not only the door-sill under the track, which bowed under the weight of the huge glass door, but also the housing in the wall for the door and its screen, a cavity that, he said, was responsible for the leakage of cold air both downstairs and upstairs. In Clayton's view, the architect had anchored the door inside the wall in such a way that it was impossible to get at it without taking down the addition's whole eastern wall and later rebuilding and reshingling it. He maintained that this solution was so drastic that he was not about to undo his freshly completed work, especially since there was no telling if, at the end of it all, he would be able to improve the operation of the door and make it airtight.

Throughout, I was learning slowly and painfully that, in

anything to do with the house, everything that could go wrong did go wrong. If one cared to get things right, one had to invest endless time and energy. In our case, the problems were exacerbated by ours being a remotely situated house and, furthermore, by our not being there the whole summer. By the time we caught a mistake in construction, alerted the contractor, tried to have the mistake corrected, and often recorrected, months would have gone by. In fact, the door was one of many points along the years of construction when I became so dispirited that I would imagine that I had built an uninhabitable house and that my role as a householder was under threat. The only explanation I can come up with for such bouts of despair is that I felt besieged by forces beyond me—that I couldn't control them the way, for instance, I marshalled words when I wrote. Alternatively, the house was like one of my books—every comma had to be in place. The truth was, I was a perfectionist. I wanted to do right by Ed, and by my family, but at every turn I had to dole out money for new, unforeseen changes, as if the more I was financially whipped, the oftener I was doomed to return to the whipping post.

In any event, I was so distraught with the problem of the door that I told Clayton to do whatever was necessary, regardless of the expense. In time, he found a way to open up the eastern wall from the inside, fill the hollow wall and pack the cavity in and around the housing with insulation, close the wall, and repaint it. At the same time, he buttressed the doorsill from below with a steel girder in the basement crawl space. Magically, once these remedial measures were taken the drafts stopped, the new fireplace started working properly, the door rolled along its track easily—the entire house became warm. I realized the truth of what Ed had once said: "An architect can make perfect drawings, but you need a good contractor to solve the problems that crop up on the site."

THE ORIGINAL ARCHITECTURAL plans had called for a stepping stone along the foot of the glass pocket door. That had

Addition, interior, 2002

seemed a simple, rustic, and inexpensive transition from the new living room to the outside. But now, as an afterthought, Ed came up with the idea of a deck to connect the outside of the addition to the deck of the original house. We embraced the idea as a final flourish. But since the new deck had to be in proportion with the addition, it turned out to be huge—twenty-six by twenty feet— with a whole set of wooden steps spanning the full width of the new door. Once Clayton started building the deck, he came up against a boulder at the north end of the steps—the one originally used to site the house. Looming out of the land as if to protest further encroachment, it wouldn't be budged, for all Clayton's efforts to dislodge it or, indeed, to chip away at it. After much discussion back and forth between New York and Dark Harbor, Ed agreed to narrow the width of the steps by a foot or so and extend a little elbow railing over the boulder. The first time I was in the house after Clayton had supposedly finished his work, I ran along the deck and down the steps and, to my horror, discovered that the last step was hanging three feet off the ground. I fell and was lucky not to have broken a leg.

When I complained to Clayton, the most obliging of the contractors I had worked with, he blamed the treacherous steps on the architect, saying that he was only following the drawings he had been provided with. The truth was, so much time and effort had been consumed by the addition and then by the door that afterward, Clayton, like Ed, seemed to lose all patience with us and our house. Still, he did take care of the steps expeditiously.

Whatever our frustrations over the addition, it had one, wholly unexpected, boon. The acoustics became muffled and there seemed to be breaks in the way sound travelled from room to room. That no doubt had to do with the expansion of size and volume, with the corresponding change in the air flow and the geometric configuration of the structure. In fact, the whole house became quieter and more serene, as if I had finally got my long wished-for plaster walls.

Somewhere along the line, I said to Linn, "When our children grow up, I'm going to tell them, 'Never go in for a

Addition, exterior, 1994

custom-built house. Buy something already there, however imperfect, and adapt to it and enjoy it. Leave building dream houses to other people.' "

"But look at the bright side," Linn said. "Our house may turn out to be a great investment, and, meanwhile, we've got a wonderful summer place for our children to grow up in."

IX

FAMILY

U NTIL GOING TO DARK HARBOR, NEITHER LINN NOR I had much experience living by the sea. Although Cooperstown did have a lake, she had enjoyed mostly inland pursuits there, like horseback riding and running or walking through the fields. Also, although she had been on the diving team at Yale, she was much more excited by skiing, hiking, and mountain-climbing, something she had done in Switzerland, Germany, and Austria when she was a student abroad. In any event, she had little experience of sailing, the sport for which the island was mainly known; situated in its protected bay, it had some of the best sailing waters in the world. Although she had learned to play tennis as a child, she hadn't spent much time playing since. As for golf, she had no interest in it. I myself was ruled out from most sports.

I frequently thought we might have done better with a house in the Hamptons, where we had a community of friends from New York. Moreover, the sandy beaches and smooth seafloor, the relatively warm waters and wonderful surf of the Hamptons always seemed enticing; the Dark Harbor beaches and seafloor, in contrast, were covered with crustaceans, shells, and sharp stones and rocks. People had to wear sneakers or flip-flops to walk on the beach, or even to go in the water, and some people even wore wet suits to insulate themselves from the cold. Indeed, it seemed only eccentric bathers would seek out the beaches and waters of Dark Harbor. But once we had spent more time on the island we came to appreciate the benefits of its rugged, hearty character, and then Linn and the girls would not have traded it for life in the Hamptons. I, for one, came to think that sailing would develop in our girls much more mental and physical stamina than swimming or riding the waves in the Hamptons would have done.

There was, however, no place to learn sailing—or, indeed, tennis or golf—except at the Tarratine Club. Soon after we started building our house in 1984, the question of joining the club had come up. Founded in 1896, it formed an island within the larger island. The first summer we stayed in our house, Linn had been preoccupied with Sage and did not meet many summer people, and I myself had had no interest in joining any country club. Anyway, the ethos of the Tarratine Club was formed by the old Dark Harbor families. Certainly, the islanders, by and large, were excluded. While we both wanted Sage to grow up enjoying everything the island had to offer, the thought that she might have a privilege that children born on the island were denied or could not afford further confused the whole issue for us. But we felt we had little choice. We needed to be members of the club even to have a place to moor a boat. If our house had been on the west shore, we could have had our own dock. But we were on the east shore, where the rougher waters made that impossible. As it happened, I found friends among the Dark Harbor summer people who were acquainted with my writings in *The New Yorker*. And some of Linn's Cooperstown friends had their own connections to the community. Thanks to them, we were proposed and elected to the Tarratine Club in 1985.

The club seemed to me a summer playground for the well-to-do, but with a difference, in that their activities were single-minded and purposeful. From morning to evening, the members participated in organized competitive sports, including a day-long triathlon for the children toward the end of the season. During the summer, there were tennis championships—for Mixed Doubles, Ladies Advanced and Intermediate Doubles, and Gentlemen's Doubles—and golf tournaments. Every Wednesday and Saturday afternoon, there were boat races, with trophies that had an almost incantatory ring to them: the Aldrich Cup, the Doughdish Cup, the Prescott Metcalf Cup, the Howe Cup, the Crane Cup, the Daniels Cup, the Derby Cup, the Bering Cup. At the end of the season, winners were presented with these silver cups, on which their own names had been inscribed. The following year, the cups were passed on to new winners.

Linn started playing tennis and taking sailing lessons—indeed, for a few days, even I went out for a group lesson. Later, when Sage and Natasha became old enough for club programs and didn't require a mother's helper, they were enrolled in sailing classes on Monday, Tuesday, Thursday, and Friday mornings. Wednesday and Saturday mornings, they had golf clinics, and Wednesday and Friday afternoons, tennis clinics. Outside these programs, children, like adults, could also schedule private lessons. Like many parents, we had trouble getting the children out of bed for golf, but their resistance to the game was somewhat overcome by the fact that, at the time, the golf pro, who had two small children, took particular pleasure in teaching kids. Once the girls were seven or eight, they fell into their own Dark Harbor routine. In the morning, they would stay in bed as late as possible and would have to be woken up several times in order to make the sailing program, at nine-thirty. We were reluctant to wake them up too early; they seemed so small and so much in need of sleep. But if they overslept and missed sailing class, they would feel left out of the doings of their friends and would fuss and be out of sorts. Once we were able to cajole them out of bed, they would pull on swimming suit, shirt, and shorts; grab their flip-flops and a fuzzy jacket; run down the stairs to the kitchen at the last possible minute; quickly eat a blueberry muffin or two that Linn would have freshly baked; and race down to the garage and the car. As Linn drove them the short distance to the yacht club (the tennis and golf clubs, the other two Tarratine constituents, were located elsewhere), they would slather on suntan lotion and get into their life jackets, which every child was required to wear when on the dock or in a boat. They would be dropped off at the parking lot of the club, where about sixty other children were also arriving, and run with their friends to the floating dock, or floats, where they would sit down wherever they could find a place. On the south side of the dock was moored a flotilla of boats owned by club members. On the north side was a cove with a mooring for dinghies (rowboats and small motorboats), which were used to ferry people to their boats, and, beyond them, "turn-abouts"—sort of floating tublike boats with one main sail and, depending on the wind, perhaps a spinnaker—on which children first learned to sail. It took the children a few years to learn to handle a turnabout and to gain confidence in the water. They then graduated to a "420," a boat four metres and twenty centimetres long, with three sails—a main, a jib, and a spinnaker. The 420s were moored on the south side, with the larger boats. Each day, two or three children would be assigned a boat by the sailing instructors, themselves teenage graduates of the program, who would try to make sure that novices were matched up with children who were somewhat more experienced. The sailors would be ferried to the turn-about moorings, and would clamber into their individual boats. They would put down the centerboard, put in the rudder and tiller, and rig and raise the main sail. Then they would untie the boat and practice sailing in the sheltered sea-lane. To allay the children's fears, to infuse them with confidence, and to give them a helping hand, the sailing instructors and the sailing master would be all around, in rowboats or motorboats. At the end of their sail, the children would have to reverse the process of getting their boats ready and, once the sail (or sails), rudder, and tiller were stowed away, they would be ferried back to the floats.

If it was a becalmed or foggy morning, with no prospect of the sun breaking through, the children would be put in rowboats and have a race to a designated buoy; or would be shepherded back to the clubhouse, essentially one large room with a kitchen, pantry, and deck, and each given a line to tie a clove hitch or other sailing knots; or would be taught the rudiments of sailing charts, compass directions, or wind currents; or would be organized into games of Red Rover or Duck, Duck, Goose, or Sailing Jeopardy, which they would play in the clubhouse or on its deck. Sometimes they would be sent on a beachcombing mission, to collect treasures like sea stars, limpets, mussels, midget glass, and purple and blue beach glass; or on a scavenger hunt, which might involve the children's taking a wooded shortcut to the Dark Harbor Shop to make lists of all the flavors of ice cream in the store that day or of the shoe sizes of the teenage summer helpers working behind the counter. The prize for a scavenger hunt might be a bag of candy or an ice-cream cone, or maybe nothing—just the excitement of being the first to run back with a completed list. Occasionally, they would be shown a movie that had something to do with sailing. But, however windless or cold or clammy or foggy it was, they would be kept busy, and along the way absorb things to do with boats and the sea.

At eleven-thirty, they would all run into the clubhouse and line up in front of the food counter and fill out slips for their lunch, which would be charged to each family's club account. A child could live a whole summer on the island without ever using money. Indeed, no one seemed to carry any cash, because everything in the club, in the Dark Harbor

Shop, and in the grocery store was charged, and the bills didn't catch up with the parents until the summer was over and everyone had returned to their regular life. After the children had handed in their lunch orders, they would hang around on the sofas in the clubhouse or at the picnic tables on the deck, waiting for their names to be called over an indoor-outdoor loudspeaker, so they could pick up their lunch from the counter. They would be served on paper plates hamburgers or grilled-cheese sandwiches or small or large orders of french fries—the club menu was limited, its only specialty until recently being clam chowder, which was popular mostly with the grownups. The children would get their own drinks from a refrigerator in the pantry and sit with their friends wherever they could find a place in the room or on the deck. By one o'clock, children had to clear out, so that adults could have their lunch. In the afternoon, while waiting for the tennis clinics to begin, at five o'clock, they might sit or stand around the yacht-club dock, splash around in the bay, or play on the few swing sets or jungle gyms or trampolines at private houses. Sage and Natasha might bring their friends over and swim in our swimming pool or sit around our deck or the pool house reading or horsing around. Evenings would be spent at home, perhaps with friends, in front of the fire, playing card games like Go Fish, board games like Monopoly, or charades. I remember that Natasha once acted out "hypotenuse" (which her mother guessed, only after many tries) and Sage did "Great Expectations."

During the week, for children and grown-ups, there would be occasional teas, town picnics, dances, garden tours, amateur play productions, and weekly forums. Sunday was reserved for church, to which I always went if Linn was singing a solo, and for picnics at neighboring, uninhabited islands. Whenever a boat was to go out, whichever children happened to be on the dock would pile in and vie to sit not on the sheltered part of the boat but right in the bow, where they might be sprayed with seawater. Once on the other island, everyone spent the time eating snacks, walking, exploring, swimming. Everyone except me seemed to find the icy water invigorating.

Linn, though she'd encountered sailing waters only in Maine, had become so proficient at driving *Natty Bumppo*, the twenty-two-foot motorboat we had acquired, that she had become part of the island's pack of "water rats," a group that was dominated by summer people who had been coming to Dark Harbor since childhood. Similarly, our children raced around town, on bikes or on foot, as if they'd been born to it. Indeed, the rocks and waters of Maine were now in their blood and bones.

At night, after ten o'clock, everything seemed to shut down. Without streetlights, Dark Harbor's darkness was almost palpable. Some intrepid souls who were still not ready to sleep, however, would take out a rowboat to watch the phosphorescence. Sometimes when the water was stirred, especially in the sheltered sea-lane, plankton would glow like fireflies and the water would drip in sparkling sheets off an oar. The boat itself would leave a beautiful, glowing wake, as if to belie the very name "Dark Harbor."

THE GIRLS' SUMMER friendships were different from their friendships in the city. Dark Harbor children lived in one another's pockets twenty-four hours a day, and were free from the pressures of tests and homework—of city life, generally. As soon as we drove onto the island each summer, the girls would want to stop at the Dark Harbor Shop, to see which of their friends were already on the island and to have their first summer ice-cream cone with sprinkles—or "jimmies." Or, further along the road, they would jump out and run into, for instance, the Low house, to see their particular friends Jessie and Frances, whom they had not seen since the previous summer. More likely than not, the four girls would later get a ride to our house from Tony or Pauline Low, Jessie and

Frances's parents. Our daughters' friends would stay for dinner and have a sleepover, or, alternatively, Sage and Natasha would grab their toothbrushes and nightclothes and go over to the Lows', and we might not see any of the four until sometime the next afternoon. In New York, we had to keep tabs on our girls—know exactly where they were, what they were doing, and when they were coming home—but in Dark Harbor they, like all children, roamed from house to house, from the Dark Harbor Shop to the tennis courts, from the yacht club to its dock, like free spirits. They never had to tell us how many friends they were bringing home for dinner. All the island children had meals wherever they happened to be. It seemed to be no trouble for people to put extra hamburgers or hotdogs on the barbecue. In our own house, if we ran out of charcoal for the barbecue, extra pasta, vegetables, or salad would appear in the kitchen. It was the Dark Harbor version of the parable of the loaves and the fishes. Linn enjoyed that informality—it reminded her of her grandparents' ever-extendable Cooperstown teas. As for me, I was reminded of what my father used to say to the seven of us children—"The more, the merrier." In my bachelor days, I had not been able to live up to that saying. Even after I got married, it was hard to add guests to the table in New York, but in Dark Harbor our facilities seemed to accommodate all comers. The whole ambience of the island was open and hospitable; people never did lock their doors, it turned out, and once the daytime policeman was off-duty, a caretaker moonlighted as a policeman, driving around after dark to see that youngsters were not drinking and causing trouble.

Of course, there were certain formal events—junior regattas and tennis round-robins, fancy-dress and talent shows—but our girls were casual and relaxed about such contests and entered into them in the spirit of fun. For one fancy-dress party, they arrived at the clubhouse dressed as a telephone. They had spent the day enthusiastically cutting and painting cardboard boxes for the costume—Sage was the dial

and cradle and Natasha the receiver, and the two were connected by a rope. They were thrilled to get the first prize.
Another season, the girls and a few of their friends came
dressed as Gibson Girls, spoofing the perfectly coiffed hair and
hourglass figures of the famous illustrations of Charles Dana
Gibson, who lived from 1867 to 1944 and had been a resident
of Seven Hundred Acre Island, a constituent of Islesboro township—his family still summered there. As for the annual talent
show, it was always an occasion for grown-ups and children
alike to make fun of themselves and the community—to think
up an idea, to scrounge the materials, to rehearse a skit. The
point was not so much to win as to do something amusing.
One season, the girls and their friends sang a song they had set
to the tune of Woody Guthrie's "This Land Is Your Land," but
with the words changed to "This Island Is My Island" and con-
cluding with the second to last verse of the original:

> As I went walking, I saw a sign there,
> And on the sign it said "No Trespassing."
> But on the other side it didn't say nothing,
> That side was made for you and me.

As the girls' earlier lyrics had made clear, the verse was poking
fun at the division of the island into west side, where people
owned nineteenth-century mansionlike cottages and liked to
sit on their docks and have cocktails, watching the sun set over
the Camden Hills across the water, and east side, where we had
comparatively modest houses and enjoyed sitting on our decks
with coffee as the sun rose.

Perhaps the most festive summer event was the Dark
Harbor Dog Show, which was conceived of in 1945 by Apple
Parish, the ten-year-old daughter of Henry and Dorothy
Parish, as an entrepreneurial alternative to setting up, say, a
lemonade stand. Like Annette, the summer people were so
devoted to their pets that, if possible, dogs were even more
numerous on the island than boats. As the innovation took

root, children drew posters announcing the date of the dog show and put them up in places like the Dark Harbor Shop and the yacht club. Every effort was made to pair each child with a dog and each dog with a child, so that no handler or pet owner would feel left out. Held on a Saturday morning, generally in mid- or late August, when the island weather was at its most glorious, it often took place on the freshly mowed lawn of the Parishes' cottage, on the west side. Outside, tickets were sold, and inside, ice cream—the proceeds going to charity. While people sat on the grass or milled around, the young dog handlers busied themselves primping and grooming their dogs, controlling and calming them. A prominent summer citizen served as the master of ceremonies, and the grandes dames of the Tarratine Club served as judges. The pets were entered in different categories: Puppies; Large Sporting Dogs; Small Sporting Dogs; Large Non-Sporting Dogs; Small Non-Sporting Dogs; Miscellaneous—for mixed breeds; Trick, Obedience, and Costume; and Championship. If a dog turned out to be too big for the child to handle as it was being walked around the ring, an adult rushed in to help. The prizes were awarded as much on the child's looks and behavior as on those of the dog on parade. The judges made a great to-do about their deliberations, heightening the sense of drama. The whole pageant had the atmosphere of a spirited English county fair.

In the early years, when we went to the dog shows, our girls were only spectators, but in 1997, when Natasha was ten years old, Philip Ladd asked her to walk his Airedale, Baxter. The Ladds were one of the oldest summer families on the island and, by virtue of that, a Ladd dog had a claim to be noticed and honored. In any case, Baxter was an impressive-looking dog. Natasha and Baxter came away with the grand championship prize. There was great excitement when the dog was presented with a silver bowl—the dog-show version of a sailing trophy, passed down from dog to dog from year to year. Natasha, as the handler, was presented with a multicolored ribbon.

I myself associated such events and awards ceremonies with the British Raj. Like the British colonists who staved off the boredom of a faraway outpost by engaging in schoolboy antics, the summer residents of Dark Harbor lightened their experience of a remote resort by indulging in their own communal capers, the most eager participants being the families that had the longest tradition of coming to the island. We, for our part, dutifully fell in step, delighted that our children would have a rich store of summer memories.

Whenever we got back to New York, Sage and Natasha couldn't wait for their next Dark Harbor summer. They talked about their island friends the way I talked about my family in India—with longing and affection. They would look forward to "the Overnight," which took place in July, when about thirty or forty girls and boys would sail out to Warren, an uninhabited island, with just one adult—the sailing master—and three or four teenage sailing monitors. They would gather wood, make a bonfire, cook themselves hotdogs and hamburgers, and toast marshmallows. There, they would set up tents and spread out their sleeping bags but stay up all night, running around and telling ghost stories by the campfire, eating candy they had collected for days in preparation. The sailing master dreaded the Overnight: he didn't like supervising a twelve-hour party of hyper children. We parents, in our own way, also dreaded it, because the children would come home at six or seven o'clock in the morning like zombies: muddied and drenched, tired and out of temper, with insect bites and sleepy heads, and not return to normal until they had slept most of the day and woken up and taken a bath. But for the children it was the high point of their summer.

As the girls grew older, became trained sailors, and served as monitors at the Overnight in their turn, their perspective shifted. When Sage was in the eighth grade she wrote a school essay about graduating from a turnabout to a 420 and then skippering the bigger boat for the first time. Her essay showed how much she had learned from sailing, not only about the wind and tides, but also about herself. That experience had become a rite of passage for her, as for so many children before her.

ALTHOUGH IN THE early years we had had to struggle to be accepted into the tight-knit Dark Harbor community, in more recent years we both had the impression that the moment we arrived for a summer stay we were welcomed by the friends we had made on the island, as if they had become our surrogate family. All the same, Linn and I had our differences in the way we felt about the island. Linn was to the manor born, and athletic; she could hold her own socially and sail and play tennis. If she had certain ambivalences because, as an intellectual, she couldn't completely fit into the summer community, she kept them private. By contrast, I was born and raised in one of the poorest parts of the world. Some of my earliest memories were of being at Dadar School for the Blind in Bombay, where my relatively well-to-do father had sent me when I wasn't yet five, imagining that it was an English-type boarding school when in fact it was an orphanage-cum-asylum. I was lucky to escape alive after three harrowing years there. Then I was uprooted from India when I was fifteen and spent ten uninterrupted years studying, first in America and then in England. Afterward, I settled in America and became a working writer. At first, my well-meaning friends periodically urged me to go back to India and throw myself into work for the poor, but the vocation of social work, I felt, was not for me. All the while, however, I felt sad that I had certain material comforts denied to most of the people in the country of my birth. Indeed, it didn't seem fair to me that I had made a place for myself in the West while my Bombay schoolmates, perhaps equally promising, had been left behind without a future. I continued to be haunted by my experiences at Dadar School. Possibly as a result, I came to identify with the poor or with people who

Family, 1987

failed in life through no fault of their own—even to find in that identification the source of my tragic outlook on life. I now realized that, in a sense, I was only trying to bandage an unconscious childhood wound. Whenever I felt unworthy of being among successful people, especially when I was among the rich, as at Father D'Arcy's eightieth birthday party at the "21" club, I put on a greater outward show, so that I would appear to be worthy of the likes of Annette. When she took my performance at face value, I rushed headlong, as it were, into her arms and Dark Harbor, much like Don Quixote supping with the duke and duchess. Thereafter, it was only a matter of time before I was swept up by my fantasies and was conducting myself like a rajah, lending my ear to a Realtor, hiring architects and contractors, and building, as it were, my own palace on sand.

It was a strange undertaking, since my identity has always been fractured and splintered by my confusion of tongues (English is my fourth language) and of cultures (Indian, American, British, and blind), and in this sense I've never belonged anywhere. My chosen vocation further entrenched me as an outsider. It was as if in Dark Harbor I were condemned yet again, and in a new way, to fit my multi-cornered self into the proverbial round hole. My facial vision was so acute that in New York I was able to walk from my office on West Forty-third Street to, say, my apartment at Eighty-fifth and Fifth Avenue, relying on paved sidewalks and streets and on the walls of buildings, shops, houses, and suchlike, from which traffic sounds, footfalls, and voices bounced off. I took buses alone to the office and elsewhere and, when I was younger and more of a daredevil, subways. In the woods of Dark Harbor, however, my facial vision was paralyzed—so much so that I couldn't even walk down from the parking area to our house without stepping off the narrow, snaking peastone path and sometimes taking a spill. In fact, everywhere on the island the trees were scattered higgledy-piggledy in the woods and had no consistent shape or order capable of casting sound-shadows;

there were no discrete groves, hedges, fences, or bushes—no set variety of birdcalls and birdsongs—to serve as pointers to help me get around this countryside. Sound on the island disappeared into the brush, banks, and woods like a stone tossed into the ocean. The only place on the island I could negotiate by myself was the macadamized town road. And that I took full advantage of, walking alone in the evenings from our house to the southern tip of the island, as far as the dirt road to Pendleton Point, or north a mile and a half to the Dark Harbor Shop for an ice-cream cone. It was as if I'd created the house, the swimming pool—indeed, the whole private campus, as it were—for others to see and enjoy, as a monument to my ability to visualize, to be as good as Everyman.

I often thought that, if left to myself, I might have long since written off the years of emotion and time spent in building the house and pulled up stakes. If I had needed to get away from New York, I could have chosen to visit Linn's family's country places for weekends to indulge my senses, instead of bowing to some hazy notion of the pleasures of a second home. Still, now, as a family man, I had to think of my wife and children—their interests, their needs, and their enjoyments. As for myself, in time I was able to make arrangements to bring my regular amanuensis with me for the few weeks a year I was in Dark Harbor. Once I was settled with a helper, I was content to sit at a desk in the corner of the old living room, writing and rewriting, revising and polishing—sticking to my last, as I did on Manhattan, the island where I spent most of the year. Again, as on the other island, I tried to partake of such enjoyable activities as I could easily fit into my writing day and tried not to worry overmuch about the rest. Whenever I was around Linn or the children, whether in our house or in the boat, I had no doubt that it was right for us to be there. Even if we quit the island one day, we'd always have fond memories of the place. I was glad that I was in a position to give my wife and children some measure of what a sighted husband and a sighted father might give his family.

That did not stop me from wondering how it was that I ever found myself at the table, as it were, of the Dark Harbor rich, for whenever I visited India and a beggar approached me, holding out a scabrous hand and croaking for a pice to purchase perhaps one morsel of bread, I would weep inside and find myself repeating, "There but for the grace of God go I." "Scram!" someone was sure to shout at the beggar and then, turning to me, add, "If you give him a pice, you will be besieged. For every one, there is a horde waiting to pounce." And yet I had gone to school with those hordes—in fact, sat in kindergarten with grown boys and girls corralled from the streets by the police for begging and for making a nuisance of themselves. They had been brought to the school for training.

I recalled that some of them had walked to meals with their hands outstretched, sometimes trailing a hand along the wall, feeling out the ground underfoot, for fear they would stumble and fall. For this they would have their ears boxed until, using whatever facial vision they had, they had learned to walk confidently, like the sighted, with their heads held high and their hands at their sides, relying on sound-shadows alone for navigation. It was perhaps from those moments that I grasped that if I failed to live up to the standards of the sighted—indeed, to surpass them—I would be condemned to live, grow old, and die unmarried and childless like the permanent denizens of Dadar School, who were left behind and discarded even before their lives got under way. The realization made me all the more determined to avoid their fate, to rise above their lot, to erase the traces of Dadar School—to defy the accepted notion that the blind must keep to their pitiful place in a world that is organized and run by the sighted. It might then be that the foundation stone of the beautifully designed, light, and airy house in Dark Harbor was laid long ago in faraway Bombay, at Dadar School.